CONVICTION

CONVICTION

by Janet E. Lemmé

236906

W · W · Norton & Company · Inc ·
New York

SBN   393   05401   2

FIRST EDITION

Copyright © 1970 by W. W. Norton & Company, Inc. All rights reserved.
Published simultaneously in Canada by George J. McLeod Limited,
Toronto. *Library of Congress Catalog Card No. 79-103967.* Printed in the
United States of America.

1 2 3 4 5 6 7 8 9 0

Introduction

MY STORY IS TRUE, though names have been changed to protect the innocent. In confinement I took clandestine notes on scraps of toilet paper and sewed them into the hem of my skirt. My clothing was, of course, searched, and I was fortunate that the paper escaped detection. Those notes, together with vivid memories, form the basis of this narrative. Immediately after my release I wrote a long diary detailing the experience so that I would be capable of reconstructing the most accurate sketch possible.

I hope that through this account the reader will have a better insight into one aspect of the international scene as it affected this American housewife and as it affects all of us. Just as brother is bound to sister, black is bound to white, youth to the aged, rich to poor, Protestant to Catholic to Moslem to Jew, so are we "*Amis*" bound to all peoples of other nations: through the tentacles of the human heart.

Acknowledgments

I WISH TO THANK Mr. Pierre Divényi for his help in correcting my pidgin Hungarian, and Mrs. L. B. Kemmis, my superb mother, for her perseverance in ungarbling my misspelled English.

Part One

I

IT WAS IN THE SUMMER OF 1961 that Busso sat in the living room with my parents and announced, "I have asked your daughter to marry me."

"Well," my father questioned, "what did she say?"—even though he knew the answer.

"She said yes," I burst out. I was sitting right there; why should they speak of me in the third person? Why was everyone so serious?

My father began talking about our family and what a good child I had been, and my mother seemed to go off on a tangent about something to do with steadfast love, and Busso agreed with everything they said, and I could not understand a word of it. They intended it to be conversational, but it had the effect of a lecture.

"Mo–ther!" She did not seem to hear my restraining pleas. "Dad, why are you telling us all this?"

Mom finally came to the point. "Busso is from East Germany. We want to know what his plans for returning home are."

"Home? Canada is my home now," Busso said. "And as a matter of fact, I like Seattle very much and could easily remain here permanently." He smiled as if at a joke. "You mean to tell me you are worried about my leaving Janet in order to go back to my motherland?"

"No," Dad said, "we are worried about your taking Janet back with you."

"It never entered my mind. When my mother is sixty-five she can visit me in West Germany, perhaps, and the same goes for my other relatives. I have no desire to return to the Zone."

"Aren't parents funny?" I commented to Busso when we left for a movie that night. "They think of the darndest things to worry about."

But by 1963 I had changed my thinking about my "funny" parents, about our whole family, and about East Germany. It was true that Busso had no yearning for his motherland, his *Heimat* as he called it, but I did. I wanted to meet his mother. I wanted to see the town he had grown up in, a town and a country with much history to reveal. I wanted to see, not far from that town, the Berlin Wall.

"Write to your mother and tell her we are coming," I insisted, and I enrolled in a basic German course in Kitimat, Canada, where we were living.

My husband objected; he was not enthusiastic; he stalled. "You can't just decide to go into East Germany from one day to the next. You must have permission, proper papers. It takes months. Think of the money. Do you realize how much you are talking about? Where do we plan to get it?"

"I saw an ad for a waitress [Kitimat, an aluminum company town, did not offer much opportunity for women.] We could live on my wages and save all yours. If you take that tow-truck job on weekends, in ten months we would have enough to fly over. If we get stuck, we can work in West Germany awhile."

He said he would think about it. "What about your parents?" He cocked his eyebrow at me.

"I'll talk to them. When they know how I feel, they'll understand."

While he was "thinking about it," Busso found a good position as a landscape foreman in Seattle. We moved to the States, and I took a technician's job in a laboratory. After a year and a half, when we had begun making a better living than ever before, we decided it was too early to settle down, so we both quit.

In December 1964, we entered East Germany to spend Christmas and New Year's with Busso's family. I found his mother and almost everyone I met to be surprisingly congenial, not nearly so sinister as I had expected the people of a one-time Nazi regime to be. My mother-in-law, an elegant woman in spite of the numerous tragedies she had experienced in her sixty-four years, was a gracious hostess, but she had been embittered, understandably so, by the war years and the loss of her husband and oldest son. In her daughter, Birke, I could see the outlines of the aged woman become young again.

Birke was impressive. She was a small young woman, just two years older than I, with excellent taste in clothing even though the available selection was scant. I thought her judgment was well-balanced in everything, and I particularly noticed the careful combination of affection and discipline she and her husband, Kurt, applied to their toddler daughter, Susann. Birke was intelligent, with an extra measure of ingenuity that seemed to give her an ever-renewed sparkle, a special savor for life. She was a sensitive, thoughtful woman: when words failed me, she often seemed to have an immediate perception of what I wanted to say. We understood each other without language, and we became friends.

Early in January 1965, Busso and I had to leave his family and friends in the Zone because our visiting permit had expired. We had made no definite plans, but we wanted to travel as far as our shoestring budget would allow; so we bought a used Volkswagen and began driving. Our travels took us through more than twenty-five different countries. We slept in the car, ate native foods, survived snowstorms in Turkey and the heat of the Eastern Sahara Desert in an eventful trip across North Africa. We arrived back in Europe in early April.

It was in Nice, France, with marshmallow clouds dotting a velvet sky and warm sunshine radiating in the smiles of bikini-clad girls, that we picked up our first mail from home in almost ten weeks. We sat silently together in the car, Busso reading the letters written in German and I those in English, until suddenly Busso gasped, "My God, no." He stared at me in horror. "It's Birke and Kurt's daughter. Susann is dead."

If they had had a telephone, we would have called, but words would have been inadequate anyway. We knew how much this child meant to her parents, how much such a baby would have meant to us. In stunned mourning we sent a telegram to express our sympathy and on the same day applied for permission to re-enter the Zone.

In June the visa was granted. Depression was heavy in the air as the last armed guards finally waved us through the checkpoint and we entered the German Democratic Republic for the second time. We drove for hours without pause until we reached their town, the quiet, small town where Kurt and Birke were waiting at the window of their upstairs apartment. Birke was dressed in black; even her stockings were black. Kurt wore dark colors, too. Deep lines creased their young faces in evidence of the pain of losing their daughter.

Any doubts I had had about coming were dispelled in our emotional greeting. The couple was glad to have us and relieved to talk out the ache of the many weeks during which Susann had suffered a long siege of pneumonia and died. When the story had been told, there was a prolonged pause as if a silent prayer would bring the little girl back to life, but the silence in the room made death's reality undeniable, and we had to turn to other thoughts.

Birke made coffee and cold sandwiches and we sat long into the night talking of the past. Kurt and Birke seemed little interested in looking to the future. Around four in the morning, Birke put the teakettle on a gas burner to heat water for our sponge baths—hot running water is still a luxury for the average family—and we prepared to go to bed. "You two will take our beds," she insisted, and no amount of protesting could change her mind. She and Kurt had arranged with the landlady to sleep in a bunk bed stored in the attic. I walked into the kitchen to say good night to Birke after she had finished washing, and I stopped in mid-sentence.

Birke was shaking pills out of a bottle, which she seemed to want to hide from me. I asked if she was ill, and she turned her back, saying no, I should not worry. I persisted in trying to find out what the tablets were for. Reluctantly she admitted that she had been taking sleeping pills since Susann's death and that the original dosage was no longer sufficient. She begged me not to make a fuss, because Kurt objected, and although he often knew about her taking the sleeping pills, she did not like to make it conspicuous to him.

"But it has been months now, Birke. How long do you intend to depend on these?" I held up the small bottle, feeling the potency it contained, and spoke as gently as I could.

"As long as I have to," she said with timidity, yet with a stubborn look that denounced my lack of understanding.

"Promise me you will try to stop soon," I insisted, because I feared such "medicine." She nodded.

"If you're worried about my committing suicide, you needn't be. One attempt was enough." Her words stunned me. "Don't be shocked. It seemed the best thing to do at the time. I was completely broken when Susie died. Believe me, it's not an easy thing to live through." She held up the sleeping pills. "One feels compelled to take some action. Suicide seemed the easiest, not dramatic at all."

"Thank God you changed your mind."

"I didn't. Not then, anyway. By coincidence, Kurt came home early that evening. He never comes home early; just that one time he happened to. I had turned on the gas in the kitchen. When I came to in fresh air and realized what it would have done to my husband if he had lost both the baby and me, I knew I had to go on living somehow."

As the days passed, with the help of a German-English dictionary purchased in West Germany, I came to know my sister- and brother-in-law well, and there was no formality between us. I could ask any question I had, and I had many. Once, I asked why Birke had not left the Zone when her brother Busso did.

"I was only fourteen then," she said, "and just beginning to forget the smell of the hospital. I had been in the hospital for half my life until they finally arrested my tuberculosis. A few years after my cure, however, I tried getting out." She was silent for a long time, and I thought she had closed the subject, until she said, "In 1959 my brother Christoph, who was twenty years older than Busso, died of TB. They never helped him much here. Good medicine is not available. It was horrible to observe his slow decay, hard on both of us, and before he died, he made me promise to find a better fate for myself."

Busso had told me about his older brother. He had tried to send Christoph the necessary medicine from Canada, but it was not allowed through the controls.

"After Christoph died—that was before I knew Kurt—I met a man who agreed to lead me on foot by a secret route across the border. The night before I was to leave, the police came to me and said I was under surveillance. They made it impossible for me to take a single step."

"How did they know? The man told?"

"No, not he. It was I. I went to someone, someone I held very dear, to say goodby—and she went to the police."

Another story of foiled escape. I had heard many by now, but none had saddened me as much as this. "Now there is no way out," Birke said, ending the conversation.

We did not discuss politics much, but there were some questions I could not contain. "Do they force you to join the Communist Party, Kurt?"

"No, not overtly," he answered cautiously. He looked around the room, at the door, the window, at his wife. The window was half open. Birke moved quickly to close it.

"Oh, no," she said in a low voice. "They don't force you to join. But if you do not, you will never amount to anything here. For a woman it is not so bad. I shall never join. But *Kurtlschatz* [Kurt darling] wants to progress. *Wer vorwärts kommen will muss eben in den sauren Apfel beissen und in die Partei eintreten.*" I remember the sentence because I have heard it from many

East Germans: If one wants to go forward, he just has to bite into the sour apple and join the party.

They asked about life in the United States, especially about the prejudice against Negroes, and about the standard of living. It was hard for them to imagine that a couple could own their own home. "Maybe some day we can see it," Birke mused.

We made many short trips to Susann's grave, and I recall that it was July fifth, the day before our scheduled departure, that the four of us visited the baby's grave site for the last time. The solemnity of the cemetery followed us back to the apartment. All at once we seemed to have run out of conversation.

"Well, what's the matter with us today? Come on, this isn't a . . ." Busso stopped short of saying "funeral."

Abruptly, Birke left the room. In the bedroom, she hid her face in the featherbedding, and I went to her and tried to console her by saying she could have another child. "No, I don't think I can," she cried, and then she said that she would like to have another even though it would jeopardize her own health, and even though she could not rely on East German medicine to save her baby if it became ill; but that, she said, was not what depressed her at the moment. "I just hate to think that you and my brother must leave us tomorrow."

The men came into the bedroom then, and we talked about the fact that we had to leave but would write often and perhaps could even afford another trip in a few years. "Why does it always have to be you who has to save for a trip?" Birke said, sounding like a defiant little girl. "Why can't we visit you just once?"

"That would be an expensive trip," Busso chuckled, referring not only to the money but to the armed sentries who would block such frivolity. "But it *has* been done," he added as an afterthought, almost to himself.

That evening the air was electric. An idea had been born. How, who first put it into words, I do not know. But it was clear. We were a family. We were more: we were friends. Two people needed help, and two friends would give it. Kurt and Birke would escape from East Germany.

"It is no longer possible to flee on foot over no man's land." Kurt contemplated bits of news of other escapes he had heard about via sparse underground rumors.

"No, the security is tight. They shoot too many of them there," we agreed.

"One needs papers, official papers," someone said.

"Yes, that is the only sure method. I'll get them for you," Busso promised.

I glanced around the room, suspicious of an eavesdropper, already adapting myself to the precautionary habits of the people who dared to express opposition to their suppression. "There has to be a way," was my simple encouragment.

But what way? How? We had not a single answer in mind, just a goal. We planned our correspondence, code names, and words, and kept it simple. As Busso and I sat in the car and said good-by, he reiterated, "We will only carry through if it's a sure thing. If you change your minds, let me know immediately."

He revved the engine once more, and Kurt smiled, perhaps thinking about the car he would have in the West. He would have to be on a waiting list for five to ten years to buy a car in East Germany.

It all seemed to have begun with the echoing promise of *"Auf Wiedersehen."*

2

EIGHT MONTHS had passed during that first trip to Europe and North Africa, and when we arrived back in Seattle, we were somewhat weary and very broke. I returned to my previous work at the lab where, by coincidence, there was an opening; and Busso went into business for himself, the landscaping business. For several months we did little besides save money and remain rather overwhelmed with the magnitude of the promise we had made. I had not the slightest clue where to begin, and Busso, too, was at first perplexed about the problem, so that sometimes, when we puzzled over it after a tiring day's work, I secretly wished we could somehow gracefully renege. I could not see how an escape could be planned from across the ocean, but I did see the ever-increasing strain it had become on my husband. He had enough on his mind trying to manage a business, I thought to myself, but thinking then of my sister-in-law and her plight, I never spoke these ungenerous thoughts.

After Christmas 1965, however, the wheels began turning in Busso's head, and he seemed thereafter to be automatically propelled from one step to the next. I typed a few letters for him to gather necessary information. All I did otherwise was occasionally to feel guilty because I could not help more. I asked questions from time to time, but it all seemed so complicated, with visas and passports, entry stamps and exit stamps, declaration papers and currency exchange rates, passport pictures and additional identification to consider.

When he was sure of the initial plan, Busso sought out a faraway friend, and by February, the first major hurdle was scaled: we possessed two official passports for Kurt and Birke.

Meanwhile, Busso instructed his sister and brother-in-law to try to get permission to travel out of the East Zone. We waited for word from them. It took time, because it is not easy for an East German to get permission to travel—anywhere outside his town or district, let alone out of the country.

The waiting was discouraging. Although Birke wrote regularly, she had no definite word during January or February as to whether or not they could travel. Early in March, we decided to abandon the plan: Kurt had sent word that Birke had had some kind of heart failure.

A couple of weeks later, however, Birke wrote that she was in a convalescent sanitarium and that she felt better than ever. She asked Busso not to "postpone engagement plans." Along with that she wrote, "Yesterday we received permission to take a vacation. As yet, they have not specified where or when."

The pressure began to mount. We waited expectantly as each day passed, knowing that at any moment the authorities could tell them where and when. It could happen so fast that we would not have time to carry out the escape. Once again Busso coded a message to ask if they were sure about it. Was Birke strong enough? Was Kurt prepared to give up his position and all they had built together? Yes, came the reply, there was no stopping now.

Late in May came the final word: "Hungary, one of the three preferences we listed, has been assigned to us. We'll arrive in Budapest on June twenty-eighth."

So there it was. We had one month to close up shop in Seattle, fly to Europe to make final preparations, and get Birke and Kurt out safely. "On June twenty-fourth we will take the train to East Berlin," Birke had written, "and spend two nights before joining the group there and traveling on to Hungary."

There seemed to be a flurry of decisions to make: whether or not I should go; I could get a leave of absence; of course I would. Why not?

Should I tell my parents our plans? The way they felt about communists and Communist countries, they would panic, perhaps even try to stop us and ruin everything. "We are taking a short vacation to Europe," I informed them. I made jokes when they asked about going behind the Iron Curtain and assured them we did not have time. After all, it was not really lying, I told myself; we would return in three weeks with Birke and Kurt, and then they would understand.

What about money? "Two thousand ought to cover our air fare round trip and theirs one way, plus miscellaneous unexpected expenses," Busso calculated. Our savings account showed about thirty-five dollars. "I'll go down tomorrow and borrow the money from the bank. We will begin paying it back the minute we return," he said, already figuring out how he could increase business in order to pay the debt. "Do you think everything is ready?"

At that moment I decided that there comes a time when doubt and fear and indecision must end and faith must lead. It did not matter that I did not know all the answers; I knew enough to affirm, "It's perfect."

We departed from Seattle and landed in Frankfurt am Main on June 13, 1966. The following days were tense and hectic. There was the car to rent—the vehicle that would accomplish the escape—a duplicate stamp to secure that would be a match for the Hungarian one and, of course, each step of our planned route into and out of Hungary to trace. In Budapest, Busso selected a rendezvous spot where we would meet Birke and Kurt.

When everything was set, we had to skip a night's sleep in order to keep the appointment we had made to meet the Zoners in East Berlin. This meeting was essential in order to cover one final briefing and to complete all details. We left Vienna and, to avoid unnecessary traveling in a Communist country, drove around the southwest side of Czechoslovakia during the night and through Hof, West Germany, the next morning. Hof is a crossing point from West to East Germany; following that road, with a special permit, one may drive directly through East German (or should I say Soviet?) territory to enter West Berlin. "An island in a swamp," Busso commented. After being cramped in the Volkswagen for seventeen hours, we checked into a hotel in West Berlin. The mid-morning temperature had already hit eighty-five degrees Fahrenheit, but there was no stopping for a shower. Our luggage had to be unloaded from the car and two suitcases repacked with enough clothing to look reasonable but at the same time leave sufficient room for the valuables we planned to bring back with us.

Ironically, we met our two "comrades" at the "Monument to Victims of Fascism and Imperialism," near the street Unter den Linden. The four of us spent hours talking, reviewing, deciding. Since the beginning, one question had gnawed at the back of my mind: were Busso and I helping, or were we tampering with lives left better off alone? Now I learned that Birke had not needed sleeping tablets for many weeks, and I felt reassured.

"Keep your eyes open," Busso warned, as our twenty-four-hour pass was running out. "If you think you have become suspect, we must abandon the plan."

When there were no more questions, nothing more to re-examine, no discernible loopholes, we said our farewells. Just one year before, that first *auf Wiedersehen* had bound us. This time a quiver of trepidation gave it a new intonation.

Fifteen minutes later came the first concrete step in moving two people out of the German Democratic Republic: the smuggling of their possessions into the West. With a little luck—please, dear God—we could do it.

Birke had removed the label from her lamb coat, but most of the other things were recognizable as East German. The six crystal goblets and the silver dinnerware were forbidden cargo under any conditions, no matter where they were made, without a sales slip and police authorization. If the guards came across these, we were lost.

Being checked through the border is an involved process when entering, and even more so when leaving East Berlin. If East Germany were the Chase Manhattan Bank, East Berlin would be the vault itself. The guards measured the trunk carefully, examined under the seats and around the engine, and with long-handled mirrors inspected underneath the vehicle to see that no one and nothing was fastened to the bottom of the car.

All was well until one guard ordered, "Display the contents of your baggage!" Busso took the brown one, I the blue, and we proceeded to open the various compartments in the large, fold-over bags. A fork tine had worked its way through the cloth wrapping and prickled my finger. I held my breath for fear that the inspector would notice its pinpoint glimmer in the sunlight. His eyes were studying the clothing intently, as if x-raying it. He jabbed into the center with his fingers, and I had to distract him somehow; "We found East Berlin very interesting to visit," I said excitedly, hoping my German was intelligible to him. He took his eyes momentarily from the suitcase and looked at me. By his expression of surprise I saw that few tourists are anxious to converse with such as him. "Yes," I continued more slowly, slightly shifting the suitcase to a different position, "it certainly is a big change from the bright lights of West Berlin." I had not intended to be impertinent; it just came out that way.

The guard pulled his hand from the clothing so abruptly that I winced. "*Fertig!*" he said coldly and moved on to the next traveler. He could have had a stronger reaction. He could have torn my suitcase apart. I should always be so lucky.

Busso and I spent the remainder of the afternoon, the only unharried few hours of our whole trip, walking around West Berlin. He filmed Checkpoint Charlie and the Wall while the sun was high, and I wandered along the street. At the checkpoint there is a refugee museum that displays many of the methods people have used to escape from East Berlin—in rebuilt cars and trucks, through tunnels, over the Wall, across bridges between buildings, anything to get out.

One of the most recent successes had been a kind of trapeze stunt. A man attached a strong wire to a pole on top of an East German building near the Wall and tossed the other end over to the west side, where his brother drew it taut and secured it. Concealed by darkness, the man sent first his wife, then his son sliding down the wire over the Wall into the West, and it was not until he himself slid safely over that the guards spotted the operation. Ingenuity combined with good fortune in such escapes was encouraging. It could be done.

Standing beside the wall that afternoon, I could see my hus-

band about a block away filming the Eastern Sector, so I mean-
dered toward him. A little boy chasing his dog ran toward me,
tangled his feet, and fell at my side. After helping him up and
dusting him off, I looked for Busso again, but he had disappeared
from view.

A feeling of desolation spread over me. It was a big city with
crowds of people just two blocks away, but where I walked there
was nothing. Once a row of apartment houses had stood there,
but their ruins had been scraped away, probably forming a
mountain of rubble somewhere else in the city but leaving a huge
empty lot here. The Wall, with its rows of barbed wire and broken glass along the top, seemed as out of place dividing a city as I
felt standing there alone beside it. Why this testimony to man's
determination to construct barriers between himself and his fellow being?

Without considering where I was headed, I turned to cross
the open field. A muffled sound behind me halted my step. I
turned back; no one was in sight. Now I stood farther from the
Wall, however, and could see a square cement building just on
the other side, about fifteen feet from the Wall. It was small and
completely sealed except for four slits near the top. Was the
sound coming from there? Were there men inside? I strained to
see, but the holes were so narrow that nothing was visible in the
black void. I turned again to go. This time I distinctly heard a
man's voice call to me. I turned slowly toward the voice and saw
only two hands holding a pair of binoculars out of the "window."

So. He wants to see my face. Well, why should I let him? He
is the man who would murder Kurt and Birke if they tried to
climb that wall to come to me.

No. If he wants to see my face, let him come over like a man
and look; but not from his beast's cage with spyglasses. My back
was to him, but I could hear what he said:

"Come here a minute. I won't hurt you."

"You have guns. Why should I believe you?"

"So does that West guard over there. Come on. Turn

around."

My curiosity was aroused. Would an East German guard actually grow so bold, or so lax, as to carry on a conversation with a girl on the west side of the Wall? Their regulations emphatically forbid such encounters. I wanted to see how it developed.

"Put down your binoculars," I said, shading my eyes with my hand and trying to see into the fortress.

He put them down. "What's your name?" He leaned just enough so that I could see his chin and cheekbone touched by sunlight.

"Janet. What's yours?"

No answer. Then, "Take off your sunglasses."

"Why?" It was fun to tease him a bit.

"Because. I can't see you behind glasses."

"And I can't see you without them. Come out of your box." It seemed to me that standing there even talking to him was concession enough. I debated about the glasses. "How old are you?" I asked. Younger than I, I bet silently.

"Twenty-four." He paused. I think he made a quick check on all sides before each sentence. "And you?" he asked.

"Twenty-five." I too looked to see if anyone observed us. "I don't think they leave you alone in there, do they? How many men have to sit watch in that tiny cell?"

"Two. And we don't sit. We stand most of the time."

"How long?"

"Eight hours." Another pause. He must be very careful. These few words could cost him a lot.

It was queer. We faced each other mutely for long moments.

"It must get kind of—lonesome." I felt somehow drawn to him suddenly; strangely, without vindictiveness.

"Yes," he replied, "very. I wish——"

Three old ladies were coming toward me from across the field. The shadowy face in the opening disappeared. Why did these old women have to come right now? I had to know about the young man. How devoted was he? Could a Westerner, a woman, influence him? What did he *Wish?*

The old ladies kept coming. They didn't seem to notice me or the guard's cabin on the other side. They headed straight for a small pile of bricks stacked next to the wall. There they seated themselves, holding their wrinkled faces to the sun and exclaiming about what a pleasant day it was. I walked around the vacant lot, hoping they would leave. They remained. I knew the guard was watching from his cubbyhole, and when I at last turned to go across the lot to find Busso, I sensed the soldier's eyes on my back. Reaching the street a block away, I turned, raised my hand, and removed my sunglasses for a moment. From the hole in the cement guardhouse, a hand came forth, just for an instant, then was gone.

He was the enemy. Why did I feel so melancholy?

3

MONDAY WAS A LONG DAY OF driving back to Vienna. Silently, I debated whether or not to register with the Embassy my intent to go into a Communist country, as I had always done before; but I dismissed the idea. It would be such a brief trip, only a day.

Tuesday morning we checked out of the hotel in Vienna and at the same time reserved two double rooms for Thursday, when the four of us would return. The manager agreed to hold our baggage at the hotel, since each of us took only one change of clothes in a single suitcase.

There was not much to talk about en route east from Vienna toward the Hungarian border that day. Our spirits were high, but we were tense, acutely conscious of the scope of our assignment. It was June twenty-eighth, a busy day at Hegyeshalom, the checkpoint to enter Hungary, with at least two dozen cars in the large parking area. We were directed where to park, and Busso went into the barrack office to present our two legitimate passports. He was gone a long time, and I began to grow nervous, but eventually he returned with two bottles of Hungarian liqueur and some trinkets. "Just so they will see that we are typical tourists," he explained.

A guard approached our car, studied the license plate, and told us to open the trunk. He glanced at our one suitcase without interest and told us to close the trunk again. After checking the picture, he handed my passport to me. He did the same with Busso's. Then, holding a third passport in hand, he looked for a third person. He spoke no English or German, but he seemed to understand our affirmation that only the two of us were traveling in this car and that we had naturally given him only two passports. Perplexed, the guard showed me the picture in the third document, a United States passport belonging to a middle-aged, nondescript man I had never seen before. I shrugged my shoulders and shook my head no, I did not know the man. Still puzzled, he walked back toward the office, motioning that we were allowed to continue through the next watchpost.

On the road, I examined the stamps. We were in luck: they had the same code number, same design, same color ink as before. Our fabricated rubber stamp was exactly as it should be.

That night Busso checked into two hotel rooms in Györ; two rooms in order to secure four hotel validations on four passports. In Eastern Block nations, the police hold the passports of hotel guests "in safekeeping." The next morning, however, when we wanted to leave Györ so that we would reach Budapest as scheduled, our passports were not granted us.

"They said the police station does not open until nine o'clock," Busso reported, and we spent an apprehensive hour wondering if that was the only reason they did not return our passports to us.

At 9:05, Busso received the documents. Ninety minutes later, we parked by the National Museum of Budapest and casually encountered Kurt and Birke. There was some complication about securing their luggage from their room at the Hotel Palast, but Busso organized a scheme whereby he inconspicuously removed their bags and packed them into our trunk.

With our two passengers settled safely in the back seat of the car, we proceeded en route to the Hungarian-Yugoslavian border, and Busso handed their new passport identities to the two emigrants. We helped them learn the vital statistics and gave them Western currency so that they would begin to look like tourists. A mood of anxiety engulfed us. We were beyond reasoning, planning, conniving. We were in the action, heading for the front lines, and, strangely, I was not frightened as I had been at Checkpoint Charlie. On the contrary, I seemed to be without emotion, in a state of suspension.

There was a fork in the road. The right branch led to the Hungarian-Austrian border where we had entered at Hegyeshalom; the left, to the Hungarian-Yugoslavian border, at Letenya. Busso took the left fork, reasoning that if we crossed from one Communist country into another, there would be less suspicion of an escape. He drove carefully, not taking any chances on the narrow, cattle-traveled road.

Birke tried to maintain her usual good humor, but I felt the earnestness beneath. "My boss will have a fit," she commented in amusement mixed with regret.

"Send him a telegram from Vienna," one of us advised, "saying 'Wish you were here.' "

The border came into view about five o'clock. We slowed to pull up behind two other Western cars at Letenya. On the other side of the barricade, maybe a hundred yards away, we could see the Yugoslavian flag flying over the border station. It was a good sight—when we reached that flagpole, our passports would all have been validated with a legal Hungarian exit stamp, and it would be easy from there.

The guard collected our documents, and Busso pretended to be interested in the souvenirs on sale in the office, while the three of us remained in the car. Birke and Kurt had until seven o'clock before the tour group would reassemble and find them missing. We waited. Six o'clock arrived. Six-ten ticked past. Six-twenty. We found less and less to talk about. All eyes were fixed on the office. What was the delay?

About six-thirty, the car ahead of us was permitted to cross the border to Yugoslavia. We watched silently, enviously, as the barrier was raised for them to pass under. Tension abated for a moment. Now that they were through, we would be next.

Busso was ordered to move our car to a side parking lot. He didn't say much, and the desperate look I discerned in his eyes frightened me as he returned to the office to "scout."

"They know! Oh, *Kurtlschatz*, they know!" cried Birke, at last uttering the unspeakable.

Her husband looked at her compassionately, without answer.

"Maybe not. Maybe there is still a chance," I said, not believing it myself.

About six-fifty there was suddenly a ray of hope. Busso appeared and slid behind the wheel. "They told me to move the car back in front of the office. Now they have got to let us through, they've got to!" He left us again but was back shortly. He moved heavily into his seat, then reached back and took his sister's hand. I covered theirs with mine, and Kurt covered all of ours with his. It could not have been more natural if we had rehearsed it, like a children's game of co-ordination where you stack your hands, then pull out from underneath as fast as you can— only this time nobody wanted to pull away.

"They have called in a passport and stamp expert," came my husband's low, slow statement. Any remaining doubt dissipated: our hoax was ended. The four of us sat dumbly, knowing we would not eat dinner in Austria as planned, knowing we would never cross the Hungarian border together.

We argued with the police and acted the role of indignant tourists in order to postpone the guillotine's crash as long as possible, but when the soldiers, a whole battalion it seemed, readied their guns and artillery, and the officer enunciated carefully in German, "You must come with me. You have no alternative," it was with finality.

4

MINUTES LATER I sat with Busso in the back seat of a police limousine, overwrought with emotion difficult to describe. Out of the back window I saw Birke and Kurt as they stood in the middle of the street watching the limousine rend us from them, and my heart ached. Tomorrow, I thought, I would be in the West, while they were destined to go through hell.

How could we possibly have failed? I was incredulous, angry, anesthetized.

The vehicle bumped to a halt at a high barbed-wire fence. A gate was opened, and the car rolled up beside the first barrack in a project of units at an army encampment. A soldier opened the rear door and ordered us out. He was leaning on the door, and as I stepped from the car the bayonet of his rifle brushed past the hair on my temple. The sensation was numbing. I groped for my husband's hand among the many soldiers milling about. Holding to Busso like a child, I felt safe.

We were ushered into a small waiting room where we sat on a wooden bench against the wall. A table separated us from a young soldier who was to guard us. He was no more than eighteen or nineteen years old, and a pistol was strapped to his side. At short range pistols are more useful, I knew, but I was glad not to have to look at more machine guns.

"What will they do to us?" I hated to speak the question. It was the only question in our minds, but uttering it made it too real and the consequence too irretractable.

"I don't know. I just can't believe that we failed."

"How did they detect the stamp? Ultraviolet lights?"

"I thought of that. No, I don't think so. They would be sure then, but they are not sure. They know that there is an escape in the making, but they don't know who is escaping from where or how it is organized. Our passports are legal. They had to call in this stamp expert to be sure the stamps were faulty. No, I think they called Hegyeshalom—no, even that is unlikely. I don't know." He shook his head sadly. "Oh God, what a mess we're in now. Honey—" He looked at me apologetically, fear turning his hazel eyes black.

"That stamp expert seems intelligent enough. I think he must listen to reason," I tried to be positive.

"What are you saying? We should tell them the whole story?"

"First let's see what Kurt and Birke think. They must help us decide."

"We may not see them soon."

The telephone rang. Our guard, who had avoided looking directly at us, did not turn his eyes from the table as he reached for the receiver and answered in a soft voice. I listened intently, but the sounds of the Hungarian language were so strange to my ears I could hardly imagine that people were actually communicating in these odd phonetics. The boy listened, grunted, listened, said something, and hung up. Then he returned to his relaxed position leaning against the wall, resting one elbow on his raised knee and his head on his fist, all the while staring at the table.

"*Sprechen Sie Deutsch?*" I ventured. He did not seem ignorant; maybe he could tell us something. He looked at me blankly. "How about English? Do you speak English?"

He glanced at me again, this time with an expression of "Who, me?"

"*Habla usted Español?*"

"Give up, will you!" Busso burst out at me in exasperation. "Can't you see he's just a stupid Hungarian? And even if he could talk, he would not tell us anything. Now if worse comes to worst here, don't you start thinking these people are 'just ordinary, nice folks.' They're not. They're our enemy, and they'd skin you alive if it would give them an advantage in the Party. Besides, he's just a punk. He can't help us."

"No. But maybe he can tell us what to expect. They're not barbarians, you know."

"They're not? Let's not test them."

The phone rang again. Now the soldier came alive. It must have been new orders, because he hung up, stood abruptly, adjusted his gunstrap, and went into an adjacent room, leaving the door open behind him.

A few seconds later he was back. This time he eyed us cautiously. That phone conversation had evidently made us more dangerous than we had been before. The boy called back through the door and received a groan and shortly a grumbling reply. Another boy, maybe two years older than the first, stumbled sleepily into our room. Our guard began talking to him rapidly. The new one yawned, scratched his head, turned his back on us and stretched, turned around to examine us, and scratched his head again. He let his shoulders sag and bent slightly to view us more closely. Then, noticing that his fly was open, he stood erect and zipped it.

"Of all the pigs!" exploded Busso. He jumped from the bench in anger. "Don't you have the decency to turn your back when you zip in the company of a lady?"

"Busso, please. Who cares about his pants!"

"I do! I'm not going to sit here and watch swine parade in front of my wife. What are they doing here anyway? Guarding us? O.K. Let them guard." The two young men stared at him warily. "Now don't tell me you don't understand what I'm saying," Busso yelled, pointing at the soldier's fly and zipping an imaginary zipper up and down under the guard's nose. "But why should I expect you to have manners in this place? Where are we? And where is my sister? Why the hell—" Now he was getting to the root of his anger: his anxiety about the two who had entrusted themselves to us. But the two guards were not going to listen to more. They were young, but the weapons in their hands put them in authority. Both had drawn pistols, and the older one looked incensed enough to squeeze the trigger. Busso came to his senses, and the younger watchman returned to his chair, while the older paced the floor, eyeing us the whole time and repeatedly adjusting his holster. Once, he halted his march and pointed to our rings and watches, and my purse. I clutched my handbag tighter.

"He's trying to take our money," I gasped.

"He wants us to remove our jewelry. Maybe he has orders to confiscate it, maybe not. Don't even look at him." In reply to the guard, Busso tapped his finger against his forehead, a sign that seems to be taken with the utmost gravity in Europe—many a brawl has begun with just this gesture. I gritted my teeth and waited, but the guard let the insult pass. "We've got to get out of here," my husband was speaking through his teeth, mostly to himself. Then all at once his eyes grew wide as he stared directly at me. "Do you realize that not a soul in the world knows where we are? None of us. It will be days, maybe weeks before they realize."

A car pulled up outside. It sounded like our VW. A few minutes later, Kurt and Birke entered the room. Their faces were grim and frightened, but they were glad to see us. The four of us huddled together on the bench.

"Janet thinks we should tell them the whole story."

"Oh yes," cried Birke, "I couldn't stand prolonging this any longer."

The men were more hesitant to give up. "How did they catch us?" Kurt pondered.

"I wish I knew," Busso replied solemnly. "We must have been trailed somewhere, perhaps on the whole damned trip." We still had not decided what to say when the door opened and the "stamp expert" entered. He had removed his overcoat now, and we saw that he was dressed in a military suit with brass on his shoulder.

"I am a Hungarian officer," he introduced himself in German, "but I am here nonprofessionally tonight to advise you. You are in serious trouble, you know. You can gain nothing by lying or being silent. One way or another"—he paused to give us time to think about his words—"we will find out exactly how and why you are attempting to cross our frontier with false entry stamps."

"I want to die!" Birke burst, "I'll kill myself!" I threw my arms around her while she buried her head in my shoulder and sobbed.

"Don't talk nonsense. Don't even think it." I tried to offer hope and gradually loosened my grip. Her anguish was shattering to witness.

The officer was a good-looking, even kind-looking man; about forty-five years old, tall and lean, with receding gray hair. He had a gentle, well-trained, persuasive manner, and his voice was quiet but strong. He spoke fluent German, though his accent was strongly Hungarian. For at least half an hour he told us about the advantages of our cooperating with him.

"You need not be frightened," he said. "You are not the first to commit such an act on our frontiers, nor the last. You seem to be intelligent. It is unfortunate that you have attempted to violate our laws. My job is to find out the truth behind this. The easier you make it for me, the easier I can make it for you. Will you co-operate?"

"Listen," pleaded Busso, "nobody need be hurt by this. Couldn't you simply let us return to where we all came from and forget the whole thing? You are in command here. Who would know the difference; who would care? Please! It could mean little to you, but it's our lives, our futures we're dealing with."

"No. I'm sorry, I cannot do that. It's too late. Too many people know you were at the border, for one thing. A possibility might have been—There are means to—" He glanced up at a hole in the wall, near the ceiling, where a stovepipe had once been. He was speaking in a very low voice. What had he begun to say? Why had he stopped? "No," he continued more firmly, "I'll do all I can for you, but you will have to be formally charged. It is the law."

"But what difference does it make to you, as long as no crime has actually been committed?" I urged plaintively. "We haven't injured anyone. Nobody will suffer if we go back where we came from. You are the only one who can help us. Please. We have nothing to do with Hungary. We just wanted to pass through. Let us go back."

He glanced at the hole in the wall again, then toyed with something in his pocket. "You have heard what I have to say. If you are wise, you will consider my advice carefully."

"I think he wants us to bribe him," Busso whispered to me.

"No! If you're right, it's just a trap," came my immediate reaction.

"Is it money you need?" Busso overruled my objections in a hoarse whisper. "Look, I have five hundred dollars here. You could do a lot with five hundred dollars."

"Yes, that is a lot of money. You must understand, I have a family, too, a wife and two beautiful daughters. I must do what I have to do for their sakes." His voice was barely audible. "Too many people have seen you. Too many know."

I surveyed the officer's face quickly, trying to probe behind that disciplined, unrevealing placidity. "I don't know," I whispered to my husband, "I almost think he wishes he could help us. I think there is a microphone in that hole up there in the wall."

"I have the same feeling. He knows or at least suspects someone is checking on him." Then in German, to the officer, Busso said, "Could you give us time to confer?"

"Five minutes." He left the building.

"It's hopeless," Birke said.

"No, no, it isn't" retorted Busso. "If we tell them the truth, they must notify the American Embassy of our detention. We'll insist on it."

"Yes! The Americans would give us asylum, I know they would," Birke affirmed with renewed hope. "But what if we can't get to them?" She plunged again into despair. "I'm afraid it's over for us, Kurt."

"No, not yet," he said mildly. "As long as we're in Hungary, we still have a chance. It's the East Germans we have to fear most. It would be better if the Hungarians punish us here, then let us find means for asylum in the West."

The officer returned, and we told him we would answer his questions if he would keep his side of the bargain and help us as much as he could.

"Yes," he promised, "I shall help you. Now it's late." It was after midnight. He told us to enter two separate chambers, but we begged that the four of us stay in the same room, even though there were only two cots. He said that of all the people he had arrested, few had placed such importance on being to-gether.

"What's going to happen to us tomorrow?" Birke asked.

"Don't you worry. It won't be so bad. You will just have to answer a few questions. Tell me now, where are you from?"

She looked hesitantly at Kurt. He nodded. "East Germany." Her head sank. The worst was out.

The officer shook his head, "I suspected it. I don't know why so many of you try to use Hungary to escape."

"Many?"

"Yes, we get more East Germans trying to flee through here than we do Hungarians."

We were astounded to hear him speak so freely, but to him it was old news. "How often? One a month, one a week?" I in-quired, not expecting an answer.

"More like one a day. Sometimes it will be a single person, like the boy in the cell down the hall; sometimes a whole family. The other day we caught a family—father, mother, and three children. They were Hungarian. But, on an average, I would say three out of five are East Germans."

I could not believe my ears. We knew there were a lot of at-tempted escapes that one never heard about, but one every day! And this was only a single crossing point. So we were not the only ones who had thought that by crossing through a series of Communist countries we would reduce suspicion. Others had reasoned as we did. And others had failed just as miserably. A new weight depressed us—the knowledge that so many innocent and desperate citizens of these countries had suffered by exactly the same route we were taking. Where did it end?

"You had all better get some sleep now," said the officer, turning toward the door.

"Wait." Busso stopped him. "Can't you give us some concrete idea of what to expect?"

"Well, if you abide by your decision to co-operate, your wife seems relatively uninvolved and will probably be on her way home in a couple of weeks, and——"

"A couple of weeks!" I repeated. "But I can't stay here a cou-ple of weeks. I have a job waiting. My parents expect me home in one week. Can't you speed things up a little? And what about my sister-in-law?"

"That is not for me to decide."

"I would like to call the American Embassy," Busso requested.

"Not tonight."

"But——"

"Good night." He turned briskly and was gone.

5

THE NIGHT WAS SLEEPLESS and very long. We discussed the situa-tion over and over. Of where we had failed we were still uncer-tain. But our failure was clear. Even regret seemed futile.

Birke could not stop crying. She wept enough for all of us, but we all ached equally. "Birke," I said, "you have cried enough tears in the past year to fill buckets."

"Yes." She wiped her wet cheeks. "Enough to swim to America in. Janet," she implored, "promise me that if I am sent back, you will keep my crystal goblets." She was generous even in her misery.

It was cold in the cell. Birke took a heavy gray wool blanket from the bed and stretched out next to her husband, pulling the blanket over them for warmth. I lay beside Busso and put my icy hands under his side as he reclined with his back to me and faced his sister on the opposite cot. Reaching across the narrow aisle between the cots, Busso stroked Birke's head. "What have I done to you?"

She slapped his hand, then held it hard and sat up. "Now who is talking nonsense? Let's have none of that. If it were not for me——"

'Stop it, *Schätzchen*," commanded Kurt in his strong, controlled voice. "You will make yourself ill. Nobody blames you. We knew the risk involved. We knew the penalty for attempted escape. But don't even think about that right now. Don't give up yet; there is still hope. You'll see."

The rock of Gibraltar, Kurt. His face was chalk white. His eyes were clouded with doubt, worry, fear. But his wife was not looking at these signs. She was listening to his resonant, confident voice, feeling the strength of his arms around her, and she was less desperate.

Our door had been open throughout the night and the dim light left on. A guard looked in on us occasionally, the young dark-haired one who had first guarded Busso and me, and I felt more compassion than persecution in his glance. About six A.M. he brought us some warm milk-coffee and rye bread. No one could eat the bread, but I drank half my coffee, glad to warm my hands on the tin cup. One at a time, we were escorted to the rest room. The floor was wet, there was no paper, and the guard insisted that the door be left ajar, but splashing cold water on my tired face felt good.

Some time later, the officer, the stamp expert who had arrested us, came to our room. "You will be called in soon to give your story. Please do heed my advice and tell the truth. It will save you much trouble and this whole matter will be over before you know it. I further advise you to arrange among yourselves as to who is responsible for instigating the entire plot. All of you will suffer less if one of you takes the blame."

He left us puzzled. Why should he say such a thing? In order to help us? Did he really think we would fall for it and push the responsibility onto one person?

"He is trying to divide us," I conjectured.

"Yes, he wants each of us to point the finger at the other one," Birke agreed. She stood up. "Well, I'm the one. I got you all into this, and I'll take the blame. It's better than all of us getting punished."

"Don't be stupid," I objected. "This wasn't all your idea. It simply evolved among the four of us. Any one of us could have thrown a damper on it at any time. How can one person be accused of the whole thing?"

"That's right," the men supported me.

"You wanted to leave," Busso said, "and I made the arrangements with Janet's help from the other side. We are equally to blame. It doesn't make sense otherwise. Agreed?"

"Besides," added Kurt, "you don't actually believe that officer, do you?"

Our debate was interrupted by the entry of several new guards. Busso was called away. The three of us waited impatiently, and I have no idea how long he was gone—it seemed forever. When he returned, he sat on one of the cots and buried his face in his hands. "I told them the whole story, exactly as it happened. I told them why, too, about Birke's TB, and her heart condition, and of course about little Susie. I told them how I planned the escape, but I don't think they believed me. The officer just kept asking me questions and translating them for the secretary to type in Hungarian. I think they think there is some organization behind us. It was so well planned, the officer said." His voice trailed off, then he became optimistic. "I can't quite figure that officer out. He seems sincerely to want to help us, but on the other hand, I know damned well you can't trust these people. If he does want to help, he has the rank to do it."

I was called next and taken to the interrogation room. The officer sat beside his desk and offered me a straight-backed wooden chair in front of him. On the other side of the desk sat a fat, uniformed man who spoke only a few words of Hungarian to the officer throughout the interview. A secretary recorded what was dictated to her.

"You must relax. Just tell me the facts. Where were you born?"

"Seattle, Washington, U.S.A."

"How many years of schooling have you had?"

"Fourteen." At this point he evidently translated my answer to the fat man, who peered at me more intensely and grunted. I wondered how many years' schooling he had had, apart from political or military indoctrination.

"What is your work?"

"Lab technician."

"The name of the company?"

I hesitated. It made me uncomfortable to give names, as though I were pinpointing the building on a map so they could bomb it, but it occurred to me that perhaps this was their way of checking to see if I was truthful.

"Crescent Foods Company." I began to feel nauseated.

The questioning continued. "Mother's maiden name?"

"What?"

"The name of your mother before she married?"

Mom? What did they want her maiden name for? What were they up to? I don't want Mom to hear about this. She'll worry herself to death. She'll know I lied. With a certain horror I remembered the day I decided not to tell my parents the truth. No, I couldn't let the police contact and alarm them. I had to explain it myself.

I began to cry. "What good is all this information to you? Why can't you just let us go back home? You're splitting up our family as it is, condemning them to live where they don't want to. Isn't that enough?" I had lapsed into English.

"I can certainly understand your concern for your family. But you should have thought of that before," he said dryly. "Please control yourself and answer the question." He had lost his cordiality and was speaking in stern command now.

No, Busso, this man is not going to help us one bit. And he will not allow anyone else to, not the Consulate, not anyone.

The questions continued, but my mind was in turmoil: If we tell the exact truth, they will not have to go through a long tedious investigation. They will know then that just the four of us are involved and will let us go sooner. I forced myself to concentrate on answering as clearly as I could. My German often failed me, but the officer understood quite a bit of English, so I injected explanations in my own tongue.

"When did you first meet your relatives in East Germany?"

"In December 1964."

"And is that when you decided to help them leave their country?"

"No. No, it was later, much later."

"When?"

"We never really decided in East Germany at all. We didn't have any idea whether we could help them or not until we returned to the States."

"When did you actually decide for sure?"

"For sure? That was not until we knew they were going to take this tour to Hungary. It was confirmed in May, not quite two months ago."

"Your husband mentioned your sister-in-law's health. Tell me about that."

Tears flowed unchecked down my cheeks now as I thought of Birke and Kurt. It was so unjust.

"My sister-in-law had TB for many years as a child. Now she has a weak heart. She lost her baby——"

"Who planned the escape?"

"All four of us."

"But it was mainly one person's idea. Which one of you encouraged the others and did the actual organizing?"

"Nobody!" I shouted, "all of us!"

"But you don't speak German well enough to plan and carry out all these details. And I doubt that you are so familiar with Europe. Your husband did, didn't he?" His voice was not exactly soft, either.

"We did it together," I replied flatly. What were they after? What did they plan to do, execute Busso?

"Look, I am trying to help you," he said in English.

I stared at him. "Help me? Then let me go!"

He shook his head. "Did your sister-in-law first ask you and your husband to help, or did you make the plan first and tell them about it?"

He was trying to trap me. Even if I did answer well, what was he translating into Hungarian for the secretary to type?

"All four of us thought of it at the same time. And you must believe me, there was no organization behind us and no political connection to it."

By the time the officer had examined me to his complete satisfaction, I was empty. There seemed to be nothing left inside me except pain, and for the first time since our arrest, a raw fear. Up to now I had somehow insulated myself against the real danger of the situation. Now it hit me. Whatever I said would be used against me. Against all of us. We had fallen into a pit, and the more we scrambled, the more the sand slipped away from under our feet.

I was still weeping when the guard brought me back to our quarters. Busso jumped up anxiously. "Sweetheart, what did he do to you?" He had never seen me so unraveled before. "What's wrong?" he implored.

"Nothing. Nothing," I sobbed into his chest. "It's just that—I —we— They are really going to send Birke and Kurt back to the Zone. Nobody can help us. There's nothing we can do to stay together. We— We'll never see each other again!" I was saying it, but it still didn't seem possible. How could people do this to other people? How could we all be helplessly controlled, chastised just for wanting to cross a line?

Kurt and Birke were each called in turn to give their versions of the story. Then we were told that a car was coming to pick us up the next morning at eleven A.M. We would be transported to Budapest.

And then? The officer was reluctant to predict our future. "There will be an investigation." What good had it done to cooperate? "The East Germans may face charges in their own country."

"If you deport them, then deport us, too," I pleaded. "Send us to our own country to be dealt with." It was a ridiculous try, but I said it anyway.

He smiled tolerantly. "We have an agreement with the G.D.R. We do not have one with the United States."

"But that is political. We are not fighting a political cause. We're just a family seeking to be together," I argued, knowing how ludicrous my words were to him.

"Well, it's out of my jurisdiction now. I've done my best for you. Good luck."

"Thank you."

We thanked him. I later looked back on those thanks with acrid irony: It was like the lamb ingratiating himself to the slaughterer.

For a short time, in spite of my husband's objections, I tried to talk with the guards. The older guard brought a Hungarian-German dictionary in which we looked up words to express ourselves. Military service is obligatory for all Hungarian men for a

two-year period after their eighteenth birthday, they told me.
The older boy would be finished soon and planned to be married.
The younger was unhappy at the prospect of another eighteen
months' duty. I also learned something else from the boys who,
merely through a little communication, seemed to undergo instant metamorphosis from savage captors to average young men
like young men the world over. If we had been caught in Yugoslavia, they told me, we would have been detained in jail for fifteen days.

And in Hungary? "In Magyar?" I asked. They shrugged;
neither boy would commit himself.

Fifteen days. Maybe, just maybe I could endure that, but no
longer.

We remained lying on the cots, one couple on each cot, as we
waited through the endless night and into the next morning for
the Budapest envoy to come for us. He didn't come at eleven
A.M. or later at one o'clock. Then they told us six P.M. for sure.
He still didn't arrive. In a sense we were glad: Who knew where
he would take us? And yet we were impatient: Let's get it over
with.

It was after nine o'clock that night when the car from Budapest finally arrived. A tall, sandy-haired officer came to survey us.
He spoke a poor German, worse than mine. Birke and Kurt were
ordered into the car in which he had arrived.

"Wait!" I threw my arms around Kurt as Busso did around
his sister. "We'll see you in Budapest." Kurt simply nodded, perhaps sensing that I was fooling myself. The depth of pain in his
eyes was indescribable. Birke and I embraced without a word,
and then the officer took us each by the shoulder and told us to
get moving.

Busso and I were ordered into the back seat of our rented car.
A Hungarian chauffeured. Beside him rode an obese guard who
kept an eye on us. The driver was not familiar with the shift
sticks of Western cars. He started out in second gear.

"Clutch it, you fool! Stop! Put it in first gear first," Busso instructed. Neither the driver nor the guard understood German or English. Both looked uneasy as we jolted forward. As the driver stepped on the gas the car gradually picked up speed. He stepped on the clutch to shift but couldn't find third. Busso, ready to bound into the front seat, reached forward and shifted into third gear. The driver nodded gratefully and grunted something. It went on like that halfway to Budapest before the chauffeur mastered the gears. If I hadn't been so benumbed, I would have laughed.

We had been forbidden by the blond officer to talk, but in the back seat, I rested my head on Busso's shoulder so that I could whisper into his ear the whole time. How often in the endless lonely days and nights that followed did I remember with acute poignancy those last moments we shared.

Part Two

6

At last our journey halted in front of two giant doors on a street in the middle of Budapest. A guard stood on each side of the passageway, which ended two car lengths ahead at another double door. We waited behind the officer's car for the door behind us to be closed and the one in front to open. On the other side of the second door our chauffeur, again with Busso's help in finding reverse, parked among at least a dozen different foreign cars, and then we were ordered out.

Climbing from the car, like an animal sensing danger, I tensed. I looked around and saw above me, on a platform about twenty feet high, the danger I had sensed: A guard stood with a tommy gun strapped to his shoulder and the barrel pointed at me. Four high brick walls prevented me from doing anything but stare. We were in a prison, a top-security prison.

Get hold of yourself, girl. What difference does it make where they complete the red tape?

My nerves did not respond. I felt snared between despair and anxiety, completely isolated. Again I looked around. Where were Kurt and Birke? I had seen them getting out of their car, and I had seen a guard motion Busso to hurry and open the trunk of our car. Then I had to climb back into our car to get my overnight bag, and abruptly everyone vanished. My heart pounded wildly. Never, not once in the past two days had I been so frenzied. All of a sudden I was alone—alone—helpless—terrified.

Don't let them take Birke and Kurt away; help them!

My head was pounding with the beating of my pulse. I followed the guard into a hallway. Halfway down, on the left, was a row of low, green wooden doors. A second guard opened one of them and revealed a small closet, about three by three, with a board dividing it about knee high. The guard made a motion toward the bench and said something in Hungarian. Understanding the gesture, I placed my overnight bag on the bench and stepped back so he could close the closet door. At the end of the hall I noted a black iron gate with a third guard watching us from the other side.

Suddenly I felt a yank on my arm, and before I could resist, I was sitting on the bench beside my bag in the closet.

"Hey, wait! What are you—?" Oh my God, they can't lock me in here!

In that moment I knew what hell it is to have claustrophobia. I was trapped. Everything in me said get out! Unreasoning dread seized me. What kept me from shouting and pounding the walls I don't know. I tried to change position and couldn't. There was no space. Minutes must have passed. I recall my weak voice finding itself, "Busso, where are you? They have locked me in a closet." But I said it half to myself, not expecting him to hear me.

Footsteps quickly approached and the closet door shook with the hammering of the guard. *"Nicht sprechen!"*

After several seconds, a reply came through. "I know." The voice was faint, filled with remorse, scarcely recognizable as that of my husband. "I'm in one, too." When the guard again clamored for silence, both our vertical coffin doors shook so that I thought the man's fist would pierce the wood. Time seemed interminable before my closet door was opened. When the latch was finally released, I stood up and walked into the hall feeling only a simple gratitude to be out of the cage.

The guard indicated that I should go to a room down the corridor. I obeyed like a robot. Just inside the doorway stood my sister-in-law. She was wearing a dark blue, long-sleeved flannel dress that didn't belong to her. Her eyes were downcast and her face wet.

"Oh Birke." I embraced her, not knowing what to say.

"No. No," she said in a monotone. "Don't touch me. I——"

Her words, her withdrawal struck me as the manner in which a dying animal instinctively crawls away to be alone when it knows death is near. Her distraught eyes searched my face momentarily, then, finding no answer, no help, no consolation, hid themselves quickly under glistening, dripping lashes.

I was ushered into the room, she out, and the door closed. Three men were in the room. One was in a guard's blue-gray uniform, another also in uniform but covered by a faded blue smock, the third in a filthy white smock that hung sloppily on his body, allowing the unbuttoned front edges of the hem to dust the floor as he shuffled about. Not one of the three men spoke more than a few words of German.

At a desk near the door sat the one in the blue smock, a chubby man. He could not pronounce my name, but it was unimportant. I was only going to be here a matter of days—wasn't I? Why so much red tape?

The man pointed at my watch, bracelet, locket, and wedding ring. He showed me an envelope in which they must be put. Obediently I removed all but the wedding ring. The tall guard, the one in full uniform, reached for my hand and I stepped back quickly, demonstrating for all three that the ring would not pass over my knuckle. The guard took a firm grip of my arm and pulled me toward a sink at the back of the room. He swept a bar of soap into the sink and turned on the water.

I pleaded. The guard picked up the wet soap and slapped it insistently into my hand. He won. I lost my ring, but it would only be for a matter of——

As soon as that was finished, the short man in the dirty white smock took me by the arm and led me to the other side of the room. He had little hair, and his red face was pock-marked—more from grime than from any illness, I surmised. He drew a gray blanket across so that it served as a curtain. It was held by safety pins to a wire running from one wall to another. I sat on the only wooden chair behind the curtain and braced myself, unwillingly conjecturing what was coming.

"*Stehen!*" the dirty man commanded, making motions to show that I should remove my clothes.

No. No, not this too. Haven't you stripped me of enough without taking my clothing?

I sat down again, shaking my head. The little man threw up his hands and raised his voice. He could curse as long as he pleased; I would not comply. The uniformed guard came behind the curtain, his hands on his hips. He glared ominously at me and licked his lips. "If you don't take them off, I will," his look said. Slowly, I stood and began to undress. The two men left me. When the "doctor" returned a minute later, I sat in my underslip. Exasperated, he shouted at me and indicated that I was to remove everything.

Repulsed by his gaze, I stood naked before the dirty little man.

This is a doctor? This foul-looking, grunting ape crouching with impatience and goggling? If he touches me, I'll vomit.

As though he read my thoughts, he stood at some distance and studied my form. He came close then and peered at my breasts. With his finger tips, he took my arm by the wrist and examined the pits. Recoiling, I closed my eyes. When I opened them a second later, he was squatting a little, his hands bracing his arms on his knees, and studying my pubic hair for scars or disease. He motioned for me to turn around, grunted, then threw a dark blue dress into my hands. My panties, nylon stockings, and shoes were also given me—but no garter belt for the stockings, and no bra. I was left alone to dress.

In the same kind of uniform Birke had had on, I followed the "doctor" out of the room and down the hall. The guard at the gate opened it.

I was led through more iron gates, up stairs, down hallways. The corridors were always vacant except for a guard at each end. The tour ended in a narrow room with lots of bottles on a table. It was not only cluttered, but unclean. I recognized it as a laboratory only because it was on a par with the shabby doctor who made use of it. He handed me a bottle, like a pint-sized milk-bottle, and grunted.

You expect me to urinate? Now? Here?

There was neither a toilet, nor tissue. The doctor walked past me and into the hall, closing the door only halfway behind him. I looked at the bottle. Surprisingly, it was clean. I had needed to urinate ever since the journey over rough roads, and though I had consumed no liquid, my abdomen felt bloated and turgid. I could not see the doctor at the door, but I could hear him whistling to himself nearby. I had to go.

But I can't! Not here, not in a milk bottle! Wait a minute; have they got me so scared that I can't even function properly? You're going to burst. Do it, Janet.

I found some paper on the table and completed the necessary task, feeling a certain strength return to my limp body as I realized that I still could control its functions with almost dainty precision in spite of crude facilities.

In another room the doctor sat down at a desk and told me to sit in a chair beside it. Copying my name from a piece of paper, he asked in German, "*Geburtstag?*"

"June 14, 1941."

"*Mutters Geburtsname?*"

Why do they always ask for my mother's name, and her maiden name at that? What are they up to? Oh Mom, Mommy.

Tears rolled down my cheeks—whether or not they had stopped during the past two hours, I didn't know. I felt very tired.

A guard then took me down the hall, down some stairs, through more gates, until he knocked on a door. A short, squat man opened the door wearing only his undershorts. The guard talked to the little man as the latter pulled on his trousers and shirt. Both of them turned to me and directed me to stand in the middle of the room. I watched as the sleepy man went to a closet. There were pictures of nude women on the walls and under the desk's glass cover. A snapshot of a woman and two children stood on top of the desk. Nothing else decorated the small chamber.

The two guards were doing something at the closet, and I had but a foggy interest. This really wasn't happening, not to me. From the cupboard the little guard handed me some cloth articles and ushered me outside and down the hall. It was a wide hall, but the walking space was narrow because a railed-off area cut through the middle. Dark-brown doors punctured the white walls at even intervals on each side of the corridor.

We stopped at the fifth door on the right, number sixteen. One guard opened the door, and the little one rushed in, snatching the articles from my hands as he did so. Taking one—it was a heavy, yellowed cotton sheet—he showed me that it must be spread out on the bed, the other sheet over it, the two blankets that lay folded on the end of the bed over that, and that I must then lay myself in the bed and sleep. I stared at him, unmoving.

Now that he was fully awake he was energetic, with the mien of a bantam rooster. The man was not unkind, but I had no interest in his demonstration. The bantam rooster looked a little perplexed, but not perturbed, and so repeated the bed-making lesson. Halfway through, he realized that I was not responding, so he made the bed himself and dusted his hands in irritation, and both guards left the cell. The cell. I was in prison. It seemed incredible. I was in prison.

I felt as though someone had hurled a brick into my stomach. I thought I could not take another breath, so powerful was the blow. Throwing myself on the cot, I believed that life would drain from me, that I could not endure the agony inside me, that I must suffocate from heartbreak.

For a long while I lay face down before realizing that I could no longer cry. My face was dry and stiff. Gradually I rose and took notice of my surroundings. This was no cell as I had imagined a cell. This was a dungeon. The door which separated me from existence had been bolted at the top and at the bottom, and also locked twice in the middle. Plated with metal on both sides, the door itself must have been made of solid oak at least four inches thick. The cot on which I now sat was simply a board, six feet long and two and a half feet wide, or maybe a little narrower. An aisle not much more than a foot wide separated it from a second, identical berth. The cots were each supported by four steel legs cemented to the floor. Under my cot were flat radiator pipes; they were cold, not in use in July, in spite of the dank atmosphere. Opposite the door, above the end of the beds, was a window. The glass was opaque. Its wooden frame was attached to the sill at the bottom so that the window opened about six or eight inches at the top. The tapered opening was then protected by a wide board on each side which protruded out several inches into the room. Stretched from one side to the other, screening the already masked window, was a heavy black wire mesh-work. With all that fortification, one had to look twice to note that there actually was a window in the cell. Needless to say, there was no way to see out.

Next to the door was a very old, cracked and rusted cast-iron toilet bowl with neither seat nor cover. No water container was visible over it. Can't it be flushed? I wondered abstractly, and it took me a long while to realize that the water was contained in a vessel sealed inside the wall. A rusty steel pedal on the floor released the water to flush.

My funereal setting was visible now by the dim illumination of a light bulb over the door. A wire screen had been attached to the wall to shield the globe, but the screen hung ajar. One glance at the cell—in a much shorter moment than necessary to describe it—sufficed. After that my eyes concentrated on the door. Shivering, I huddled under both wool blankets, which themselves felt damp, and sat leaning against the wall facing the door. About five feet from the floor, in the door, was a round hole perhaps two and a half inches in diameter, covered by a piece of metal with small holes cut in it as in a colander. It has an appropriately insidious name, which I learned later: the *spy*. I spent the remainder of the night staring at that orifice.

7

ABYSMAL DEPRESSION NOTWITHSTANDING, that first night in solitary somehow passed. I knew it was morning only by the sounds of activity in the corridor, sounds of metal keys in locks, sounds of footsteps approaching my door quickly. My light went out, I was left in semi-darkness, and the footsteps hurried on. Soon there were other steps, different feet. These didn't stop at my door. These feet were not clothed in jailer's boots. Were they prisoners' feet? A woman's feet? Birke's feet? Pressing my ear to the metal plated door, I listened intently.

"Busso! Birke!" Cleated boots advanced toward my cell and a fist pounded on the door. *"Pofa be!"*

I could hear water at the end of the hall, evidently falling a long distance into a pool. The footsteps returned more slowly and passed my door again, then more steps, this time from across the hall—boots and soft soles too. Maybe this was an overnight station and the guards were now releasing the prisoners. Yes, it must be something like that. The officer has said this was just a formality, that as soon as our story was officially recorded, we could go. He said I would be released in no time.

Why do you work yourself into such a tizzy, Janet? Be patient for a day or two. But what exactly did the officer say?

Co-operate and it will go much easier for you. What will go much easier? What day is this? June twenty-eighth? No, it was June twenty-ninth when we drove to the border. June thirtieth has passed too. July first—today must be July first. Our plane will fly from Frankfurt on July sixth. Oh God, let us be on that plane. In conscious prayer, I knew we needed a miracle now.

The door opened and I sprang from my cot. The little man who had put the sheets on, the bantam rooster, was there with a tall, towheaded, seedy-looking guard. *"Kommen!"*

"Where to? To my husband? Please let us send a wire," I pleaded in German.

"Momént. Nem szabad beszélni!" he commanded, making motions to show that it was forbidden to speak. He looked about my cell, then pointed sternly at my cot. In no uncertain terms, though the words sounded like a 33⅓ record played at 78 rpm, I understood that one folds one's blankets first thing in the morning. It was The Rule.

"I must see my husband. I don't care about the damn bed!" It was obvious that he understood no more German than he spoke. *"Meinn Mann, mein Mann! Bitte!"*

"Momént. Nicht sprechen! Kommen!" The tall guard spit the words at me and started to close the door again.

"Nein, warten Sie," I couldn't let them close the door on me again. They had to take me out of that cell no matter where I should go. With my hand to my lips I promised to be silent.

The bantam rooster led me down the hall toward the end opposite where I had entered the building.

Schnell! Schnell!" He insisted I hurry. It must be important.

By the sound, I knew we were approaching the source of the running water. At the last door, we entered. It was a shower room. There were two spouts at least seven feet from the floor, and water fell from one into a round metal pan. That was what I had heard. The little man moved quickly to demonstrate to me that I must take a round, battered tin pan from a stack near the wall, scoop water into it, take a gallon-sized, crusty pail from another stack, take an old rag from a pile beside it, and carry everything back to my cell.

Was that all he was taking me to? Not to Busso? Not to answer my questions? Whatever I had expected, this wasn't it. My eyes clouded in disappointment. Stumbling about the work, I did as he had directed. The water was cold. It sloshed out of the pan onto my dress as I struggled to put one leaden foot in front of the other. At the door of my cell, I hesitated. Looking at the two guards I wanted to scream. "No, please don't make me go back in there!"

The tall one grinned. *"The Grinser,"* I dubbed him silently. His lips were thin, maliciously curled at the corners. The short one showed none of the patience he had constrained himself to use the night before, and he took the pan of water from my hands to place it on the floor of my cell. He rubbed his hands over his face and arms in the manner of washing, then pretended to pour the water from the pan into the bucket and take the rag to scrub the floor. They left me. I fell to the bed, weak with frustration. God, I can't take this. I will die.

But I didn't die that desolate morning—a fact which chagrined as much as astounded me. I put the wash vessel on the unused cot and splashed cold water mechanically on my face for a long while. Somewhat revived, I told myself that the busy work of washing the floor would help save my sanity—perhaps. Two thin cotton towels had been given me the night before, and I rubbed my face and arms hard with one of them. Then I got down on my hands and knees and washed the floor as best I could with the gritty, stinking rag and unclean water. Although I had resolved never to sit on the porcelain toilet edge, which was etched by thousands of cracks, I rubbed it all over with the rag too. It was the best I could do, which seemed to count for something.

Unexpectedly, the door opened again. This time I didn't entreat. It was useless. The little rooster hurried in and poured the dirty water from my pail into the toilet, slopping half of it onto my "clean" floor, then beckoned me to follow him with my two containers and the rag. Doing as I was bid, I replaced the bucket and rag on a stack, rinsed out my wash pan, refilled it with clear, cold water, and carried it back to my cell.

The cell was cold. I sought warmth under the damp blankets

of my cot, but continued to shiver. How long had it been since I had slept? A day? More. Two days? Since the night of the twenty-eighth in Györ. That seemed months ago. And before that, the hotel in Vienna—that seemed another world. Our home in Seattle, another existence entirely.

My mind was muddled. It needed rest. At last I closed my eyes, but a key in the door soon roused me. The door didn't open. Instead, a square hatch about eight inches by eight inches, carved in the middle of the door under the round peephole, opened. It swung down, forming a table on which someone now placed a large chunk of brown rye bread. I took it and crouched a little to look through the opening.

"*Nein, verboten!*" An angry voice forbade me to look through, and a hand pushed a shallow metal bowl of dark liquid at me. I took it, and the hatch was immediately slammed shut. Breakfast. This was my breakfast. And probably all I would get until tomorrow morning, I guessed. The liquid was lukewarm. Holding the bowl in both hands, I raised it to my lips to taste. It was semisweet, the color of coffee, but with no similar flavor. After trying it again, I placed it on the floor beside my wash basin, the bread next to it, and returned to my cot.

Not much later, perhaps ten or fifteen minutes, the guard again opened the hatch. I rushed expectantly to him, but all he wanted was the pan of liquid. I gave it to him, and the bread too, but he pushed the rye loaf back at me so that it fell to the floor, and he slammed the hatch. A second later it was opened by someone else who set a blue plastic cup on the door sill and poured water into it. He waited for me to take it, then bent himself to see my face through the space. He was dark, not unpleasant-looking, and he smiled just a little. Taking note that the cup he gave me was crusted with dirt in the bottom, I turned my back on his gaze until he closed the trap door.

Like a monkey in a zoo. He should look at himself if he wants to see a strange sight.

The aching in my body was intense. I lay down and slept at

last.

It was around noon when I was roused by the sound of the guards opening my hatch. They passed two bowls to me like the one I had seen that morning—one containing an orangish water soup with a couple of slices of potato, and the other with about a cup of green beans in it. With the tablespoon they had given me, I tasted the food. It didn't interest me. I felt sick. I had to make a plan of action. When the guards returned, I decided, I would withhold the pans until they listened to me and tried to help.

The hatch opened. "*Mein Mann, wo ist mein Mann?*" I crouched to look up at the dark-haired guard. "*Sprechen Sie Deutsch?*"

The blond intervened and demanded the utensils. "But——" I wanted to throw the food in his face. Before I knew it, I had given the bowls back; the hatch was closed and my plan to make contact shattered.

Panic enveloped me: it started in my toes and grew steadily, inflaming my entire body. What could I do? How much longer? How could I contact someone who would get us out of here? *Could* someone get us out?

Outside I heard the chant of Hungarian numbers. Men were practicing something. *Egy, kettö, három, négy! Egy, kettö, három, négy!*

It's probably the guards drilling. Preparing for what?

Weakly I assembled my throbbing bones under the blankets and, turning toward the opaque window, stared at the design of it. On the outside, in the middle, were two wooden rods, one horizontal, one vertical. They formed a cross. I looked at it, thinking of Him. I believed in His justice, but where was it? A lump grew in my throat.

It was uncanny how I knew suddenly that someone had crept silently to the door at my back and was watching me through that insidious peephole. Uncanny, but I knew it. I could feel it without even turning around. A shiver ran through me, and the lump in my throat became a knot in the pit of my stomach. I turned to face the unknown eye that watched me. "I would like to curse you," I said directly, "but I can't think of a word foul enough." As if in reply, I heard an almost inaudible short scraping sound and felt the eye leave me. The cover had been placed over the *spy*.

Rage filled me. "Hey, peeping-Tom! Hey, eavesdropper! I want to ask a question. Tell me, why am I held incommunicado?" It did not matter that he couldn't understand English; I resented his leaving. I needed an audience; someone must hear me out. I wanted to tear the prison down. Instead, I hurled myself onto the bunk, grasping the blankets and forcing my face hard into them. All the yelling, all the cursing, all the screaming accusations I wanted to verbalize to my captors congealed in a garbled, smothered groan, long and unburdening. And when at last my pent-up energy was spent, and my inner wrestling with man's injustice to man and my outward pounding of the blankets subsided, I sat erect and faced the door again. Clearing my throat, I said simply, "What I should like to point out, sir, is that your laws are not just." That ended the matter. At a dead end, empty of emotion, I refolded my blankets and arranged my bed.

Keys rattled behind me and the door opened. "*Kommen!*"

Hope sprang to life again. Eagerly, I followed the guard. At the end of the hall, he paused and gave two short whistles. A whistle came in reply, and we proceeded around the corner. He took me down two flights of stairs and along a hall. We passed through a heavy iron gate and then by a row of green wooden doors. I recognized them as the closets we had occupied the night before. We were returning to the room where I had last seen my sister-in-law. Maybe she would be there. Maybe we could all see one another now. I entered. Only one guard was there at the desk. My heart sank. "*Sprechen Sie Deut—*"

"*Nicht sprechen!*" the man commanded. He pointed across the room to where our suitcases stood and indicated that I must separate my possessions from the others'. I did as I was told, my tears leaving dark spots on my husband's shirts. The entire bottom of the suitcase was covered with dozens of rolls of eight-millimeter film, movies Busso had taken of the Berlin Wall, of Hungarian youths digging ditches; behind-the-scenes pictures and illegal shots of guards, borders, and installations. I covered the film quickly with clothing. What would they do to us if these movies were exposed? It occurred to me that I might never see Busso again. My God, what if they tried to send *him* back to the Zone too?

It didn't take long to complete the division. The guard ordered me to go behind the curtain then and put on my own dress. He took all the other things from me so that I still had no bra or garter belt. After allowing me to change in private, he pulled the curtain aside so that he could keep an eye on me as he and the other guard itemized all my belongings in a record book on his desk.

Resentfully I watched the standing guard pick up each of my things, examine it curiously, describe it in Hungarian, and go on to the next article. I couldn't dwell on the impertinence of his grimy fingers handling my lingerie, because I was trying to conceive of a means to contact Busso. The guard held up my ballpoint pen to itemize it. I rushed over and begged him to let me have it and a piece of paper. To my surprise, he allowed it. Scribbling rapidly, I told Busso not to worry about me, and that in a few days I would contact the Consul, just as soon as I was released. At the top I printed Busso's name in bold letters and then implored the guard to give it to my husband. He nodded and put the letter on his desk, then offered my hairbrush, toothbrush, and toothpaste to me and sent me with the other guard.

Feeling somewhat rueful, I returned to my cell: in my hand, between the hairbrush and the tube of toothpaste, I concealed my ballpoint pen.

8

IN THE CELL, I reviewed what had happened and wondered what would happen next. In contrast to the excitement of the previous week, prison isolation left me with nothing to do, absolutely nothing. I lay down on the cot and closed my eyes. The sounds of solitary confinement hummed in my head: the same sound that a heart makes when it skips a beat in uncertainty, or when it slows and sinks in grief, or when it breaks.

Again I felt eyes watching me. I did not even raise my elbow from its resting place over my face to let the intruder know that I knew he was there. All at once my observer started banging on the door and hollering. I bolted upright and stared at the *spy*. The hatch in my door opened and the blond, thin-lipped guard peered in.

"*Nem szabad——*"

A flow of Hungarian, which I was sure no one on earth could understand, followed before he slammed the trap shut again.

Confused and a little shaken, I returned to the bed. Suddenly there came more pounding on my door. I had not sensed the eye watching, for the pounding at the door had come too abruptly this time. There were footsteps leading rapidly away.

What the devil? What is he clattering about?

The footsteps returned. Two pairs this time. I crouched on the corner of my cot, tensed for action. Keys rattled. The door swung open. The bantam rooster and the vicious towhead stood there. The blond had a triumphant smirk on his face; the bantam looked scornful.

Not knowing what the problem was (Had I kept the executioner waiting?), I remained where I was sitting, my legs tucked under me with a blanket over my knees, and looked wide-eyed at my guests. The blond looked ominous, but I tried to feign confidence. The bantam rooster waved a finger at me and lectured me in rapid Hungarian. At the same time, he tugged at my arm, patted my cot and shook a finger. "*Verboten, verboten.*"

By the time I got the message, my nerves were completely jangled: I was not allowed to lie on the cot, or in fact to sit anywhere except directly on the foot of the cot and face the door. The rooster demonstrated in stilted posture how I was to sit. I nodded understanding, and finally they left, not without re-emphasizing, "*Verboten!*"

I can't lie down. Not even that. There is no chair. There is nothing to do. There is no window to see the world outside. There is no change, no action. I can't lie down. What a ridiculous rule. And the guards get so worked up about it. What ridiculous men.

I had to urinate and examined the cracked, rusted iron funnel which served as a toilet. The thought of using it was repugnant, but I reached the point where I had no choice. At that moment I made my first major adjustment to prison life.

Gradually the gray illumination of dungeon-daylight faded. The shadows of the window bars vanished, and the gloomy atmosphere corresponded to my dark meditations. I heard occasional footsteps outside, then nothing. Later my ears were alerted by new sounds in the hall. It was dinnertime. At least they wouldn't starve me. That was some consolation, but I lacked the appetite to be honestly thankful.

The guards reached my door. The light went on, and my hatch was opened. A tin plate of noodles was thrust at me, and as I took it the dark-haired guard I had seen before leaned toward me with a half smile and offered water. Having washed my plastic cup as best I could, I held it up.

"*Deutsche?*" questioned the guard in a low voice. He had seemed to want to talk to me before.

"*Nein. Amerikanerin,*" I replied, yearning to have a communicant. "*Sprechen Sie Deutsch?*"

Holding his palm up as a sign of ignorance, he answered, *"Nicht sprechen. Nem, csak Magyarul."*

I had no idea what his subsequent words were, but I knew they meant that he spoke no language I could understand. He closed the hatch quietly, and I struggled with the feeling that he was as disappointed as I was.

You're always looking for a friend, Janet. Don't be so soft. Remember Busso's advice. A guard is a guard and you are his prisoner.

The cold, yellow noodles lay limp, dry and untouched in my pan.

The light, about a twenty-five-watt bulb, made new patterns on the wall, and I studied them absently. I sat very still, as if the aching would cease, the terrible thoughts of recrimination would quiet themselves if I did not move a hair to stir them. I must have sat like that, motionless, for at least two hours, until I heard a voice down the hall calling, *"Doktor?"* and a few minutes later, *"Schlafen!"*

There must be all Germans on this floor. The guards always use German commands. Could Busso be in the next cell? No, that's impossible. I would know from the knocking.

Knocking on the walls was one of the first things I had tried. From one side came no sound at all, from the other only a short reply. I repeated the effort many times, but the prisoner next door was reluctant to respond. That was not my husband. How many cells are there on this floor? At least twenty, probably thirty. And how many floors? I have counted six, but there could be more. And this was only one wing. How many more wings were there?

There was no doubt that hundreds of prisoners were being held under top-security guard here. Why had they been arrested? Had they all been helping someone escape? (Smuggling money or goods is more likely. Everybody does that between East and West.)

A man placed his mouth near the peephole and commanded, "*Schlafen!*"

Sleep. How can I sleep? I've got to figure out what to do.

The impulse to do something raced in a circle with the question, "But what?" A vague gladness that the day was over soothed me; yet at the same time I dreaded the night. When I was sure the guard was down the hall, I slipped off my dress and put on the old shirt they had given me to sleep in. I sat at the head of my cot and with my arms around my knees, leaned against the wall, and waited for the light to be extinguished. I waited a long time. The busy footsteps in the hall diminished. Nobody came to turn my light out.

"*Schlafen!*" came the repeated command from the other side of my door, this time with insistence.

"*Aber das Licht,*" I said, pointing to the light.

"Uhhhh?"

"*Das Licht. Machen Sie bitte das Licht aus.* You forgot the light. Please."

"Uuuhhh?"

I got up, mindless of my bare legs and underpants, and went to the door to explain.

Evidently deciding that I had something important to tell him, he opened the door. Now, I felt self-conscious of my shorty pajamas but pointed again at the light to show him it was on, and then returned to my bed.

"*Licht?*" he imitated stupidly. I had not seen this guard before.

"Turn it out, please!"

He shook his head from side to side and left. The light remained on. A moment later, the bantam appeared.

"I just want you to please turn out the light."

He understood my gesturing. "*Nein. Licht aus verboten. Schlafen.*" The light was to remain on. That was the final word, and the guards left.

What kind of a lunatic asylum is this? They leave me sitting half the day in darkness and at night they leave the light on! Sleep, they keep ordering me. Why do they pester me so? If they want me to sleep, why don't they turn out that damned light?

That was not the end of the commotion over the light, but by the time the guard had issued at least five commands for me to sleep, I decided that the only way to end the harassment was to pretend I slept.

From a distance, I could hear a whimpering woman in another cell. Then came a louder cry, but it was soon muffled. By a guard? Poor woman. What had she done? Maybe crying would help.

How lonely prison is. I knocked on the right wall. No answer. I got out of bed and knocked on the left wall. *Knock, knock.*

Knock, knock, came my neighbor's reply. From the sound of the knock, and from the alcove where the door was recessed, and from the width of the window sill, I could tell that the walls were two feet thick. I was in a vault. How much longer? Several days? A whole week? But I was lucky. What about the others? For Birke and Kurt, it might be a month. Maybe six, or a year. My thoughts churned on. What about my mother-in-law and Kurt's family in East Germany? What would happen to them?

At last, Saturday morning dragged itself out of the sleepless night and the light of dawn inched into my cell. Sounds in the corridor indicated the beginning of a new day.

"Today something will happen. Relax, kid. Something must happen today." I was now speaking out loud to myself. It helped. I still felt anxious and fearful, but less confused, more prepared to wait a few more hours until they were ready to come and release me.

Passing out the bread seemed to take longer than it had the day before, but when the time came, a piece of odd, dark-red, sweet pectinized substance was passed through the hatch on top of the bread. I guessed it was supposed to be plum jam. The imitation coffee was the same as before, but not even warm. I forced myself to drink three swallows before setting it on the floor. I held the bread loaf in one hand and the sweet jellied square in the other. The jelly was sticky and looked to me as if someone had played patty-cake with it. I ate a few bites. The flavor was that of un-flavored gelatine, with sugar and lots of red dye added. The bread was tasteless too.

Then came the waiting.

If only there were paper and pencil. If only I could read. They must call me before noon. They must.

I made a concentrated effort to organize my thoughts and pass the time constructively. I wrote oral letters to my parents. I prac-ticed speaking German and French. I recited poems by Robert Service and passages from the Bible, but I usually floundered in the middle and could not remember half. I did calisthenics. Mostly, I worried about everything, even about my own mental state. I shuddered, a new vision coming to mind of how I would look as a lunatic: a wild-eyed me digging my nails into the walls and into my own flesh, tearing my hair out and screeching for help.

God no. No, best not. Use your inventiveness. Find something to do.

Not until near-noon did I realize that on Saturday I had little chance of being seen by anyone. It is true that they work on Saturdays, but just half the day. That meant no one would do anything until Monday. Could I last? I saw no alternative.

What to do, what to do! Time was unmoving, and Saturday afternoon was endless. Something tickled my cheek. An insect? A web? I brushed it aside and found it to be only a hair. I pulled it out and played with it idly. Maybe I could weave something with my hair. I pulled two more hairs out and began to braid them. It was not as easy as I had expected. Hair is not pliable as yarn is. In the dim light I could hardly see the strands. Finished, the braid was about seven inches long and did not look like a braid at all. It was too thin. I tried nine hairs then, grouping them in threes before braiding. One still could not discern that it was a braid, but at least when I dropped it, I could find it again, whereas the first braid had been too fine to see on the floor. By the third braid, though I stood at the window so that the most light would be shed on my work, my eyes were tired. I decided to make three braids a day for something to do until I was released. Sardonically, I pictured myself hobbling, a bald old lady, from the cell.

I searched the room for something new to inspire me. A spider, black and about the size of a large pea, legs included, was slowly making his way from the direction of my cot toward the ceiling. I watched him for a moment, then took my shoe and squashed him. Immediately I regretted the killing.

Under the circumstances, couldn't you have demonstrated a little mercy, Janet?

I stared at the six tiny legs now plastered to my wall and contemplated the nature of brutality, the plight of the weak, the domination of the strong, and the victimizing of all of us by circumstance. I reached no profound conclusion but decided to leave the dead spider there on my wall. Some people paint pictures of spiders. I had the real thing. Besides, I told myself, I want to have one small piece of evidence that a living thing can actually exist in this desolation, even if it is only an insect. It's reassuring.

Or was it? He had not, after all, managed to cross the wall.

9

SUNDAY followed much the same pattern as the days before it. At one point I was startled when a guard slapped a bar of brown soap into my hand and said, *"Dusche, dusche!"*

A douche? Good grief, not that too. But then I realized he

meant that I could take a shower. The warm water was briefly refreshing, but by the end of the day I was again tied in knots. I dreaded going through another sleepless night like the last ones, so I knocked on the door and begged for a sleeping pill—I, who had once been shocked at the thought of consuming such a drug. But that was a hundred years ago. The guard could not understand and was about to brush me off in irritation when I hit on a word he recognized: *"Schlaftablette, bitte, bitte."*

"Tablette?" he questioned, and I nodded wildly. *Moment,"* he replied, and was gone.

"Moment." That was the answer they gave to every question. *Moment.* May I see my husband? *Moment.* May I send a wire home? *Moment.* When will I be released? *Moment.* That word meant simply, "I've heard you out, so shut up and don't bother me." But this once it was different. To my joy, the guard returned with two small brown pills. They looked like vitamin pills to me, so, as it turned out, sleep seemed as elusive as ever.

Whether the tablets were fake or my own doubt hindered their effect I'm not sure, but Monday was slow in coming and equally slow in passing, no better than the day before.

Once, a guard peered in to see me brushing my hair, and he took my hairbrush and toothbrush away from me, saying, *"Verboten."* He placed them in a plastic bag and hung it on a nail outside my door.

I grew increasingly anxious through the plodding hours. I jumped at every sound. Each time a guard approached, I sprang to the door in hopes that it would be opened. For once in my life, I had time to meditate, but I didn't use it. I did a lot of thinking, but my thoughts were generally scrambled and unwholesome.

I remember counting the days that morning, and all of the sudden, I forgot everything else. It was the Fourth of July, Independence Day! I sang *The Star-Spangled Banner* and marched up and down my cell. It had been a long time since I had felt so good, so proud. Damn it, but I wish I could watch the fireworks at Greenlake tonight.

The celebration could not last, however. My stomach began to bother me, so I lectured myself and resolved to eat, no matter what was served. I lectured myself on innumerable subjects, particularly on the folly of not being prepared for this predicament. But for what purpose? I remained in the same inert state. How good is hindsight?

On Tuesday, July fifth, I could hardly force myself to rise from the cot. I had no symptons of physical illness, but the heartache I felt was a very real ailment. My emotions fluctuated between dejected despair and passionate indignation and wrath.

I can't go on like this. I must force them to do something about me, to take some action! Someone has to answer my questions or I'll go balmy. They have no cause to keep me in solitary confinement. Why? Someone must help!—Who?

Footsteps again approached, different from the others, heavier steps. I stood tensely, my ear pressed to the door, ready to entreat aid from any passerby. My door opened so fast I hardly had time to jump back and avoid being hit.

"*Kommen!*"

At last!

The guard turned to me and gave a command of some sort. I did not understand. He stomped up to me, turned his back, and with a sharp snap slapped his right hand into his left behind his back to demonstrate the posture in which I must walk. Reluctantly I followed his example and clasped my hands behind my back, more conscious now than ever before of my prisoner's status.

I followed the man down the hall, where he paused for a moment to give a short whistle; then he led me to the left, through a gate, down the stairs—three flights of them—and out a door into what I now saw was a chambered courtyard. I was led along a narrow sidewalk, the wall of the prison on my left, the wall of the courtyard on my right, to the fourth door. The guard told me to enter and latched the door behind me. "*Spazieren!*" he called through the *spy*. "Walk!"

I found myself not in a room where I could expect to meet another human being, but in another cell. The only difference was that, here, part of the roof had been omitted and through about a six-foot space I could see the sky. How long since I had seen the sky? How beautiful it was, clear and blue and so boundless. I was astonished at how bright and sunny the day was. The cell was dismal, with no hint that it could be warm and lovely outside. A bird flew across the open area, and I felt a poignant sting of envy.—More than envy, I felt disappointment, weary, exhausted disappointment.

The guard returned in a short time, not more than ten minutes later, and led me back to my cell door. At the door, however, I did not enter as I was expected to do. It was not my plan to cause trouble, to fight; but I could not go back into that cell. I could not sit there any longer and wait. Uncontrolled trembling took hold of me. I felt as though every organ in me quivered spasmodically. I was in the drum of a cement-mixer, and it tossed me in a thousand directions at once. A weird pressure gripped my brain, and I searched for something to support myself, something to preserve my stability, my sanity. It was apparent that no one here would help me. The cell meant more agonizing waiting, more nothing. I refused to walk through the door, either too weak or just strong enough not to take that dooming step.

Tears filled my eyes, so that the anger on the faces of the three guards was blurred. I could not understand what they were saying and they could not understand me. It was no good asking for my husband. They didn't even try to comprehend my words.

How distraught, how frustrated must I become? How can I force them to see that I mean no harm, that all I want is someone to talk to, or I will go mad? Is that so much to ask?

The only thing the guards understood was that I was rebelling against their authority, and before I quite knew what was happening, my arms were seized and I was thrust into my cell.

The door was locked and bolted securely behind me.

Nothing had been solved. My inner panic increased. I remained at the door, listening to every sound, imploring and pleading for attention whenever someone was near. How long I remained there, God only knows. Finally the bantam rooster came and opened the hatch so that I could see his face. He was perturbed: amidst the flow of Hungarian I understood the word "*Offizier*."

"Oh yes, *ja, ja*," I nodded vigorously. "*Offizier!* Anybody!"

"*Offizier*," he affirmed, "*gut. Offizier. Telefon Offizier. Gut?*" He held his fist to his ear as though he were holding a phone. "*Gut. Mománt.*"

Mománt? Did he say, "*Mománt*"? No, please don't put me off again, please! He left me abruptly and I had to bite my fist to keep from shrieking after him. "But maybe he really will telephone," I told myself without conviction.

How long can a person cling to one tenuous strand of hope? I paced the cell like a confined junkie must, praying that the guards would bring him the stuff he yearned for, tortured by the knowledge of past experience.

10

INCREDIBLY, the door was unlocked, perhaps an hour later, and I was told to follow the guard. At the end of the hall he whistled, then turned right instead of left. This was not a trip to the luggage room or to the courtyard. Something was about to happen.

I felt like someone must feel who has been buried alive and, with barely enough oxygen, suddenly hears the shovels and picks of men inching toward him. I had little thought of where I was going or what would happen there, not even a rational fear.

The guard paused before every turn in the corridor and whistled. If he heard a warning whistle in reply, we waited a minute. If not, he peeked around the corner, then continued. In one long passageway, the guard pressed a button that set off a series of flashing red lights alternating with a loud buzzer: the corridor had to be cleared so that no two prisoners could contact or even glimpse each other. My guard seemed as much in a hurry as I was. We stopped at last in front of a door on the fourth floor. I was told to stand facing the corner of an alcove, while the guard opened a second door and spoke to someone. Then he ushered me into the room.

At a single desk in a small chamber sat the sandy-haired officer who had come to the border to escort us back to Budapest. I was relieved to see him, almost happy; he was someone I recognized. I folded weakly into a chair, and without rising the officer began talking.

Tears of relaxed tension streamed down my cheeks. I couldn't speak or even listen. The officer kept repeating in broken German, "But why are you weeping like this?"

"I—don't—know, I've—been so—worried. Where is my—my —my husband? And my—my—what are you doing?" My halting words were interspersed with gulps and sniffs and spasmodic hiccoughing. Even if the officer had understood German well, I doubt that he could have deciphered exactly what I was saying— though it is inconceivable that he could not guess.

"But why are you carrying on like this, crying like a baby? I cannot understand what you are saying. Don't you have a handkerchief?" He searched his desk and handed me a few sheets of newsprint to blow my nose on.

"What's the matter?" He gave the appearance of dismay. "Are you ill? Are you uncomfortable?"

"No—no—I'm just worried sick—about my family. And nobody . . . understands a word I say and . . . It's awful—all alone—and every time I lie on the bed—or sit—the pounding drives—guards peer in—" I looked at the guard who remained in the room with us and who gazed at me blankly. "I can't sleep.

The light— Why are you doing this to me?" My words seemed insufficient, trivial. "Where are my——"

He interrupted me with "Don't you have any books to read?"

"Nothing!"

"Would you like a partner?"

"Oh yes! Please! Let me stay with my sister-in-law. Where is she? You're not going to send her back——"

"I'm afraid that is not my department, but I will try to arrange a partner for you."

"My sister——"

"No!"

"But——"

"What about food? Are you getting enough to eat?"

I could not have cared less at the moment if I were eating potato peels. Why did he dwell on trivialities? I wanted to know about my family. I had waited timeless, excruciating days for these few simple answers. Why did he continually avoid the question? "Could I please send a telegram home to—" I blew my nose again in the coarse newsprint. It refused to remain crumpled on the desk and slowly re-opened to distract me with a display of my profuse excretions of mucus.

"There is nothing to cry about," the officer said. "You are not being mistreated. You must be patient. If there is a problem in your cell, if you need something, you can come to me. I will take care of it, understand?"

I could? The gratitude that flooded through me brought new tears. I simply nodded appreciation.

"You are not allowed to lie on the bed, you say? You want to lie down?" Although I told him no, it was not that important to me, he seemed to push the favor as though conceding to my most urgent request. "All right. I'll give you permission to lie on the bed three hours a day. That is all, though. You are not allowed to lie all day or more than three hours, understand?"

"Yes. *Ja.*"

He succeeded in shaming me for my sobbing. I blew into the

paper with all my might, swallowed forcefully, and took deep breaths. The hiccoughs continued, but the tears subsided, and I began to control myself as the officer questioned me.

After many ordinary questions, he said, "Now tell me, where is the man who was with you at the border?"

"Pardon me?"

"The man. When you entered Hungary at Hegyeshalom. Where is that man now?"

I was puzzled. "Man? You mean my husband?"

"No, you know very well I don't mean your husband. The other man. The third passenger in your car."

I stared at him, instantly sobered. What could I answer other than the truth? "But there was no other man. My husband and I entered alone together, just the two of us."

Before I had time to think further on the question, he moved on to another subject. It was all so jumbled, so confusing; it happened so fast. In one breath the investigator was telling me not to cry, I had nothing to fear. In the next he asked in a most felicitous manner if there was anything I needed. In the third breath he was standing over me showing me exactly where to sign the papers that had appeared from nowhere in front of me. And in a final sentence, immediately after I had signed—having heard only the part of his speech which said my family was fine and perhaps I could see them soon, as soon as all the formalities such as this signing of statements and what-not was over—I was ushered out of the room.

Before the door was closed, he called me back briefly to say, "By the way, your husband sent you this. You see, he is just fine." He extended two 100-gram chocolate bars to me. Busso had sent them? I fingered the bars tenderly as I followed the guard back to my cell. Where did Busso get chocolate? In the wrapper he had scratched three X's with his fingernail. I would ration this gift over a long period, relishing each bite.

Again I was in cell number sixteen: the same four walls, the same locked door. I reviewed the scene that had just transpired,

and a fog seemed to lift from my mind. What had I learned?
What had I accomplished? Nothing.

You're back where you started. But at least you know Busso
is alive and here—or is he? How long ago was that candy sent,
and did Busso really send it? He could be anyplace by now. Sent
back to East Ger— No, God, please no. Sick depression settled in
me. I felt I had squandered my one chance. What more could I
have said? What more could I have done? Nevertheless, I had
failed. A new realization spread over me of how completely at
the mercy of my jailers I was.

Wednesday arrived. It was July sixth, the day we were scheduled to fly home. Exactly one week before, we had met Kurt and
Birke in Budapest. Exactly one week of my life had been consumed behind prison walls.

About mid-morning I stretched out on my cot, feeling a little
thankful, in spite of myself, for the officer's permission to lie
down. Within twenty minutes came the now-familiar banging
objection at my door. It didn't surprise me, but it angered me beyond reason.

"Get off my back!" I shouted back at the intruder. "*Offizier
sagt liegen erlaubt. Verstehen Sie?*" Or is that just one more hol-
low promise? The man spat a retort in his own tongue, to which
I replied, "*Telefon Offizier! Offizier sagt* O.K.!"

He was still muttering as he left me. I huddled under my
blanket, sitting with one shoulder supporting me against the wall,
too nervous now to lie down. Voices could be heard at the end
of the hall, discussing me, no doubt. Eventually the guard returned with another policeman. In order to emphasize the message, the two opened not simply the hatch but the whole door.
The man who approached me and began to speak looked amazingly like Hitler; he had the same mustache and spoke better
German than I had yet heard here. "You may lie down," he said
stiffly, "but only for three hours. Only three hours, no more!
Understand? No more than three hours!"

"*Ja, ich verstehe, danke.*" You shouldn't thank him, Janet. That's so weak.

He grunted and left. I returned to the sanctuary of my blankets, wishing I could forget the Hitler guard, forget the towhead, the *Grinser* with his evil grin, forget and flee from all of it.

Later in the afternoon, my door was unlocked and I went for a walk in the courtyard as I had done the day before. As then, I was startled by the bright sunlight and the heat. It was with reluctance that I returned to the dark halls of the prison. Instead of walking up the stairs, the guard took me into an old, small elevator, where another guard lifted us the two flights to my floor. The two men whispered to each other, and I had the repulsive feeling that the short one was telling the tall one that I was a good woman for him.

For the third time that day, in pidgin German, I asked to see the officer. "*Moménts, moménts*," came the familiar reply.

"But the officer said I could see him whenever I needed anything." I received only uninterested stares.

The officer said a lot of things, Janet: he said you would soon go free, conveniently not defining the word "soon"—a promise already broken according to my definition of soon. He promised that I would see my husband and sister-in-law when the papers were signed, but so far that promise has not been kept. He mentioned books. Where were they? He said I could lie down, but look what turmoil that great privilege caused me. And what about a partner?

I made up my mind, unstable and trembling as I was, not to harbor any more illusions or false hopes. Thus fortifying myself, I was surprised when I returned from my walk to find the door to my cell open (one never saw an open cell door, never), and a girl, escorted by two guards, awaiting me inside.

II

AT THE SIGHT OF my pretty young guest, I was at once overjoyed and suspicious. What was she doing in my cell? Was she Hungarian? Was she a police agent sent to quiz me?

"*Sprechen Sie Deutsch?*"

"Yes, I'm from Vienna, and I speak English too," she said with a quick smile. I felt intoxicated—someone to talk to at last! Our smiles faded as the guards stood gawking at us, and we waited for them to leave.

The bantam rooster turned to me before closing the door. "You see? We take good care of you here," he seemed to be saying, all giddy with gladness for me. I must admit that he had appeared at moments to be genuinely distressed to see me so constantly unhappy. Up to then I had dismissed his concern as impatience because I disturbed his routine. Now I would almost have believed he was one guard with a soft spot.

I introduced myself when we were alone, and the girl replied, "I'm Gretchen." She was a petite young woman with round, large blue eyes. Her hair was streaked blonde and cut short. She wore a lavender cotton sundress and high, spike-heeled sandals. On that first day, she impressed me as being too pretty and too well-dressed to be a prisoner, in her form-fitting frock with its V-neckline that did not attempt to conceal her plump breasts, especially here where we were not permitted a bra. I complimented her on her dress, and she was pleased. "Well, thank you. It's one of my favorites. My dressmaker made it from another one just like it." She continued telling me about her clothes for a long while, and it seemed strange to me, there and then, to be discussing fashion. I thought briefly about the two inexpensive blouses I once had purchased for Birke and how delighted she had been to have nylon from the West.

Gretchen was a garrulous girl. As she told of herself and complained about prison conditions, I analyzed every word and scrutinized each gesture, debating whether or not she was a spy. Perhaps she was assigned to learn the "truth" about the "other man." Fine, I decided, let her snoop. I had already told all there was to tell.

On the other hand, some of the things that Gretchen said led me to believe she was anything but a secret agent. It seemed not to matter to her whether a subject was profound or trivial; she made no distinction and had definite opinions, delighting in her own verbosity. She complained about not being able to bathe since she had arrived three days ago, about not having a change of clothes, and particularly about her hair. It looked good now, she said, but when the set fell, she would insist they let her see a hairdresser. "I've never done my own hair," she lamented. "They can't deny me a necessity like that." But then, she did not expect to be here long, just a matter of days; and with that thought her good spirits returned. "I can't wait to tell my friends about these silly Hungarians." She winked, and as she told me about her friends she boasted, "Viennese women are the most beautiful in the world," not-bashfully including herself in that category.

She stood at the door for a time, knocking until a guard appeared at the peephole. Holding up a cigarette, she asked for a light. Instead of opening the hatch, the guard lit a match and held it up to the *spy*. Not only were the matches poorly constructed, but there was a strong draft in the cell, and it took exactly four attempts before one of the faulty matches stayed afire so that Gretchen could draw long enough to get a light. Then she seated herself comfortably on the cot opposite mine, folding her legs Indian fashion under her, and enjoyed her cigarette.

"I'm surprised they don't forbid you to smoke here," I observed, "they forbid everything else."

"Well!" she exclaimed, which seemed to be her pet expression, "they don't allow it much. It's awful! Do you know that I

am used to smoking twenty-five or thirty cigarettes a day, sometimes forty? And do you know how many I am allowed to
smoke here?" She didn't wait for my guess. "Ten. That's all.
Ten." She waved her right hand demonstratively to punctuate
her sentences, forming little circles with her forefinger and
thumb. "Precisely ten," she repeated, again making a circle with
her finger and thumb; "they count them out."

"Maybe they're helping you fight cancer."

"Well, of course! But then Hungarian cigarettes could not
possibly have half the harmful ingredients that American cigarettes have, you know. The government wouldn't allow it."

I soon found that Gretchen had a sense of humor. It felt good
to enjoy simple jokes together. We often laughed over errors I
made in German, and sometimes over hers in English.

"Why are you here, Gretchen?" I asked, on a more serious
note.

"I smuggled a woman out: and you?"

"I tried."

"You didn't succeed? That's awful. I know how you must
feel," she sympathized. "At first I was so worried about my Rolf
—he's my friend—that I hardly slept Sunday night. But now I
know he's out, thank God."

"Is he Hungarian?"

"No! Oh no." Her aghast expression was evidence enough
that we shared the same opinion of Hungarians. "He's an Israeli."

"An Israeli? Wait a minute, who were you trying to smuggle
out? How is it that your friend got out and you didn't?"

"It was a fluke. I was supposed to go out but didn't quite
make it."

It took me a while to codify the history that Gretchen proceeded to relate—partly because it was an involved story, and
partly because her Austrian accent was difficult for me. Besides,
her words tumbled out a mile a minute, and I had trouble keeping up. But we had plenty of time to talk and repeat, and repeat;
plenty of time.

She told me that Rolf, the friend with whom she lived when he was in town, had been asked by a stranger to smuggle the stranger's wife out of Hungary, and out of sheer compassion Rolf had agreed.

"How come the man left without his wife in the first place?" was my question.

"Because he and their son had been issued legal passports two years ago, but the wife hadn't."

"Oh yes, I know. That's their way of insuring the return of the traveling spouse. I'm glad it doesn't always work."

Rolf had needed a woman to enter Hungary using a rigged passport, so that the Hungarian woman would have the necessary entry stamps in order to exit legally. Naturally Gretchen couldn't turn her boyfriend down when he needed her. But that left her without a stamped passport of her own. "How were you planning to get yours stamped?"

"Rolf declared I didn't need to. All I had to do was go to the police, say I had fallen asleep on the train and that the conductor had failed to stamp my papers."

Sure, that's what Rolf had said. I could imagine the scene that must have taken place as this little girl (she wasn't much taller than five feet) insisted that she had entered legally, and the police insisted harder that she would have to come with them. I knew the story from there.

"Tell me about your Rolf," I requested, and she did. She had met him at work and detested him at first because he was so bossy, but day by day they became attracted to each other, and he began to be nice to her. They fell in love, and he stayed at her apartment when business didn't call him out of town. "He's a member of the Israeli underground," she whispered, and I raised my eyebrows in appropriate wonder. I would have disbelieved her entirely, since I judged that Gretchen was by nature inclined to tell stories, but there was always a remnant of truth in her tales. She described to me how she sometimes went on late-night missions with Rolf, trailing some suspected Arab agent: "The

Arabs are planning a war against Israel, you know."

"I know. My husband and I were in Jordan and Syria last year. Outside Damascus we unknowingly camped near a secret training site where Syrians were preparing themselves for combat," I remembered. "A soldier crept up behind and held us at rifle point until he decided we were harmless. Then he became friendly and told us how they were soon going to 'reclaim the territory stolen from our fathers,' as he put it."

"Yes, the war will come soon, within a year, I know, and the Jews will win." (One year later that war erupted.)

We exchanged stories, and I guess Gretchen felt she knew me well enough then to say, "Janet, I think I can trust you, and I want to let you in on a little secret."

Why should she trust me, I wondered, at the same time thinking I had enough to worry about without getting involved in somebody else's intrigues; but my curiosity overruled. "It's safe with me."

"I just want you to know that Rolf and I are married."

"That's great, but why the big secret?"

"Don't you see? If the police here find out that I'm married to the man who planned this, it will wipe out my whole defense. I'm banking on the fact that the judge will see me as a simple, innocent little girl who was seduced into carrying out this unlawful plan because of her love for a scoundrel. If they learn that I'm married to him, they'll never believe that I didn't know what I was doing. It will ruin my defense." She kept her voice low, reminding me that, *"Feinde hören mit* [figuratively, the walls have ears]. I think it's safer to refer to him as 'my friend,' in case this room is wired."

I wondered why she should worry about whether or not I knew she was married, and said, "It isn't a secret from your family, is it?"

"As a matter of fact, it is," she admitted. "They like him, but they think he is too old for me."

"Weren't you scared to come here? I mean, Europeans know

about these things."

"Plenty scared, believe me. I even tried to talk Rolf out of it, but he wouldn't listen. He said he promised the man."

"Was that his only motive?" People could charge a good-sized fee in that racket, I thought but I didn't want to intimate what I was thinking.

"You mean did he get paid for it? No, he would have told me."

"How old are you, Gretchen?"

"Eighteen. I mean nineteen. That is, I'll be nineteen tomorrow. Tomorrow is my birthday."

"What a place to spend a birthday. On my ninteenth birthday I was hardly aware that things like this existed. I was too busy planning a career and dating to be concerned," I confessed.

"I know. I have met many Americans in Vienna, and none of them seems to know what's really happening here. They just drive their shiny cars, flash dollar bills and think they run the world just because they may be rich enough to buy it—Oh, excuse me. I don't mean to offend you."

"No, I know that type of American. Thank God they are in the minority, but too bad it's the spoiled ones who form our reputation here in Europe." As a second thought I asked, "How old is Rolf?"

"Thirty-six. But he looks a lot younger," she added hastily, "only about twenty-eight."

In spite of my misgivings about my new partner, I liked Gretchen. It was good to have company, and I had to give her credit on one score: at least she had had sense enough to be properly frightened before entering this country. That was more than I could say for myself. We talked long, almost until dawn, that first night. There was so much to learn about each other, so many details of experiences with the police to compare, so much speculation to make on what was in store for us.

12

I REMEMBER the first morning Gretchen and I awoke together. I wished her a happy birthday and gave her the only present I could, a bar of chocolate. She commented on the novelty of spending one's nineteenth birthday in prison and ate the entire bar before getting out of bed. "I love chocolate," she avowed, "I just crave it. At home I eat it by the pound."

"Why don't you ration it here," I suggested. "We may not get more for a long time."

"Me ration chocolate? I can't. I can't resist it."

As the first days passed, we both ignored such differences of opinion. I put aside my suspicion and loved Gretchen. Her flippant disdain of the police in Hungary, her unending conversation and unscathed teen-age confidence were rejuvenating. "I have had incredible experiences," she bragged, "more than most women twice my age. Do you know, when Sukarno was still a big shot, he visited Vienna, and I attended his party. He asked me to have a drink with him and he would have asked for a lot more if I had led him on, but I didn't want to be part of his harem." At any rate, Gretchen was an entertaining diversion from my own painful thoughts.

When at last I was again called to see the investigator several days later, I realized how good Gretchen was for me. My German had improved so much that I now recognized exactly how poor the officer's was. I felt fluent in comparison and found myself helping him as he groped for simple words. Often, however, both of us were at a loss as to how to say what we meant. I asked that Gretchen be allowed to help, but the investigator would not consider it. I asked for a dictionary, but the request was denied. I appealed to him for an interpreter, but he dismissed the necessity.

I demanded to see my Consul. That petition was totally ignored.

It would take reams of paper to re-construct the mixture of Hungarian-German-English that was used, so I can only try to relate here the core of my interrogation.

Along with my persistent request to see my in-laws and the Consul, I wanted to know exactly what the charge against me was. At such moments the investigator pretended not to understand me and made an effort to look occupied with the papers on his desk. He announced that he would initiate the questions, not I, and he reminded me that if I were co-operative and truthful, I would be able to have my wishes.

"But you said that the last time," I flared. "What takes so long? I must send a telegram home or I'll lose my job!" I was growing excited again, and the officer looked uncomfortable; he did not want to go through another scene like the last one. Neither did I.

He asked me to spell my name, which he could not pronounce, and give the usual details of identification. When he asked for my place of birth, I replied, "Seattle, Washington."

He shot me a quizzical look, then glanced at the guard who sat near me. They exchanged opinions and the only word I caught was "*Washingtonban.*"

"Not Washington, D.C." My one great fear was to be labeled a political enemy and I hastened to explain, but the explanation was useless.

"Occupation?"

"Lab technician."

"What do you earn?"

"About four hundred, but I've probably lost the job. Please——"

"Per year?"

"No, per month."

He was writing figures rapidly on a scratch pad to convert the dollars to Hungarian forint. At the bank rate of about twenty-five forint per dollar, that would be roughly ten thousand forint. On the black market, which is a more reliable standard of true value, four hundred dollars would bring at least sixteen thousand forint, which is what a Hungarian policeman might make in a year. If I had not been impatient to move on to more important matters, namely visitation privileges, I would have enjoyed the questions that followed, obviously off the record, as to how many years' schooling I had had, how long I had worked for Crescent, what my starting salary was, when I received raises, what my father did for a living and how much he earned. I found myself feeling a certain pity for the poor uniformed puppet who interrogated me. Which of us was really the prisoner? He wanted to know the facts, but I knew the lies that confused him about how poor the masses in America are, and I doubt that he believed me. He probably thought I was wealthy, or paid by the government, and no oath of honor, no explaining would ever enlighten him.

When he proceeded, he said, "Tell me about your brothers and sisters."

I wondered if all this was really necessary. Nobody back home had anything to do with this. They didn't even know about it. After deliberating the harm I might do by answering, I answered matter-of-factly, until he said, "And your other brother, what does he do for a living?"

This was going to be good: "He's a policeman," I replied happily.

"What?"

"Yes, a policeman, like you." It was a poor comparison, I thought.

"Aaaahhh, yes—tell me, how long has he been in Viet Nam?"

I had expected anything but a question like that. My brother had finished his service after Korea, at least ten years ago, long before Viet Nam. What was going on here? Had Busso made up some story off the top of his head? What on earth for? I tried to stall in order to think.

"Answer!" the investigator insisted. "He has been in Viet

Nam for how long?"

I felt confused. "I don't know what you're talking about. My brother is not in Viet Nam."

"Then when *was* he there?" he persisted.

"You seem to know more about it than I do. What are you talking about?" It didn't make sense. Even in German one cannot confuse the words *polizist* and *Soldat*. This was preposterous.

The only clue I had to his line of thought was that in Hungary and other military states, soldiers and police are one and the same. Soldiers perform the police duties: an army, a police patrol, and a national guard all rolled into one.

He wrote something on the paper on which he was taking notes in longhand, then continued the questioning. Many of his queries began, "Now tell me in your own words," but more often than not he answered the question himself, concluding, "Isn't that right?" I corrected his misstatements as best I could, knowing, however, that on paper he made little effort to rephrase as corrected. Several times he read from the statement my husband and I had signed at the border, adding, "Is that correct?"

"Yes, except——"

Then he would write for a time, never glancing at the notebook in order to copy our statements exactly. An illustration of the confusion reigning was the question he put to me: "From the United States you returned to East Germany"—"to the G.D.R.," he corrected himself, "in the summer of 1965, for the second visit, isn't that right?"

"No, not exactly. It was from North Africa that we returned, not the U.S. We hadn't been in the States since winter 1964."

He grunted and continued the questioning. I never knew at such times whether or not he understood what I was getting at. He covered the same ground we had previously trod, the death of the baby, our family ties, our motivation.

"Tell me about the third party traveling with you into Hungary. What happened to him at the border? He had an American passport, didn't he?"

"There was no third man," I said between clenched teeth. God, this was unbelieveable. First Viet Nam, now "the other man" again. Where would it end? I explained that the border guard had asked us about a passport, but we knew nothing then and we still knew of no other American at the border.

A man stuck his head through the door, without having waited for an answer to his quick knock, and exchanged a few words with the officer. After that the interrogator seemed to be pressed for time, and the line of questioning was dropped. "Now," he said, looking at me for the first time during the entire interview, "who did the planning of this crime?"

I simply looked back at him. Did he expect me to say it was not I? Was I supposed to swear that I had had nothing to do with it and accuse everybody else?

"I know it wasn't you. You're not related to the others, not really. You're not even European. Was it your husband? Or perhaps your sister-in-law? Did her husband suggest the whole idea? Who?"

"We all planned it together," I replied with attempted placidity. Maybe it was the expression on my face that finally stopped him short. "Is there anything you wish to add before signing this statement?"

"How can I sign something I can't even read? I need an interpreter. My Consul should be here."

I did not imagine the concerned look that flashed across his face before he said with determination, "But you told the story to the officer at the border." I was wasting his valuable time. "Now you have told it to me and I wrote exactly what you said. You saw me."

That was rare. It became more incredible every minute. How should I know what he wrote? In Hungarian! "And if I refuse to sign it"—which was what I intended to do—"what then?"

"You will only make it harder on yourself, and on the others too. They have all signed. And of course we will not be inclined to let you see them until all the statements are completed." He held up a note. "I also have a letter for you here if you deserve it."

"When will I see the American Consul? Have you contacted him?"

"It is not our business to contact him. Your case will be published in the paper and he may ask to see you if he wishes."

I've never been slugged in the abdomen, but at that moment I knew how it must feel. They would publish it—if he read it— There was little hope for much now, except that the officer would keep his promises of visitation privileges. "If I sign, you assure me that I—"

"Yes," he interrupted impatiently. "You may see your husband, perhaps twice a week. You will certainly be allowed to write to him every second day. I shall try to arrange a meeting with your sister-in-law. Sign here." He pressed the pen into my hand. I could smell his perspiration.

Still I hesitated, "What have you written about my brother in Viet Nam? He was never there, and I can't sign such a thing."

The man standing over me took a deep breath and held it while shuffling rapidly through the pages of notes he had written about me. He scribbled out a few illegible lines. "Now, you see? I have erased all reference to it."

I shook my head in disbelief. How should I know what he crossed out? At the bottom of each sheet, I signed, a gloom filling me as though I were signing my own death warrant.

13

BEFORE I WAS DISMISSED from the investigator's office, he handed me a letter from Busso and a piece of blank newsprint with the instructions, "You may write to your husband in German, not English, so I can read it. Do not write about the case. Write only about how you are. Tell him you are feeling fine so he won't worry. Use just one side of the paper. And tell your husband he must eat more. The food is good." He gave permission to write, then told me what to say.

I had hardly been back in the cell long enough to fill Gretchen in or to read my letter when the hatch opened and the *Grinser*, the towhead I had detested since the first day, placed a pair of scissors on the hatch shelf. He spread his hand so we could view it, pretended to cut the nails, then pointed to me and said something to the effect of, "Cut yours."

"No, I won't cut my nails," I replied with a certain indignation. It seemed in no way to be a reasonable request. My long, polished nails were the last feminine possession remaining to me, chipped and ragged though they now appeared. They had taken my bra, my garterbelt, my hairbrush. My dress hung like a sack without its belt. My hair flew like a zombie's after my washing it with prison soap that I couldn't rinse out. Now, without a file, I was supposed to hack off my nails with children's scissors. No sir, I wasn't about to.

The guard and I argued back and forth, he in his language, I in mine, and there was no lack of understanding. I bent to look squarely at him through the opening and he shoved his fist at me so fast I barely escaped a bloody nose. Then he thrust the scissors with a violent sweep into the cell and slammed the hatch. Gretchen and I knew there was more to come. I let the shears lie and waited tensely for the next round. Within a few minutes the *Grinser* had brought a reinforcement agent, and both appeared at the hatch. The new guard had a louder voice and could narrow his eyes more threateningly, and we repeated the same scene as before. Included in his words I caught something about the "*Offizier.*" It dawned on me only then that this was not just the guards' whim, but that at our meeting earlier the investigator had noticed my nails and ordered them cut. Still, it seemed to me to be a totally unnecessary demand. I refused to cut and, quietly, I picked up the scissors from the floor and laid them in front of the guards on the hatch platform. This provoked them immeasurably, and the *Grinser* shouted a few oaths that I was probably fortunate not to understand, his thin tongue lashing like a snake's. He slammed the hatch.

Gretchen had not said a word since the whole thing began, and I looked at her concerned young face. Seeing her expression, it occurred to me that my fingernails were a rather trivial item about which to bring the whole prison down around my ears, and that I just might regret the consequences. Reluctantly, I took the dull instrument and sawed away at my left hand.

Gretchen was cutting the nails on my right hand when the door suddenly opened and no fewer than five guards, including one with a lot of tinsel on his uniform, marched in. We both looked up in surprise, and Gretchen's innocent blue eyes must have worked their magic, because, instead of exploding at us, the captain bawled at his men to the effect that the prisoner was cutting her nails, and why the hell had they bothered *him?*

With that episode over, I was able to take Busso's letter out from under my pillow and read it in peace. It was good to see his handwriting and to read the words many times over; then I told Gretchen of the news he sent. "I have ordered butter and *Brötchen* for you," I quoted. "You should receive one half cube (5 grams) and two *Brötchen* every morning. Write me if you don't. I'll send food as often as I can, so don't you order any. All our money is recorded in my name. Did you get the chocolates? I'll send you more." It had never occurred to me that one could order extra food in prison.

Gretchen began immediately to knock on the door to ask to see the officer. "If you can, I can order food too. I want some chocolate."

"That's not all," I continued, "he writes that he gets books too. I'll help you knock." From somewhere down the hall came a slow, "*Momént*," and Gretchen flew into a fit of cursing. It was her steam vent, and I wished I had one like it. "*Verdampte Schweine!*" She swore. "They're all a bunch of sadists here!"

"And perverts," I helped her.

"And perverts! Ignorant, cruel beasts, that's what they are." In vocal assault, Gretchen had a capacity to continue for hours.

When a guard finally came, Gretchen said, *"Ich möchte mit dem Offizier sprechen. Offizier!"* The guard looked blank and repeated, *"Offizier?"*

"Of course *'Offizier'* you idiot." Gretchen smiled and spoke sweetly. "Why do you cows always repeat everything like parrots?"

"Momént," replied the guard, returning her smile. We waited the rest of the day. On the following day, a Friday, I think, we finally received books. We could choose two from a stack of five or six, but they were all in German, so Gretch made the selection. At the same time, she was summoned to the investigator's office. I tried to occupy myself with reading while waiting for her news, but even if the books had been graded readers, I couldn't have concentrated, for it was a big event when either of us left the cell.

When the door opened, Gretchen burst in as though just coming from a shopping spree, her arms laden with packages, exuberant and anxious to tell what had transpired. "My sister was here. I got to see her for a few minutes. She brought these cookies for my birthday. Help yourself." Now I found that Gretchen gave as easily as she took. The soft vanilla *"Plätchen"* tasted delicious. We laid them carefully, one by one, on their wrapper placed neatly on the floor, and with a plastic beaker of water, enjoyed afternoon tea.

"Here's the story on our chances," my roommate reported, walking up and down the cell, clicking her spiked heels, gesturing in great circles with her arms and speaking rapidly with excitement. "The maximum for smuggling people is six or seven years."

"Good Lord," I breathed.

"But that is only in the most extreme cases and has not been applied for years."

"What's the minimum?"

"Three months."

"That's still too long in this hole," I moaned.

"In Yugoslavia we would be held fifteen days at the border and that's all."

"That's what the soldiers told me. But we're in Hungary."

"Well, if one is cleared, one goes home immediately," she reasoned optimistically.

"No," I began to think realistically for the first time. "It's impossible for them to let us go now, even if we were completely innocent. That is not the way of the People's Republic. How would they explain our imprisonment for this period, especially if it drags out? They would never acknowledge that we have been held without sufficient grounds."

"I know. Well anyway, listen to the good part: my sister has seen the man who represents Austrians here and has retained him to fight my case. I have a lawyer!"

"Is he Austrian?"

"No, he's Hungarian, but he represents all the Austrians who get in trouble in Hungary. There are quite a few. He had many connections and promised to do all he can to help me. His name is Dr. Kasti. And you know what? He is planning a vacation in Austria so he can visit my folks while he's there. They'll pay him well. He must be very trustworthy, or the Hungarians wouldn't let him cross the border."

I was glad for Gretchen, and envious too. She seemed to have everything going for her—her family in Vienna, her sister here, a lawyer working for her. We compared our chances.

"Don't be discouraged," she comforted me. "After all, what did you actually do in this escape plan? Nothing at all. You didn't plan it. You did even less than I did. I entered on a false passport, a passport that didn't belong to me. I gave that document to another woman, a Hungarian, and she accomplished her escape because of me. You did nothing so bad as that."

"But you are a minor," I said glumly.

"I have my worries too, you know," she replied lightly. "Mainly, I'm afraid that Rolf might be so upset about me that he would come in to try to help. If he did, they could gather enough charges against him to imprison him for a hundred years. On the other hand," she mused, "there is one thing that always keeps him from doing anything too rash," she thought it over before telling me, "his children."

"Children?"

"Yes, three. He was married before," she explained, and something about the dogged way she spoke told me that not everything she said was girl scout's honor. I wondered if she were really married, if Rolf were really divorced. It was none of my business, except that Gretchen seemed concerned enough to try to explain: indeed we did each have our own problems.

14

ALTHOUGH Gretchen and I were bonded by our mutual plight, there was one area where we clashed head-on: the investigator. She found him attractive and "*sympatisch*," the same tall, blond, ruddy-faced officer I despised. To me he was an unfeeling, cowardly instrument of The System. Gretchen thought him a victim of circumstance who could be her most valuable benefactor here if she played it right—and she played for all she was worth. She evaluated the result of her second interview with him: "I think he is falling in love with me."

"Love! Oh, that's priceless." I was somehow unconvinced.

But the fact was, there did seem to be some kind of game going on between the two of them. The way Gretchen said he talked to her certainly was not the same tone he used with me. He seemed to go out of his way to reassure her of her welfare and soon-to-come freedom. He had even allowed her to see her sister in person.

I didn't exactly blame Gretchen for using any means she could to get out, but still I was critical. "He is the most cold-blooded, unprincipled man I ever hope to meet."

"You think so because you're a prisoner," she argued. "I don't think he really likes this kind of work. He was probably forced into it."

"If he's such a great guy at heart, why doesn't he let me see my husband?"

"He told you why. He had his orders. He must do what he is told. He can't help himself. If he didn't do it, somebody else would, and you would hate the other man just as much. He used to be an actor, you know, and——"

"That figures. He loves playing the Big Man. You're young and romantic. Do you think he wouldn't use any means to squeeze evidence against you out of your own mouth?"

"Of course he would, just as I would use any means to fight back."

"Why do you defend him so? Just who is falling for whom?"

Saturday morning I was again taken to the officer's room. The guard who brought me did not insist, as the others always did, that I place my hands behind my back. He was a stocky, amiable, handsome man who had a smile in his eyes and appeared to enjoy life, even as a prison watchdog. He tried to strike up a conversation.

"*Allemangne?*"

"No, American."

"Ohhhhhh, *Amerikai!*" He nodded and looked more closely, perhaps to see if Americans didn't have a second head and six arms like the monsters we reportedly were.

The officer bade me sit down and asked how I was. Without waiting for an answer, he continued speaking. "I have seen your husband. He is fine, you must not worry, but he will not eat. You must write and insist that he eat." His concern was touching.

"But!" he continued emphatically, "you wrote too much in your letter. And your husband wrote far too much. I told you before, only one half page. Now I must draw a line through the other side of this new paper. Only one half page, on one side only! Ten sentences. Ten words to a sentence, maximum. No more. And you must write large. If your husband tries any more of his tricks, neither of you will be able to write again. He writes so tiny that I cannot read it. That's cheating! You will both follow the rules, or you could be made very uncomfortable, you know." Was he implying that we were comfortable at the moment?

I made the same pleas as always and asked, "Have you heard from the American Consul?" trying to sound as though I naturally expected my whole nation to be up in arms over our arrest, when in truth I anticipated only condemnation from a few acquaintances back home. I thought it unlikely that American officials would wish to involve themselves in our bungled attempt to defy the Eastern Bloc.

"No, I told you the Consul must first contact us. Do you understand?"

"Yes, I remember. Has it been published yet?"

"I do not know. Probably." He dismissed further questions and announced, "You will be assigned a lawyer by the State."

"I would like to choose my own lawyer."

"Do you know a Hungarian lawyer?"

"Of course not."

"He must be Hungarian. We shall appoint a very good one."

"Will my husband have the same attorney?"

"No." He accepted no argument, explained that he was in a hurry—when wasn't he?—and held several typed pages in front of me. "It is written exactly as you related the story to me, you can believe me." His voice had mellowed. He was anxious to convince me to sign the paper.

I did not pick up the pen that was proffered. "What about my sister-in-law? I must see her!"

He gave the same tedious postponing promises, looking directly at me, a thing he seldom did. Could I possibly believe him? Gretchen did, and I wanted to so much. He was my only link. "Now, if you will just sign here," he coaxed, leaning over my shoulder to pick up the pen and point out where to sign. I leaned forward in my chair so that his body would not touch me. His presence made me nervous, even ill. He had me at an impasse, and I knew that if I did not sign he would simply harass me, plague me with promises of letting me see the others, "if you co-operate." Why prolong the struggle?

"What about the part about Viet Nam and my brother?"

"You saw me cross it out last time." His face was reddening with anger, and he leaned closer to me, holding the pen. I scanned the pages, but didn't spot *Viet Nam* typed anywhere. If only to get away from his closeness, his odiferous sweatshirt, and his hairy arms, I forfeited further argument and signed.

Gretchen had been asking to see the officer again ever since her last visit. He had told her then that she would be permitted to obtain anything she needed from her stored luggage. We both felt desperate for deodorant and soap. In addition, I hoped to get shampoo from my bag. Gretchen was outraged that the guards would not let her lie down during the day as I could, and she defied their rules as often as she could. If I didn't hear the "bulls," as she called them, outside, and warn her in time, she received a heated scolding, and the door shook with pounding. Ten minutes later, when all was quiet, she would snuggle under her blanket again. She nonetheless resented the disturbance and intended to get permission from the officer. Most important, she was anxious to order her chocolate.

After several days of knocking and receiving *"Momént"* in reply, Gretchen was summoned. She pranced around the cell when she returned and reported to me with delight and pride in her ability to wrap the investigator around her little finger: "Hungarians aren't much different from other men," she mused. "Just a little more stupid." She had ordered ten bars of 200-gram

chocolate (about four and a half pounds), two *Brötchen* and ten grams of butter per day, a kilo of apples, and a kilo of pears. "Oh, I almost forgot. Do you like milk? I ordered a half a liter milk per day!"

I like milk, but that was one thing Gretchen would have for herself. "You must drink it. You seldom drink water, and you throw half your food in the toilet. Milk is good for you." I felt rather motherly just then. At every meal Gretchen complained vehemently about the "garbage" and very often flushed the entire portion down the toilet without taking more than a taste. "What about lying down? Did you get permission?"

"No, damn it. He skipped over the question as though I hadn't asked. But he'll give it soon, don't worry," she asserted.

The next time I was called to the office, I could hardly believe my eyes. There, with his back to me, sat Busso. I said his name and we clung to each other for an instant before the investigator coughed, *"Genug, genug.*—Enough, enough. No kissing is allowed. Sit down."

We were allowed to sit together and talk in front of the officer's desk for a few minutes. At first it seemed as though we had nothing to say, because we stared silently at each other. Busso looked very thin. I lectured him about eating and he explained, "I refused to eat until they let me see you. It was worth it."

He thought I was losing weight too, and I said, "I've been eating as much as I can, but my appetite is not what it used to be, and neither is the food."

"Isn't that the worst slop you could imagine? Nothing but noodles—you know how I hate noodles." (Yes, he had forbidden me to cook them from the day we married.) He complained about the food, about the ration of ten cigarettes and how they had to light them through the *spy*, and told me that he had been in solitary for ten days. Now he was thankful for a mate, an East German doctor who had tried to flee. As yet, Busso knew noth-

ing of his sister's whereabouts or welfare.

"Did you get my first letter, written the second day here when I separated the luggage?" I asked.

"No." I had thought as much.

"English is not permitted," thundered the officer. "You must speak German!"

We switched to German and lowered our voices. Busso cursed the investigator under his breath and I pleaded with him not to antagonize him, or the guards either, because I knew what an explosive temper my husband had. At least now, however, I knew he had not lost his fighting spirit, and that was good; but I did not like the direction it was taking, the hate in his eyes. I tried to caution him, but he was hurt, as if I did not understand his shattered hopes: "You don't know the promises they have made to me, over and over, about seeing Birke and Kurt, seeing you—twice a week he said I could see you. This ape here said I could write you every other day. He promised." I thought he was going to grab my shoulders and shake me into understanding, but then he realized that I knew and he asked about me.

"I'm fine. I have a cellmate."

"Another girl?"

"No, silly, a boy—her name is Gretchen, and she is Austrian."

"How is your cell?"

"I have a cot and a toilet."

"We don't have a toilet in the cell. We have to knock and then they make us wait. You have women guards, I hope."

"Well——"

I hesitated too long. Busso became upset, and I wished I had said yes immediately. "Those rotten pigs!"

"But they never see me undressing or anything. I'm very careful, you know that. Besides," I added, "they hardly ever look in on us."

"Do not discuss the prison!" boomed the investigator. "I have warned you before."

"That man isn't human," Busso judged. "If only you hadn't

come with me."

"Never mind that now. If we had known then what we know now, I wouldn't have, but here I am. I'll survive. It's Kurt and Birke who are the big losers."

"God, I know that," he said pathetically. "But we'll get them out, mark my words. I don't know how yet, but there must be a crack somewhere in that damned Wall."

"Yes," I agreed, thinking that he and Gretchen had something in common.

Busso gave me instructions as to what I should do if I were released before he saw me again. I should go to the Embassy and get legal help, and if the Hungarians assigned either of us a lawyer, I was to pay them. All our money was recorded in Busso's name, and he wanted to pay the bills.

"Your time is up," announced the Hungarian. "You must go."

We had been holding hands casually; now our grip tightened. "Please eat."

"I will, don't worry about me," he promised. "Did you get the *Brötchen* and butter?"

"Oh yes, I forgot to tell you, thanks. And the chocolate and also, today, the half bar of soap, plus my glasses. Thank you."

"And the milk too, did you get that, a half liter?"

"Milk? No, Gretchen got a pan this morning but it's only one glass."

"I ordered milk for you. You must get it tomorrow."

We stole a quick hug before the guard pulled Busso's arm and pressed him through the door. Busso threw a kiss to me over his shoulder and disappeared into the prison maze. The elation, the joy I felt on seeing my husband suddenly left me. He was gone. To what? Would he be all right? When would I see him again?

15

WHEN BUSSO LEFT, I expected to be taken back to my cell. Instead, I was told to wait for some time, then was led into an adjacent room. It was a barren room with no carpet or wall plaques, but it was not a cell. There were two wooden tables and three straight chairs. As I stepped into the room, a man rushed at me, his hands extended, with a broad smile which exposed a single tooth.

"Ah, here we are!" He shook my hesitant hand in both of his. "*Grüss Gott, grüss Gott!* I am Dr. Nagy," he said in German, "your lawyer, do you understand? They have assigned me to your case. *Verstehen Sie?* Do you understand? I am going to defend you."

"I am very pleased to meet you—what did you say your name was again?"

"Ah, she does speak German!" he exclaimed, beaming.

"Not very well, I'm afraid."

"Oh but you are modest. You speak very well!"

How does he know that when I have spoken only the first two sentences one learns in a basic German class? And what is he so enthusiastic about?

"They told me you are American, is that correct?"

"Yes."

"From Washington."

"Yes, but not Washington, D.C." I tried explaining, but his little blinking eyes and furrowed brow suggested, in spite of his nod of understanding, that he was puzzled. "I live in Seattle, near California."

There seemed to be a ray of light. "Ah Kalifornien! *Ja, ja. Ich verstehe.*" He looked pleased and again smiled to display the only tooth he possessed, a lower incisor. "Ah now, let's talk about your case. Tell me about it briefly. I have read your statements, both yours and your husband's, but tell me quickly in your own words. I have another appointment, so there is not much time, but I want to hear it from you, *verstehen Sie?* Tell me how it happened."

He was not young, somewhere between fifty and sixty. His hair was scant on top and his whole face was red, especially his nose. He was a fleshy man, and when he was straining to understand my speech, the muscles in his cheeks drew upward, and those over his eyes, downward so that layers of skin almost covered his small eyes.

I related the story of our attempted escape plan, as well as the motives for it. Funny how it all seemed shorter and simpler with each telling. The way Dr. Nagy listened without interruption impressed me. When my emotions began to get the best of me, he took my hand and said, "Now, now, *mein Liebes*, you are all right. You don't need to worry. This will be straightened out in no time."

There was little sense in getting choked up, and I quickly regained my composure. "But I am not so worried about myself as I am about the others. My husband is very excitable and he has not eaten well."

"Your husband is all right. I just saw him. He saw his lawyer first. He has a woman attorney, ha, ha, ha. She is very competent even so," he added.

"Even though she is a woman? I hope so."

"Oh, ha, ha, ha. Of course, of course. The woman, Dr. Paulinyi, is very competent, very. She will do everything possible for your husband."

"Like what? What can she do for him, or you for me?" There was no belligerence in my voice. It was a natural question.

"Well, first I must study the case. Let me think. . . . Oh, yes, one other thing, you will be leaving here in a few days. You are being transferred to a new prison."

"To a better prison?"

"Oh definitely. Much better, I think. I will visit you there."

"Often? Every day? I go out of my mind not knowing what progress is being made."

"Yes, as often as you like."

I was beginning to like the man. He was not what I had imagined I would have selected for a lawyer, certainly no F. Lee Bailey, but he was the best I had at the moment.

"Dr. Nagy, I appreciate your help, and I will pay you of course; that is, my husband will——"

"Now, now, never mind that. You are not obligated to pay me. Your husband said he wanted to pay us both. Maybe his lawyer will accept it, but he is not obliged to pay. We are paid by the State, *verstehen Sie?*"

"Yes."

"Well, never mind. We can always talk about that later."

"Dr. Nagy, would you please write to my parents? And can you contact the American Consul here? Perhaps you can even do something to help my sister-in-law and brother-in-law. You will, won't you?"

"*Aber, mein Goldiges,* what can I do? I can only defend you in court."

"But you can at least notify my folks and my boss."

"Of course, of course. I can do that."

"The addresses are——" I had to instruct him to write the information down, or he would have continued sitting there nodding.

"Ah, *ja,*" he sighed, putting the addresses scratched on the back of an envelope into his thin, empty briefcase, apparently preparing to leave. I couldn't let him go yet, not without taking one step closer to freedom. It was difficult to think. "Dr. Nagy, please notify the American Consul that I am here."

"*Aber, mein Goldiges,* I cannot do that. Haven't they contacted you yet?"

"Not yet."

"Well my dear girl, I cannot tell the American officials what to do. They will come when they choose to, not when we tell them to. I have nothing to say about that."

"But how will they know where to find me?"

"It was printed in the paper that you are here, was it not?"

"How should I know that?" I began to have serious doubts about my attorney's ingenuity. Where would I get a newspaper —and how would I read it? "Perhaps the Americans could bring me something in English to read."

"Don't you have books?"

"Only in German. I don't follow half of it."

"But it's a good chance for you to improve your German, *mein Goldiges,* ha, ha, ha." I didn't think it was so amusing, but I smiled as agreeably as I could.

During the interview with Dr. Nagy, another man in plain clothes sat at a few feet's distance, observing me. He had not said a word, but out of the corner of my eye I watched him. He scrutinized me unflinchingly, and I decided that this was the Communist substitute for a tape recorder.

"But I should think the American Consul would contact you by now," the lawyer said, rising. "You just wait here. I'll go check on it. It must have been published by now."

As soon as he left, the small man at the other table rose and came to me.

"You are American?" he asked, stumbling in his German.

"Yes, I am an American."

"*Washingtonban?*"

"Yes, Washington."

"Kennedy. Johnson. Ha, ha, ha."

I gazed at him. What did he expect me to say? The man leaned close to me and spoke in a confidential whisper. "Hey, what you do here?" His German was even worse than the officer's. "*Divisen?*" he rubbed his fingertips together.

Had the lawyer left the room on purpose so that this kook could syphon information from me? Did they really expect me to tell a stranger, a Hungarian, all the things I may not have told the officer or the lawyer? I had the feeling he was not nearly so simple as he led me to believe.

"*Geld?*" he said with gleaming eyes. "*Schmuggeln?*"

"No, not money. Not smuggling," I answered wearily. "People. *Meine Familie. Aus der D. D. R.* Not Hungarians."

"Ah, people," he repeated, as though this were the first he had learned of my "crime." If for nothing else, I despised him for his poor acting.

The lawyer returned. "Ah, now my dear, this gentleman is coming to have you sign a couple of papers, and then I must go." The investigator followed him in.

"Papers for what?"

"For your release from this prison so that you can be transferred." He noticed the skeptical look on my face. "*Ah, mein Goldiges,* do not worry. Just sign the papers. It is in your best interest that I advise you to sign. The sooner they finish with the red tape, the sooner you can go home. I cannot come here again, but I may visit you anytime there."

"But I cannot *read* what I am signing."

"These papers are simply for your release, believe me."

"And the reams of paper I signed before? What about them? The officer promised me that if signed those he would let me see my sister-in-law."

"Those papers were written exactly as you stated your story." (How did he know how I stated my story to the officer?) "Actually, I find nothing very incriminating in there about your participation."

The officer thrust two papers at me. I questioned the lawyer again, but he said, "It's all right. Sign." The officer stood impatiently, leaning over me and pointing at the line on which I was to sign. His perspiration was noxious.

"I want to see Birke. He promised me."

The lawyer spoke in Hungarian to the officer, then replied to me, "My dear, it is impossible today, but this gentleman assured me that when the papers are all in order, you will have your request." Dr. Nagy's voice took on a parental tone, *"Ah, mein liebes Kind,* you were very naive, you know that, don't you?" He shook his round head to emphasize his sadness and patted my shoulder. "Of course you realize that now. You were very naive. Ha, ha, ha."

I signed the papers hurriedly and was glad to be rid of the officer at one shoulder and the lawyer at the other. There seemed nothing more to say. I gazed out the window. There were curtains on it, real cotton lace, beautiful curtains, and no bars. It was sunny outside. I wished I could go to the window and feel the curtains, feel the sun on my face. When could I go home?

16

THE "FEW DAYS" Dr. Nagy said I was to remain at the State Security prison, *Staatssicherheitsdienst,* or *Stasi* as it was called, stretched on interminably. At first Gretchen and I had thought we would never run out of conversation, but after a period of uninterrupted dialogue, we seemed to reach a plateau. Few incidents ocurred to awaken us from our despairing lethargy, and they were usually negative stimulants. The only happy occassions included the couple of times we received food "from the store" and my notes from Busso, four in all, the last three of which conformed to the ten-word, ten-sentence rule. I was allowed to write only two notes back to him. Day after day, Gretchen and I riveted the door with our knocking in hopes of seeing the officer, but it resulted only in a couple of brief visits by Gretchen, visits which were less rewarding for her than the first had been. She never did manage to secure authorization to lie down.

"It's ridiculous, positively ridiculous!" she complained. "You have permission to lie down and you never do."

"I want to stay wide awake during the day in hopes that I

will sleep better at night. I'm groggy all day, yet I can't sleep. Do you think they put something in the coffee? Some type of sedative?"

"I'd be surprised if they didn't. Sure they do. '*Bróm*' they call it. It's mainly a sex retardant, or repressant, or whatever the term is. I'm sure it's in that dishwater they give us to drink in the morning. That's probably what makes you groggy and me sleepy. Isn't it crazy? You don't even sleep at night without tablets, and for me they refuse permission during the day, yet I lie down anyway and cause them more trouble because they have to be on their toes to catch me."

"It's just the system here. You know there must be a mike hidden somewhere in our cell," I said, not sure myself if I meant this facetiously or not, "so that they'll be ready in 1984 with room 101."

Orwell's *Nineteen Eighty-four* was one of the first books we had discussed. Gretchen had read every important book I had read, and many more. She read rapidly and avidly. One of her constant grievances was that we received only one book apiece every five days or so. I could sit for days slowly wading through the unfamiliar German words, since my concentration was poor anyway, while she read both books in a day and had nothing to do.

"Slow down," I advised over and over.

"I can't! That's just like telling you to speed up."

Sometimes describing the incidents that transpired in prison inflates them beyond their scope in time. The minutes ticked by so slowly, it seemed that nothing at all ever happened, yet many things now stand out in my memory, incidents such as the first day that Gretchen and I showered together. One of the younger, more friendly guards, a dark, curly-haired man who was unusually courteous and amiable, led us to the shower room. With the door closed behind us—there was no lock—we hurried to feel the clean, warm water splash down on us.

"I wonder if he will have the decency not to look in," Gretchen whispered as she slipped off her dress.

"Don't ask. There's nothing much we can do but turn our backs to the *spy*."

"Oh no!" she cried, stepping under the shower. "I forgot my soap!"

We had both forgotten soap, and I was not yet wet, so I pulled my dress over my head and, just that fast, opened the door enough to slip through—and ran head-on into our "courteous, amiable" young guard, who had not had time to peel his eye away from the peephole.

One of our most persistent struggles concerned our hair. As we were not allowed to keep personal articles in the cell with us, we found it necessary to hide what we could under our blankets. If the guards happened to catch sight of Gretchen's comb or my brush, they would menacingly order us to put it in the plastic bag hanging outside the cell door. I must admit that even when we managed to keep both the comb and brush, our coiffures were not exactly high-style. It was especially difficult because of the brown soap they gave us, which left a sticky film and caused the hair to mat.

"The sad thing is," I mourned, "I have shampoo here in my overnight bag."

"You've got to make the officer let you have it," Gretchen was determined. "I cannot endure my hair like this another day." She was in good dramatic form.

"I don't think he'll allow it."

"Why not? Tell him it's medicated. You have a skin problem on your scalp!"

"That's good. I'll try it."

"Stick with me, kid, and you'll learn all the tricks of the trade." Her eyes twinkled with new excitement.

"I'll sit and scratch my head constantly and make him worry about catching my disease."

"Yes, you'll do all right!"

As it happened, I asked him the day that I saw the lawyer. To my surprise, he wrote it down on a piece of paper and said it would be brought to me. Days passed, however, and the shampoo did not arrive.

"The shampoo is not all that bugs me," I complained. "I feel sorry for you, Gretchen, for having to share this cell with a walking sweat gland. I know I stink something awful."

"*You* do? I smell worse. It's so uncomfortable. Even if nobody else were around, it's awful to smell yourself."

"I could use a good, sharp razor too."

"Oh, that doesn't bother me. Lots of European women don't shave under their arms, or their legs either. They think you're odd to be so bare; kind of sexless, the men say."

When Gretchen was next called to the officer, she told him she needed the deodorant as well as my shampoo.

"Well, can you imagine?" she exclaimed on returning, "he didn't know what I was talking about. He did not know what deodorant was!"

"You're kidding."

"I'm not kidding. I said '*déodorant*' as the French say it. I said '*desodor*' as other Europeans do. I made up different pronunciations. Finally I simply had to demonstrate," she said, lifting her arm and pretending to spray. "Then the dawn came, as though he had read about the new invention somewhere once. He agreed I could have the '*dodor*,' as he called it, and the shampoo too."

Something like two weeks later, the shampoo arrived. With it was a package of Wash 'n Dry tissues that I recognized as those my sister had given me to travel with. Noting my surprise, the guard explained, "*Dodor.*" Gretch and I burst with laughter. "*Nem Dodor?*" questioned the bewildered guard, and he took them away, never to return with our precious deodorant.

We were delighted with our shampoo, especially since the next day was shower day. After a good head-scrubbing, we were relatively happy that morning—until our curlers were taken away. No, not commercial curlers: the curlers we invented. We had searched for a long time for an idea to curl our hair and finally came up with the foil from Gretchen's 200-gram chocolate bars.

"I knew this chocolate must be good for something," I said, twisting pieces of the foil into ropes on which I wound my partner's fine hair. But our great idea was short-lived. "Hitler" discovered our beauty salon, immediately opened the door, and removed the devices personally.

"*Verboten!*" he announced.

Probably the funniest thing that happened was the arrival of the pears. They came about a week after Gretchen had ordered them. She was called from the cell to another room where the staples were issued to her and returned beaming, her arms laden.

"Let's see if it's all here."

"Chocolate, five 200-gram bars," I counted.

"But I ordered ten," she complained.

"You probably bought out the whole store with five."

"Peaches, seven. They're small, but they look delicious." She placed them carefully in a row on a piece of paper on the floor. "So this bag must be pears," she estimated, looking in. "Or are they?"

"Let me see," I too looked into the bag. "Those little runts are called pears?"

"Of course, can't you tell by their color?"

They were pear-color all right, but no bigger around than a half-dollar piece. Some were smaller.

"Well, what did you expect," Gretchen said, holding one mini-pear up by the stem and prancing around to display it. "They're *Hungarian* pears."

We laughed for an hour over the miniature fruit. Maybe it wasn't really all that funny, but we took full advantage of rare opportunities for levity. The laughter tasted better than the pears.

Amusing episodes at the *Stasi* were few and far between, however. Gretchen was losing faith in her blossoming love affair with the officer, since he seldom called her to see him; and instead of blooming, his quasi-infatuation appeared more to be wilting.

"He can't even speak German as well as you can, and he has studied it a lot longer," Gretchen criticized. Where she had previously spent hours pointing out his possible merits, she now devoted attention to ridiculing him. "He used to offer me his cigarettes. The last time I was in his office, he laid the packet on his desk so that I had to take them myself. He didn't even light it for me. Oh well, it doesn't matter. He always gets so flustered anyway when he has to strike three or four of his crummy Hungarian matches in order to light one cigarette. And have you seen the clothes he wears? Not even a suit. Just a tan sweatshirt and baggy pants."

"Don't you think he is enamored of you anymore?"

"It's hard to tell. I think so. Why else would he always bring up the subject of my friend? He insists that I'm throwing myself away on Rolf. He thinks Rolf is still married to his first wife, you know, and is just using me. He says I shouldn't waste my love on a man like that. Why should he care what I feel for Rolf? But there has always been someone in the room with us lately. We're never alone. He wouldn't dare make any advances. Nonetheless, he still has that look in his eye."

"You're an attractive girl. At least the jerk isn't blind."

The days grew heavier and heavier. I was frustrated beyond words. Everything I saw, everything that happened or rather that did not happen, even the things Gretchen said or did, now irritated me. I kept hoping that any minute the guards would send me to the new prison. But all they did was peer in at us and forbid us to talk loudly, to sing, or to lie on the cots.

Gretchen had found that coughing brought the doctor whenever he was around—about every second or third night. She enjoyed any kind of commotion, anything that would make them open the door and gave her attention. So she coughed nightly. It annoyed me, but at least the doctor came and I could get a sleeping pill and fresh, cool drinking water.

Often at night we heard screams from other anguished prisoners, and most nights somebody sobbed himself to sleep. Frequently the noise of a fight and rampant cursing sounded down the hallway, but the prisoners were quickly subdued. And in between these vibrations of life lay the long periods of silence.

Besides not sleeping, I was worried about my health in general. My menstrual period was overdue. I had been expecting it for two weeks. Why didn't it come?

"The worst thing here is to watch your own body deteriorate. No decent diet, no proper cleansing facilities. And when a girl does have a period, what does she do? Let it drip?"

"Didn't they give you any *Watte?*"

"What's *Watte?*"

"Cotton, just plain cotton batting. I needed some when I first came."

"What do you—I mean how do you use it?" I asked stupidly. "Do they give you a special belt, or what?"

"Are you joking? They give you the cotton batting, that's all. You make a little wad and put it where it will do the most good."

"I can hardly wait."

I was beginning to fear I would be incarcerated forever inside the *Stasi* walls. Then about the twenty-eighth of July, I think, the cell door was opened and a guard called out something in Hungarian. Gretchen and I stood looking at him. He repeated himself. Seeing no response, he showed us a number on a piece of paper and asked for an indication of whom it represented. We shrugged and looked at each other.

"Do you have a number?"

"I don't know. Do you?"

"I don't know."

The guard left.

"I have a feeling this is it," Gretchen said softly. "You're leaving now."

"I think you're right. They didn't bolt the door, you know."

"I know." A dark spot appeared on her now very rumpled and soiled lavender dress. For the first time, Gretchen was crying.

I didn't know what to say. There had always been something unbelievable about this little girl. Maybe it was her too-big and too-blue eyes. Maybe the fantastic stories of what she had experienced in nineteen years. Or maybe it was her undaunted self-confidence, her defiant attitude toward any authority. I had never quite accepted that she was real. Along with everything else, I had grown disconsolate with her and had sought less and less to enter into conversation. I had even stopped asking her to explain the German words I didn't know, in spite of the fact that it was my loss and not hers. I was glad to be leaving. I didn't know what lay ahead. I didn't know what I was charged with. But I was anxious to go, ready to find out.

Now Gretchen had tears in her eyes and I was ashamed, ashamed that I hadn't tried harder to be a pleasant cellmate lately, ashamed that I had envied her her easy sleep and optimism, ashamed that I had felt sorrier for myself than I had for her.

"Hey there now," I soothed in English. "Don't be sad. You'll be leaving here soon too, as soon as your lawyer returns. And when you go, it will be directly for home, not to another prison. Think of that."

"I know. Well, at least something is happening around this gruesome place."

"Yes, it renews my hope. At least I'll get away from these leering perverts. I expect to have women guards now."

"Oh no, don't wish that. I'll bet there's nothing worse than a female guard. I'd rather have a thousand men. Women are so jealous."

"A guard's a guard."

"Janet, if I don't go home, if I'm sent to the same prison you go to, I'll do everything in my power to make them put us together."

"I will too, Gretch," I said a little guiltily, for at the same time I hoped for a cellmate more of my temperament.

"Janet, if not, remember our date in Vienna!" her breath caught a little. We had dreamed for hours of how she would show me around Vienna, and especially of how she would show me the best salon in the city where we would be beautified together, erasing all the prison grime.

"How could I forget? I can hardly wait." My enthusiasm was genuine.

"Janet—" Gretchen said my name for a third time as though I would disappear through the wall before she said what was on her mind. But she didn't say it.

"What is it, Gretchen?"

"It's that I—that is, sometimes I exaggerate. I have a vivid imagination. I— Do you want to know something funny? I thought you were a spy."

"I thought you were too. Prison incites suspicion. And never mind about your imagination. You've been good company."

"Janet," her eyes flitted around the cell as if the words she sought would appear on the cement. "It's about Rolf——"

"Your *friend*?"

"What I mean to say is, he's not——"

"I know. That is, I guessed."

"You know we're really not married? But how did you guess?"

"You're too smart to confide any real secrets to another prisoner."

A gleam came into those great, round, blue nineteen-year-old eyes. If Gretchen's conscience hurt from that small bit of prevarication, she recovered quickly. "But you let me believe you believed me. You're just as bad!"

"I'm just as bad," I accorded, knowing that in light of my low moods and disparaging thoughts, her comparison was accurate. "Look, they're coming for me soon. What about the pen I smuggled in here? Do you want it?"

"No thank you, I have trouble enough."

I would have to smuggle it back out, even though I trembled at the thought of being caught with such a weapon.

The guard returned to point at me and hand me my plastic bag. I reached quickly into it. The pen was concealed in my hand, and I dropped it at the bottom, then pulled out one of my nylon stockings to give to Gretchen. She had been using it to tie her hair back, as I did, while washing. "You keep this—to remember me by."

"Thanks. You may not have it as good as you anticipate in your new domicile. Take this peach and a bar of chocolate. Take two bars." I tried to refuse. "I insist." She pressed it into my hand. "Take at least one bar. Look, I still have four bars left" (from her third delivery). "After all, you hardly drank any of my milk, and yours never did arrive. You must get some vitamins."

"Thank you. Good-by, Gretchen,"

"*Schnell!*" urged the guard, "*schnell!*"

Before I left, another guard came to the door with a pan in his hand. He started to offer it to me, then saw that I was leaving and withheld it. I bent to examine the contents. By the odor, I knew what it was: my milk, the milk Busso had ordered for me.

Gretchen looked at it in surprise, "Ugh, it's sour!"

"Isn't that appropriate?" I responded. "I hereby bequeath this sour milk and the whole rancid barn to you, partner."

"Thanks, partner. Good luck to you too!" She was trying to be light, but her quivering chin betrayed her.

"*Schnell, schnell!*" commanded the impatient guard as he slammed the door between us.

"See you in Vienna," I whispered.

"Hurry, hurry!" Why did nothing happen for so long, and then suddenly everybody seemed to be in such a dither? At the end of the hall, another guard took custody of me and led me to the room in the basement where I had first been "examined" and my belongings had been confiscated. One of the guards snatched the small plastic bag from my hand and my heart stopped. I should have hidden the pen in my dress. What will they do to me? The contents of the bag were displayed on the desk and two men pawed over my toothbrush and toilet articles. Each touched the pen several times, but kept looking through the other items. One man began questioning me in Hungarian and I stepped back to avoid his foul breath. His voice rose and his head jerked from the desk to me and back to the desk. Then the other guard seized the wrapper I had saved from the first chocolate Busso had sent, in which I had carefully folded his four notes to me. With a triumphant grin he tore the writings in half and put the shreds in his pocket. The pen had been overlooked entirely, but something more precious was lost.

My clothing and purse were returned to me in a large plastic bag. A tag was attached with my name and number on it. I recognized the little fat man in the blue soiled coat who handed it to me. While he went to get my papers from the desk, I noticed a small mirror in the corner over the sink. I had been told to stand in one spot, but with the rare, rather defiant mood I was in, the mirror was too tempting. I walked over to look and was totally unprepared for the face that stared back at me. It was Snow White's stepmother, only worse. The eyes were sunken in dark pits. The complexion was colorless except for several red blemishes around the chin and cheeks. The hair, although Gretchen had combed and teased it for me that morning, hung formlessly. Was it *my* face? How should one react to such a face? I giggled. My face? I laughed out loud.

The fat man called me to his desk. Amusement time was over. I saw a telephone on his desk. "I want to talk to the officer. *Offizier!* He promised me that I could see my sister-in-law before

I leave here." I tried my best to convince him. He did not speak German. "*Offizier! Telefon Offizier!*"

"*Nem Offizier!*" He tried to urge me out the door. Finally he picked up the telephone and turned the dial. He spoke for a few seconds, listened a few, and hung up. "*Offizier nem—*" he explained. All I understood was that I could not speak to the officer and that I would not see Birke. The enlivenment I had felt on being released from my cell, at least for a time, suddenly drained from me. I felt sour and useless, like the curdled milk that had been held too long upstairs. Without appreciating the bright sun that struck me, I followed the guard out the door to where a small van was waiting. I did not care that it was waiting for me or think of where it would deliver me. Throwing my baggage inside, I reached up to grasp a rail. "Busso!" I breathed, seeing him, yet not believing it. "Is it you?"

Part Three

17

"I MISS YOU." He loosened his grip to sit back and look at me. "*Ach Du lieber Himmel,* you look—" Busso hesitated to say it— "awful."

I felt self-conscious now, not amused as before. Damn these bulldogs. They could have told me I would see him. They could have at least let me prepare a little. "I know. I saw myself. Looks like you've got yourself a real scarecrow." He didn't look so handsome himself. His big dark eyes were sunken deep into their sockets, and he had lost much weight. "Haven't you been eating? You weren't in solitary again, were you?"

"No, I've had three different mates. Remember the East German doctor I told you about? Just a young man my age. He and his fiancée——"

"*Nem szabed beszelni,*" the guard in the front of the van next to the driver cautioned us. He held a finger to his mouth to say we were not supposed to talk, but he was smiling.

"These bastards," Busso muttered.

"Honey, he's being nice about it. He doesn't really mind if we talk." The guard said something else to us, laughed with the driver, then turned around to face forward and didn't bother us anymore.

"What about the East German doctor?"

"He and his fiancée tried to escape. Both are being sent back. The doctor didn't want to go through that and tried to hang"— his voice caught and tears came to his eyes—"to hang himself in our cell. I was asleep. He tore the bedsheets under the blankets, so I didn't hear anything, until there came a loud cracking when the screen tore away from the window frame because of his weight. I

awoke to see him hanging—hanging there." He bit his lip to re-
strain his emotion. "I thought he was dead," he said, shuddering,
"and I screamed for the guards because I couldn't get him down.
It was horrible, a nightmare."

I held my breath, feeling sick inside me as though I had
watched the tragedy myself and lost a close friend.

"I don't think his neck broke, and he will probably recover.
He was sent to the prison hospital. But I'll bet he'll try it again.
He kept repeating that he cannot face returning to the Zone."

It made me shudder and squeeze Busso's hand tighter. Birke
and Kurt were returning to that same place. Would they endure?
Would Birke try to accomplish what she had failed at once before?

"What about your other cellmates?"

"One was Hungarian. He killed a Russian soldier who was
flirting with his girlfriend. I couldn't understand much he said.
This man here is West German, He tried to get his girl out. He's
a good sort." Busso indicated a man traveling with us. I had not
paid much attention to him until now.

The young man had red hair cropped short and a nice face, a
face like Norman Rockwell might paint, not the face of a jail-
bird. We greeted each other, and then Busso and I turned to
more pressing topics. Busso was at his wits' end over the proba-
bility that his landscaping business would fall apart. "I'll lose
every contract if I don't get home now!" he lamented.

"Don't worry," I tried to console him, "If I get home soon, I
can handle it," feeling a little hurt that he seemed to be more
concerned about the business than about me, but at the same time
feeling wifely in accepting it that way.

The truck bumped to a halt before a mammoth brick building. I later learned that it had once been a stable owned by Maria
Teresa. It was converted and has since become quite a famous
prison, the cells of which have held almost every known law-
breaker throughout decades in Hungary—the Markó Prison, lo-
cated in the fifth district of Pest.

Busso and I were abruptly separated. I had to wait in a room with other prisoners, all male, all Hungarian. The guard examined my plastic bag and, finding the chocolate bar, told me to eat it. A moment later Busso appeared. "Here." He handed me three chocolate bars with nuts. "Eat it all now. We're not allowed to take it into our cells. They won't even allow me to buy food for you in this hell-hole." The guard hustled him away again, and I sat and ate my candy. When the guard stepped out the door for a moment, I slipped a half a bar to each of the four men nearest me. They looked at once surprised, suspicious and pleased. The guard came in to catch me returning to my stool. His eyes flashed, but when he saw the others staring at the floor, munching silently on their chocolate, his admonishing look held a tincture of envy: the jailer was more restrained by rules and regulations than was his prisoner.

Later, I was called into the adjacent room, only to glimpse Busso being led away. All my belongings were laid out on a table, a fat woman guard held the articles up one at a time in her chubby fingertips as if the objects were dirty, and each was listed in a large book as had been done at the State Security prison. The guards wondered and laughed over many of the articles, such as my snap-cap curlers and my three bottles of bright nail polish. They passed a box of Tampax around to each other, trying to guess what it was. I stood silently by, refusing to let my new-found joy at having seen Busso be bruised by a few obnoxious guards. The fat lady handed me my pink and white dress and underclothes, and turned her back on me. I touched her arm to get her attention again and ask if I could have my other slip. She wheeled around, looked at me haughtily and slowly brushed off her sleeve as if to say, "You dare to soil me, you filthy prisoner?" I flinched, not at the fat woman, but at the flame of hate that singed me, and forgot my question.

Another woman guard came to the table where my things lay scattered. She searched through my wallet and pointed to a passport picture of Busso, the only picture I carried. I took it out and she closed my hand around it. *"Egy fénykép. Egy fotó,"* she said holding up a finger. One photo. I could keep it with me. Then she motioned for me to follow her, and I obeyed gladly, anxious to see my destination. She was a masculine-looking woman with a kind of sneering smile and piercing eyes. She removed her cap often and ran her fingers through her auburn, short-cropped hair, as a pitcher on the mound might do. When she stopped to talk to another guard in the hallway, she stood with her thumbs in her gunbelt, the holster of which was empty, and cocked her head to one side, watching me out of the corner of her eye. We passed through a small courtyard into another wing of the building. A half dozen men in prison stripes were painting the brick building, and they stopped working to gawk at me. I felt uneasy but could not help staring back, surprised at how normal, except for their attire, they looked.

I followed the woman into a building. Past the entrance, on the right, was a double door, and on the left a wrought iron gate. Behind the gate stood Busso. He was one of about twenty men standing in two rows. Not in stripes, they were dressed in their street clothes with their hands clasped behind their backs. Busso's eyes met mine briefly before I was pushed to the right through the double doors.

My lady watchdog demonstrated that I must remove my clothes. We were alone in the room, and I did as I was told. All at once she opened another door, ushered me through, and closed it as she left. Naked, I stood before three men and a woman, all wearing white lab coats. I watched them scrutinize me, and for a moment no one spoke.

"Guten Tag. Sprechen Sie Deutsch?" the oldest of the men who sat at the desk addressed me at last.

"Ja, guten Tag," I replied weakly. My self-consciousness began to turn to anger. What did they gain by subjecting me to tricks of humiliation?

"Where are you from?" he continued in German, ignoring my body and looking into my eyes.

"The United States of America."

"Why are you here?"

"I have relatives in East Germany and—" The way he nodded eliminated the need for further explanation. I ignored my nudity then, recognizing a chance to get some answers. "Can you tell me what to expect here? What do they plan to do with me? When can I go home? Why don't they let me talk to anyone?"

"Don't you have a lawyer?"

"Yes, but——"

"He will visit you and answer all your questions. As for how long you will be here, I cannot say." He spoke softly, almost with regret, I thought. "Perhaps it will not be long. Maybe a few months."

"Months!" I wanted to scream in protest, but he was the most courteous official, doctor, or whatever he was, I had yet encountered, and I needed him.

He came over to examine me. He asked if I had had any severe diseases, or had any health problem at present, and checked me for scars in one quick glance. There were none to be found, I said "no," and he dismissed me. The other two men, one about my age, and the woman, a bleached blonde, were still giving me an optical X-ray as I left.

Outside, after I had dressed, I saw Busso again. The iron gate was opened for me, and as I passed my husband, I tilted my head up quickly and kissed him. "Don't forget, I lov—" Suddenly I was sent reeling down the corridor by a heavy shove from behind. The female guard was shouting furiously and when I stopped just short of slamming against a wall, I turned to see her shaking an admonishing finger in Busso's face and yelling incomprehensible utterances at him. She made him turn his back to me, then pushed me into a nearby room. It was a shower room. I again had to strip. Under the pleasant warm water, I glanced up to see the guard searching my clothes.

It makes no difference. All she will find is a month's collection of prison grime.

Dried and dressed, I preceded my warder out again (Busso was gone) and up two flights of stairs. On the second floor, through the top of a Dutch door, three prisoners without guard issued me a large metal wash pan, two sheets, two blankets, a small tin pan, a tin cup, a tin spoon, a folding paring knife, and a pair of the grubbiest slippers one can imagine.

At the top of the sixth and last floor I waited, fascinated by my surroundings. So this was a real prison. It was more as I had imagined a prison than the *Stasi*—at least I saw prisoners, cement steps, metal walkways, and guards with large key rings—but it was still unlike anything I had seen in pictures. Where were the bars? This part of the prison formed a *T*, with each side of the three branches lined by solid metal doors. There was a peephole and a hatch in every door. I saw a guard at one door spying on the occupants of a fifth-floor cell. Standing on the sixth floor, I could see to the fifth floor, to the first floor in fact, though not so clearly through all the wire, because the middle of the corridor was slashed by a pit about seven feet across. The crevasse was screened with heavy wire and railed by an iron fence. On the floors below, I could see men mopping and scrubbing the walkway. On the sixth floor, women polished the rail. Most of the surveillant guards were male. A couple were female.

One of the male guards came to me and led the way to a cell at the far end of the left branch of the *T*, cell number two. At the door, he smiled, *"Német?"* he inquired. I shrugged to show that I didn't understand, but returned his smile. He had a pleasant enough face for a guard, very relaxed. Somebody called to him from the stairwell, and he left me for a moment. I waited at the door, anxious to meet my new cellmates.

I will have cellmates, won't I? They can't put me alone, not again, I couldn't bear it. Yes, someone is inside, more than one. I hear them. Will they be German? Can I hope for an English speaking girl again? Well, even if they're Hungarian, I'm sure they speak foreign languages. They can tell me what this is all about. They can tell me when I can hope to breathe fresh air and begin to live again. Why are they here?

The casual guard returned to unlock the door. I stepped into the cell where six pairs of eyes awaited me. Six women, all sizes, ages, and shapes, six women who looked like anything but a blessing. One wore only an underslip. Another had her skirt unzipped, allowing her naked abdomen to gape out. She stood nonchalantly in bare feet, toying with a knife in her hand. The third face belonged to a young black-eyed girl. It was the pert, pretty brown-skinned face of a gypsy girl. Her long black hair fell in snarls past her waist, and she was also barefooted. Beside her was a short, blonde, green-eyed girl in black pants and a black sweater which strained to cover two gigantic breasts that made her looked lopsided. She danced up to me with glistening eyes, her bosom bouncing heavily for lack of support, while she pointed her thumb at her chest declaring, "*Rózsi! Rózsi!*" and whipped her head back and forth excitedly, so that her short, straight blonde hair flew carelessly over her eyes. Two more women stood at the back of the group. They were older, around forty, and were the only ones who were not talking at me.

I stood stunned, understanding nothing of what was said. After the first wave of disappointment passed, I shook myself and began an introduction. "My name is Janet. Does anybody speak English?" No response. "*Meine Name ist Janet. Spricht jemand hier Deutsch?*" No response. "*Français? Español?*" I finished weakly.

"*En-Rózsi! Te—?*" the blonde said, standing close and looking into my face. She repeated herself until I understood and gave my name.

"Jeanette! Jeanette! *Jó, jó,*" she said excitedly, pronouncing my name as the French do. "Jeanette, Jeanette, *Németül? Hova valósi? Németországba?* Jeanette, *Deutschland?*"

"No, *nein,* I mean, *nem. Nem Deutschland.* America."

"*Jaj, jaj! Amerikai, Amerikai!*"

Rózsi and the little black-haired gypsy formed a chain around me with their arms and danced in a circle. The black haired girl stopped and looked at me, "Jeanette, *cigaretta? Cigaretta?*" I thought she was offering me one and said no, but then I understood she was asking for one and said no again, but felt more disappointed, because she was disappointed now. Rószi continued dancing around me, singing off key, "These boots are made for walkin', bum, bum, bum, bum, bum"—that's all she knew. The others were still, their faces vacant, watching the curious new prisoner who would share their quarters.

"Jeanette, Jeanette, Jeanette!" Rószi demanded my attention, bouncing up and down to the rhythm of her singing, "These boots are made for walkin'." I stared at her, this jubilant, dancing, giddy child who wanted me to sing the song for her. Sing? I reached for the post of the bunkbed nearest me, feeling my insides petrify in hopelessness. Sing? I sobbed.

18

THERE MUST BE SOME MISTAKE. This isn't a prison. This is a lunatic asylum.

I had expected something better than the dim, crowded cell with a bare toilet in the corner, a sink, and four double bunks. I had expected someone to talk with, someone less strange than the six women who pressed around me for a closer look at the American. How could I get out of here?

One of the older women patted my hand to console me and nodded her head in sympathy. "*Kati,*" she said. "*En-Kati.*"

The pretty little gypsy said, "*En-Vera, Ve-ra, érted?*"

"Vera," I repeated absently, trying to distract welling tears.

"*Nem szbad sírni, Jeanette, ne sírjon,*" Vera said gently, stroking my hair. She handed me her handkerchief, a gift she insisted I keep forever. Feeling too lost for assuagement, I was surprised to find myself consoled by the simple kindness displayed by the women. Nonetheless, some of their efforts served less to pacify and more to disgruntle me, such as the pert little Vera's attempt to include me as "one of the group" by revealing a source of her own particular grievance. She pulled her panties down to exhibit to me numerous scabby sores on her pubic area. I nodded sadly my commiseration, thinking of the toilet I was to share with her.

Eventually, a loud bell rang, and my cellmates scrambled for their washpans under the cots. Two of the girls had made my bed for me, an upper, and having showered earlier, I climbed up to crawl gratefully in between the heavy old tarp-like cotton sheets, wishing I could hide there until the nightmare ended. I thought about Gretchen and how right she had been. We had been better off in the damp cell alone together. Now I missed that little blonde imp.

Most of the girls stripped completely to wash themselves, disregarding the *spy* and possible guard behind it. In order to clean their backsides, they placed the washpans on the floor, turned their backs to the door, and squatted over the water, splashing it up between their legs. It looked vulgar. I turned over to face the wall, sure I could never wash like that.

After a second bell sounded, a guard came along to check the cell. He waited a moment while the girls rushed around, tripping over each other and swearing, placing the stools, the *"hockers,"* in line and the washpans back under the cots. When the last girl, little blonde Rózsi, in worn baby-doll pajamas, jumped into bed, the light went out.

"Jó éjszakát kivánok." Good night.

Darkness. How long had it been since I had seen darkness, felt its soothing arms embrace me? For the first time in a month, I was not to sleep with a light bulb burning overhead. It felt good. And there was a window too, an open window just beyond the foot of my bed. Through the bars, I could see the blue-black sky speckled with stars. I lay for a long while, entranced by the won-

der of the sky. Could Busso see it too? Where were Kurt and
Birke? What did my parents know of us? Had they heard anything in the Zone of our catastrophe, a familiar one to them over
the years, and one of which they dare speak only in whispers?

From a distance I heard dogs barking and wondered what tormented them so. Somebody must be teasing them. Vaguely I
wished I could pet them. There was so little tenderness left in the
world.

As the first day, a Thursday, progressed, I became better ac-
quainted with my cellmates. I had the impression they felt that,
even if I was too stupid to speak Hungarian, they would take
care of me. They said, "*Jó*," when I did something right, which I
thought meant "yes" but which actually means "good." And they
said "*Nem, nem* Jeanette!" when I did something wrong, which
was most of the time—like that very morning when I heard people marching outside. I squeezed between the end of one bunk
and the side of another and climbed up on the radiator in order
to look out the window. Below, in one section of a three part
courtyard, I saw prisoners, all men in striped suits, marching
around a square.

"*Nem, nem*, Jeanette!" the women cried. "*Nem szabad!*"

Reluctantly, I climbed down. Rószi came and explained in
careful Hungarian that looking out the window was "*Nem szabad!*"

"So what? I don't give a damn what's not allowed here. I
want to see my husband. Maybe he's out there." I went to my
cot and took Busso's picture from its place under my pillow to
show to them.

"*Aaaaa, Férjed. Értem, értem*," they said, understanding.

The little gypsy Vera took my hand; and patted it. "*A férjed
nincs ott most*," she explained. "*Később*," she pointed to an imaginary watch, "*Később, nem most.*" Later that day, when a different troop of prisoners could be heard, she carefully demonstrated
how I was to climb up and look out the window. Following her

directions while someone else stood guard, her ear against the door, I went to the far corner and climbed up on the top bunk. With one foot on the bunk and the other on a pipe attached to the wall, I pressed myself against the wall behind the right pane of glass that stood open into the cell. With the sun striking the glass on the outside, I was concealed from the view of the guards in the courtyard. After waiting for a long triple row of street-clothed prisoners to march around the cobblestoned square six floors below, I saw my man. Everyone in the cell was watching me, and from my expression they knew when I spotted him. The morning was brighter for all of us.

It didn't take long to learn the routine of the Markó, and the remainder of the day was without pleasure for me. When an ex-cruciating bell sounded in the morning, five A.M., everyone jumped out of bed posthaste. They raced around to sprinkle water in their faces and scramble into their clothes. I followed suit and could barely zip my dress when, within ten minutes, the guards unbolted the door and took roll call.

"*Jó napot kivánok!*" The first girl in line, Kati, who had a band with the number two around her arm, called out and followed with something she had memorized. She said the same thing every morning, and if she stumbled on a word, she was reprimanded. Then came the bed-making, a tedious process that took at least two hours a day, involving patting water along the edge and pinching inch by inch to make a crease in the cotton sheet, then folding the blankets just so to make the bed look perfectly rectangular and square-cornered. Some put cardboard strips in the pillow case to make sharp edges.

Breakfast usually provided a break, however, with the same barley water coffee, called *kávé*, and chunk of rye bread like that I had had at the *Stasi*. The *kávé* in the Markó was sweeter, though, and I actually grew to like it. Having seen the others either tear or cut their bread into chunks and put them in the *kávé*, I tried it for myself. One girl nudged the other and they all looked on approvingly. "*Jó*, Jeanette? *Jó?*"

"*Jó*," I replied: I liked their do-it-yourself soup, and they were pleased. When noon came, our seven pans, *csajka* as they were called, were passed through the hatch and returned one at a time with a kind of steaming, Hungarian paprika broth. The sink was filled with cold water and the *csajka* floated in it to cool the soup a minute; then the women slurped it down as though they were starving. Though cooled, it was too spicy-hot for me, and I gave mine to the brown-haired girl, whose name was Mauri. The women were not starved, however; they had to hurry in order to rinse out their *csajka* before the guards and two women prisoners who did the serving were at the hatch a second time with a pot full of mashed potatoes. Everyone was delighted with the plain ol' potatoes, except me, and I again gave most of mine to Mauri. When plain ol' potatoes were served the next time, I might add, about two weeks later, I had learned to be grateful for the fare. It was far superior to noodles, hot pepper, cabbage, pea soup, noodles, noodles, and more noodles.

The best part of the day turned out to be the "*séta*": around seven-thirty A.M. and three-thirty P.M. we heard the call "*Séta!*" and lined up in the cell, ready for walking in the courtyard. The doors of about twenty-five or thirty cells were unlocked, and women streamed out to form a single line and proceed down the stairs to the courtyard. Talking was strictly forbidden, but of course the women tried to get away with it.

"*Amerikai, Amerikai!*" I heard whispered around me. Those who got caught were ordered out of line and made to stand facing the wall after the names had been written down on a *fegyelmilap*, a discipline warrant.

In the beginning, the walk was a fascinating diversion. We formed two lines around the square. I watched the girls ahead of me and glanced behind me when I rounded the corner. There were eighty-eight counting myself the first day. Most were dressed in "civvies," some nicely so, others in a cheap fashion, generally the clothes they had been arrested in. A few girls had nylon stockings and high heels which seemed odd to me in prison. Many of the girls looked to be under twenty. Their skirts were skin-tight and shorter than then fashionable. Although some may have dressed provocatively, no one walked that way. Hands behind their backs, most shuffled along with head bowed. At least a dozen of the women were dressed in native gypsy garb. One older gypsy always swayed back and forth as she walked, in the manner of mourning. At the end of the line were about twenty women wearing prison-striped jackets and skirts.

Walking with guards surrounding us was not altogether recreational. The mornings were pleasant enough, but in the afternoon sun, with soot falling over our clothing from the large chimneys on the roofs above, the walk could be a drudgery. Across the top of the courtyard was a bridge on which two guards stood watch over us with machine guns in hand. They made me nervous, but anything was better than being in the cell.

After walking, the girls sat more quietly in the cell. Some played dominos in the afternoon, one or two read, Rószi and Vera danced, and Mauri preferred to lie across three wooden stools and sleep. Footsteps could be heard up and down the metal outside, and when they came too close, someone poked Mauri so that she could bolt upright just in time to avoid being caught.

I remember how lonely that first day was. I wished I had someone to talk to. My cellmates tried to teach me a few words of Hungarian, and I learned the names of utensils and objects around the room. But it was not conversation, and my heart was not in it. Besides, they too grew soon weary of repeating simple words, *csoika, kanál, pohár, ágy, lepedő*—pan, spoon, cup, bed, sheets, and so on.

One of the women had a lovely, melodious voice. With her arm around my shoulder she hummed the tune to *Ghost Riders in the Sky*, her sweet, haunting tone leaving me choked with homesickness.

I tried many times to ask for an officer to talk to—that had been the byword at the State Security prison—but faces remained blank. They could not understand what I wanted. It was confusing, because I had thought that *"Offizer"* was a Hungarian word, and it took me a while to realize that it was only German.

Will anybody ever listen? How much longer? Where is Birke? Why doesn't someone tell me what to expect?

I alternated attempts to talk to someone with lectures to myself on the use of self-discipline and patience. That first long Thursday came, at last, to an end when the nurse with the straw-bleached hair peeked through the hatch to ask if anyone needed to see the doctor in the morning. Benevolently, she gave me two sleeping tablets.

Friday passed exactly as the day before it. The only bright ray came when I climbed to the window and looked through the bars at Busso far below. I had the contented thought, "He is near. He walks. He is well," and an urge to crawl through the window to wave and call to him. How small he looked six stories below. How out of place. I could not look long.

I washed my dress that evening, in cold water with the sudsless brown prison soap. The dress was all rayon and bound to shrink, but after some thirty-five days, it was a luxury to be able to launder.

The week was ending. Saturday came. The hours passed slowly, and more slowly. The hatch was opened that day, however, to admit two blessed books for me. They were written in English, *The Green Hat* and *The Lost Stradivarius*. I caressed them, treasured them as precious companions.

Sunday was an even longer day than most. We were not let out to walk at all, and supper was served at noon, a cold meal to be set aside until evening. As the sun left our bars, everyone gathered near the small wooden table. Vera nominated herself hostess, and she divided the food which had been given through the hatch as seven slabs of gray-white substance. With unwashed hands, she placed each on a piece of toilet tissue and passed it out.

I picked mine up—it felt rubbery—and started to put it to my lips.

"*Nem, nem,* Jeanette!" Rózsi pulled my hand away. Vera took my piece back again and began sawing at it with her dull knife. It took a long time to cut it all into pea-sized pieces. I still had no idea what it was until, with a chunk of bread as the others were eating it, I placed a piece in my mouth. It was fat, heavily salted, raw pork fat. Since Vera's fingers were not the cleanest, and neither was the table, I thought I could not swallow the lardy glob; but everybody was watching and smiling and encouraging, and I ate.

That was not the only time my appetite dwindled. As the monotonous days passed, I ate less and less in spite of the fact that Szemetria, the guard with the relaxed smile, and other guards commanded double portions for me. I forced myself to eat as much as I could then gave the rest to Mauri, who was always hungry.

Monday was shower day. Two or three cells went together, forming a double line at the back staircase, and walked behind a guard down to the shower room on the first floor. Each girl carried her own towel and soap in her hands, clasped behind her back as always. We were, of course, supposed to be silent, but the guard was in front and the stairs turned in two places between each floor: the guard could not hear around the corners. Subsequently the women exchanged messages, even written ones, and changed places in line when necessary for their communication. A high incidence of detection was no deterrent. Someone behind spoke German to me, and I brightened, but all she could or would say was, "Do you speak German?" and nothing more.

Returning from the shower, where we all bathed in one room and I had half expected gas to pour forth instead of water, we walked down the aisle on the sixth floor toward cell two. Below us, on the fifth, a group of men waited in line. Some of them whispered up to the girls, some threw kisses, and several leaned out, craning their heads upward to see under the skirts above them. A few of the girls accomodated by stepping a little closer to the railing to faciliate a better view.

The *Vipera*—that was the name given to the police woman who had first directed me up the stairs—was the most detested guard on the sixth floor, and the prisoners had nicknamed her accordingly. *Vipera* is a snake, or more correctly, a viper. Before lunch that day, the *Vipera* came to ask us something and Kati gave my name. The *Vipera* left, and I tried to learn what was going on.

"*Civil major*," Kati explained—she pronounced it "cee-veel my-your." Did she mean major? Would that be an officer, someone to talk with?

"Jeanette!" Rózsi came to me and put her arms around me, "*Cigarettát, Jeanette. Kérek, cigarettát.*" All the girls gathered round me and begged for cigarettes. I agreed to obtain some if I could.

As it turned out, I was taken to a cell at the end of the corridor. A pansy-faced man in an ill-fitting sports jacket and gaudy tie awaited me.

Thank you, God. At last someone to talk to.

It was soon evident, however, that he could not understand me, nor I him, and all I could do was guess that he was asking me if I needed anything. Summoning my entire Hungarian vocabulary to mind, I tried to list my needs for him: "*Konzul*, please, American *Konzul*. Books, *könyvet*." (I had finished the two books given me.) "Lawyer, oh, how can I make you understand the word *lawyer*? And paper, *Papier*," I tried to show that I wanted to write a letter.

The man watched me, smiling. I didn't like his look. Why was he grinning like an idiot when I was trying to tell him something important? "Don't you comprehend? I must see someone! Someone with whom I can speak!" He merely grinned and nodded, not understanding a word. A package of cigarettes lay on the table. I hadn't taken a cigarette since I was fifteen, but, remembering my companions, I eyed them, and he offered me one.

I accepted, and he struck a match to light it for me. The match went out. He struck a second. No flame. He struck a third. Holding my breath, I managed to draw properly and light the nasty thing. He gave me the remainder of the package, about six more, and motioned for dismissal.

Caught in the excitement in the cell as the girls lit and passed around the prized cigarettes, and as they danced around me, singing and hugging me, I almost forgot for a moment that another day was passing and I was still no wiser.

19

MY DRESS HAD SHRUNK with the first washing, even though washed in cold water, but since I had lost weight, it fit better that way. The cloth was still damp in the morning, and there was no choice except to wear it wet. I wanted to save my only other dress, the pink, for something better than a prison cell. Besides, I told myself, it would be cooler wet.

By Tuesday I knew the routine in the "Markó Hotel," most of it being a long, monotonous void for me. Except for watching Busso for two minutes each morning, there was little comfort, little that was familiar to me in the prison. Even seeing my husband had its drawbacks: his stooped shoulders, his bowed head, his heavy step tore my heart out. Once, however, I looked down and saw him obviously out of step with the others in an exaggerated limp, swinging one arm aimlessly back and forth at his side, deliberately disobeying the rigid rules. That was the real Busso. He must have been in a good mood that morning. I wished I was too.

In short order, I learned to occasion a little variety for myself by signing up to go to the doctor. He was the only one who talked with me at all. One had to have a legitimate excuse, of course, and mine was a sore throat. It was true. I had always been susceptible to sore throats, and my larnyx was particularly raw now. In the outer office with a group of patients on my first visit, the *Vipera* ordered me to remove my dress—for a sore throat, mind you, but at least I had my underclothes this time. In the inner office, to the doctor, I said, "Has my husband been to see you?"

"What makes you think I know which one is your husband?" he asked cautiously.

"I know you do. He is a foreigner and speaks German too. Besides, you have the names and records."

He nodded.

"How is he? Has he asked about me? Please tell him I'm fine."

"I cannot transfer messages, but I assure you that you need not worry. He is well. He asks about you too."

"But if he came to your office, he must not be completely well. Please tell me."

"Are you ill?" He asked, not committing himself further. "What is your problem?"

"My throat hurts."

He leaned over me in the antique dentist-type chair and swabbed my throat with an orange ointment.

"Come back if it gives you more trouble," he said kindly.

"Thank you. *Auf Wiedersehen.*" He was the first Hungarian to whom I had volunteered, "Until I see you again."

The group, women from several different cells, was watched closely en route to and from the doctor. Nonetheless, ways were found to talk to each other. Now and then, when we were close enough in line and when we rounded a corner so the guard couldn't see, a girl would risk speaking to me. I learned that there were a few who really could speak German, but unfortunately our conversations were necessarily brief. I had noticed one woman in particular and was anxious to converse with her because she seemed different, more intelligent than the average convict, and nice. I thought she told me she was a nun, but I must have misunderstood. A criminal nun?

Some of the women could cry all day long. You could hear them wailing in other cells. One day Szemetria, the guard, had said, "*Rózsi, holnap bíróság!*" and *Rózsi* cried for eight hours straight. I thought it meant that she would be transferred and must leave our cell where she had been happy, where she loved Vera and mothered me, and where she enjoyed dancing around in bare feet on the asphalt floor singing, "These boots are made for walkin'." I could not remember much of that song, but I sang others for her, and she filled in with an off-key *la, la, la,* and kept dancing. She had tried more than anyone to talk to me. She was my favorite, and when she grieved I was saddened.

Vera and Mauri liked me because they both had hair long enough to sit on and I had a brush—the only hairbrush in the whole prison, I think. They helped themselves, never bothering to ask, casually taking it from where it was tucked under the springs of my bunk. Since it was, by democratic vote, one might assume, community property, I volunteered to brush their hair for them. I shortly became the cell's official hair stylist. It helped to pass the time, but unfortunately, *I* used the brush too, and I had seen women in the doctor's office with half their scalps bald and painted with purple medicine to rid them of lice; my head always itched when I thought about it.

If time permitted, I combed a fancy up-swept style for the girls. It was not easy without spray or pins, but we improvised. When the guard had passed our cell to make the rounds and the girls knew they had a few minutes to hunt, they searched under the upper bunks for the end of a wire. It took a long time to unwind a short length, twist and break it, but when they were successful, *violà!* there was a hairpin. Hairpins were forbidden in the Markó, only rubber bands permitted, but hairpins were one thing the guards, even the *Vipera*, would overlook when they chose to.

I should not give the impression that we were free to brush hair any time we pleased. There were strict rules as to the use of each hour in the day. Cleaning the cell took most of the morning. Besides the ritual of the bed-making, there was general housework such as dusting, straightening the two shelves so that large and small articles of clothing were folded in matching dimensions, polishing the *lavors*, the washpans, with cotton batting and tooth powder, scrubbing the sink and toilet, and washing the floor.

Cleaning the floor was the job I disliked most. It was black, made of a soft asphalt material, and pitted with heel marks. Each morning the asphalt was swept with a broom that looked like a dilapidated relic of the days when witches were jailed. After sweeping the floor and dousing it with water, one mopped it on hands and knees, with a filthy rag that must have been in use almost as long as the broom. There was no need to sop up the water, because it soaked right into the floor.

Generally we took turns on the chores, but washing the floor was used as a punishment. Once Mauri was caught sleeping during the day while sitting on a *hocker* and resting her head on a lower bunk. She was sentenced to scrub the floor for five days in a row. Another time Vera was sassy to the *nevelőnő*, the women's director, and was ordered to scrub for ten days. As this chore was always booked in advance, my turn came only once.

Although the cell never looked any different to me, always dirty, we felt we worked hard enough to deserve a coffee break. After the beds were made to the cell captain's satisfaction, we usually cut a slice or two of our respective chunks of bread, sprinkled a pinch of salt on it if we were fortunate enough to have salt in the community jar, and drank tepid water to wash it down. I and a couple of the other girls usually saved one beaker of *kávé*. It tasted better than the water, and I had learned not to drink all of my *kávé* before the morning *séta* anyway since, probably because of nervousness, my bladder could hardly hold two cups until I got back to the cell. I tried to build the illusion for myself that the break was like old times at work with the girls. It lifted my spirits, and I gradually developed a taste for rye bread with salt and imitation coffee.

Unfortunately, I had to return to drinking water with my

bread because one morning I came back to the cell after the *séta* to find that my *pohár* containing my saved *kávé* was not in line on the shelf where I had placed it. The tin cup was on the floor and the brown barley water splashed across the sink and asphalt. At first I thought it had fallen. The others moved quickly to put things back in order. "*Nevelőnő*, Jeanette," Rózsi said, demonstrating that my drink had been thrown out by the guards, "*vagy Vipera*." I gathered that saving food or drink was another breach of prison etiquette.

Just then the *nevelőnő* entered. She was a husky officer with shoulders like a quarterback. She was in charge of the sixth floor, and she spilled forth a lecture to which, standing at attention, someone responded, "Jeanette."

"*Nem szabad! Érted? Érted*, Jeanette?" the female warden said, waving her forefinger at me.

"O.K.," I accorded. "I won't save any more," but of course she could not understand me, so I tried to ease the situation with a smile. I couldn't see what she was so upset about: I was the one who was going back to water with my bread, not she.

Ten A.M., which is late in the morning when you arise at five, was the deadline for having the cell shipshape. At that hour the warden, the *nevelőnő*, or sometimes a visiting personage, inspected. More often than not, two or three girls had to make their beds over after the inspection.

After ten o'clock it was time to study the prison rules chart. I did not know until I was told some weeks later that it was against regulations to do anything except study the rules between ten and eleven-thirty; but that is another story. It was even forbidden to use the toilet during this hour and a half. The reason I didn't know was that no one ever studied the rules chart. Mauri usually took it from its hook on the wall, laid it on the table, then folded her arms over it and rested her head for a nap. The others sat on the hard *hockers* talking, squabbling, and daydreaming. I usually spent my time gazing out the window at the sky or sitting in the one cool spot in the cell, on the toilet cover. It was the only place where the wall was smooth cement instead of stucco. I could unzip my dress and press my bare back against the cool concrete. Often I brought my feet up and rested my head on my knees so that I didn't have to look at people I didn't understand or a cell I hated, and could lose myself in private thoughts.

The girls would do anything for a cigarette. Because they made no attempt to ration or save, they had to devise ways to obtain a smoke. They begged for tobacco from other girls when we walked, and if another was generous and if she had some, she passed it down the line the next day. Often, even when we had cigarettes in the cell, we were out of matches, and those had to be begged too. Matches could sometimes be had from one of the better guards like Szemetria.

Few women smoked filtered cigarettes because it left them with no butt. Butts were called *"chicks"* and were as prized as the cigarettes themselves. *Chicks* were saved, because when a girl had three or four, with a piece of toilet paper she could roll another cigarette. When all tobacco was exhausted and the *chicks* of the *chicks* had been puffed to ashes, there were the mattresses. A hole had to be made in the old canvas cloth so that the straw stuffing could be removed, which in turn was rolled into toilet paper weeds. Weeds they were, indeed. I tried one and gagged for ten minutes.

Besides passing cigarettes and notes, looking out the window, lying on the bed, tearing straw from the mattresses and wire hairpins from the springs, there were additional rules to break. Vera's favorite trick required employment of that most versatile of assets, the toilet. With the rag designated for the floor, she sponged water from the toilet then leaned as far down into the bowl as she could. Rózsi or someone was posted at the door. Vera tapped gently on the pipe to get the attention of the men in the cell below, and if and when they risked responding, she talked to them. Most of the conversation consisted of asking what the other had said, I think, because all Vera seemed to say was *"Mi?*

Pardón?—Mit mond?"

What a picture that made: pretty wild-eyed Vera hugging the toilet bowl with her hands to brace herself, her face pushed far into it as she talked, her long, blue-black hair falling carelessly around the bowl and into the remaining water that she hadn't pumped out. It was repulsive, yet comical. Vera was having the time of her life. "Jeanette, Jeanette, *telefon!*" she laughed to me, patting the john lovingly.

Another necessary communication link was the water pipe. In the *Stasi*, all pipes had been buried inside the walls, but in the Markó they ran along the back walls of the cells. A pipe and a tin cup made a pretty good intercom. News traveled fast.

There was so much bickering in the cell that at times I thought my head would explode. I did not have to understand the language to know what it was about. It concerned trivial, ridiculous things like who got to use the gallon of hot water that, if someone had her period, was passed into the cell in the evening. The silly part was that eight women could not begin to wash themselves in one gallon of water, so why not give it to the one it was intended for? But this wasn't always fair, because when three girls happened to be menstruating at the same time, still just one can of water was issued. It was also unfair because when no one had a period, someone lied and said she did. It might fool the guard, but not the women in the cell, so the hot water became community property. (When the *Vipera* was on duty, the women knew better than to try to fool her because she made everyone, Vera in particular, pull down her panties and show the bloody cotton; otherwise, no water.) But there were hundreds of other things to squabble about, so that it seemed to be one continuous battle. When it got too loud or came to blows, a tin spoon on the metal door reverberated and a guard came running. Usually a girl was transferred out and a new one transferred in, and tension abated for a short while.

Once the fighting was because of me. Mauri started it. I had learned to count in Hungarian, so the women asked me about prices in the States. We used all kinds of charades to understand one another, and some words were similar in both languages, such as "auto."

"Auto, America, 1966, two thousand five hundred dollars," I said. "Man, one year work, five thousand dollars."

Mauri said I was a liar. The others ignored her and asked me more prices. I told them as best I could, mooing to show that I was giving the price of beef, oinking for pork, but Mauri continued to deride me. I had not noticed her resentment before then. She had always eaten my food, unfortunately ruining her pretty young figure, and used my hairbrush, never saying much. Now with galling clarity I saw myself as Mauri saw me. Even in a prison cell, I was one of those conniving, capitalistic Americans whose tongue, above all, was not to be trusted.

"Mauri, there are the extremes, the terribly rich and frightfully poor; if only I could explain to you—" She turned away from me with disdain, and it hurt.

20

KEEPING TRACK OF TIME was becoming next to impossible. From the first week I had been making mental notes about my prison experiences, notes that might be useful in writing a "short article" if I were ever able. But as the weeks passed, the sequence of events grew clouded. I needed a calendar.

Since there was no paper or pencil, one made do. Having watched someone else, I learned that in a pinch a piece of common toilet paper, something like newsprint, and a burnt match serve the purpose. With these implements I made myself a calendar, beginning with the twenty-ninth of June, the day of our arrest, through the thirtieth of September. Three months would be enough, I was certain. I crossed off the passing days and circled special ones, the few uplifting days. On the back, I jotted key words to help me remember strange happenings and people. A concise word or phrase was enough to recall scenes clearly.

More than once was I afraid of having my "diary" confiscated because of the unannounced *hipis*, cell raids, that the guards rejoiced in perpetrating. Eventually, when a needle was passed in, for one hour only to sew torn clothing, I sewed the thin rolls of tissue into my skirt hem and seams and did not wash my dress thereafter. Of course seams are checked when one leaves, but I was lucky.

One person who is easy to recall even without notes entered my life after I had been in the Markó several days. Her name was Mary. She was in her mid-twenties, not bad looking, but thin to the point of emaciation. She was an extremely nervous person with jerking mannerisms, ill manners, and incessant chatter. Mary needed help, astute psychiatric help.

She, Crazy Mary as I thought of her, found it a tremendous lark that since I could not speak Hungarian, I was evidently retarded. When she was excited about something, she would come to me and jabber excitedly, her eyes gleaming overbrightly, her face only inches from mine. Often she hung her thin arms around my neck and, placing her face even closer to mine, gave out with a raucous laugh. She called me *barátnőm*, meaning "my friend," and I was never sure whether it was intended as a compliment or a jeer. A certain instinct told me that she spelled trouble: she was too unpredictable to be trusted.

By Wednesday cell two had become too much for me. I had been there almost a week. How much longer must this lunacy go on?

Rózsi had been called after breakfast, her eyes red and fearful, to go to the "*bíróság*." The others discussed something intently for a while and the discussion gradually developed into the familiar tone of quarrelling and crying. With the increased tempo of bickering, I managed, without relating to the squabble, to work myself up into quite a dither. My Hungarian cellmates were confounded: the morning had almost passed without a peep from the mute American, and suddenly she was shouting and speaking in tongues, splashing tears all over everything.

A spoon was rapped firmly on the door, resounding as though it would bring the whole prison down. To the hatch came a wrinkled old guard who looked at me with concern and sounded as though he would talk to somebody about me.

Within an hour I was in the office of the *civil major*. We were alone, and he seemed to be telling me that three years ago he spoke fluent German, but now he had forgotten it all. I thought maybe I misunderstood what he wanted to say. We sat and looked at one another, he with the same senseless grin he had worn at our first meeting, and I on the verge of tears, trying to speak slow, precise German in the hopes that his memory would return to him as suddenly as it had left.

"*Auto?*" He pointed at me, then to a window where, through the curtain, I saw a yard full of foreign cars covered with tarps.

"*Igen.*" Yes, I had an automobile here, unfortunately. What would happen to it? Would we be charged by the German company at the regular fee of seven dollars and fifty cents rental for each day even though the car was idle?

He had offered me a cigarette, and knowing the other prisoners wanted them, I couldn't tell him I did not smoke. I was on my second cigarette when he motioned me to the window to point out my car. I went to it and pulled the curtain partially aside. It took a concerted effort to keep from swaying, for the cigarettes were strong. As I pointed to our red bug, I felt the man's hot breath on my neck. I stiffened, turned quickly, edged past him and sat down. His presence had transcended the effect of the nicotine, nauseating me much more than the tobacco did.

When the interpreter arrived, a well-tailored, attractive policewoman, she sat in a chair next to mine and graciously translated every word that both the major and I said. He reaffirmed that three years ago he had spoken fluent German, but now it left him. "Don't you speak Czechoslovakian?" he asked, "Or Russian?"

Impatient to make progress, I stated my needs briefly. "Please tell him that I must write to my family," I said to the policewoman. She was very gentle in telling me to be patient, that all the things I asked for would be taken care of in due time, mostly by my lawyer.

"But I have only seen the man for five minutes. Why doesn't he come?"

"Our lawyers are very busy," she interpreted the major's words. He was anxious to change the subject, curious about my personal life.

"Your husband is here too, isn't that right?"

"Yes. I would like to see him. Could you please arrange a meeting for us? Why shouldn't we see each other?"

"I'll see what I can do. Yes, I'll see what I can do about everything. How long have you been married?"

"Four and a half years."

"Do you have children?"

"No."

The major made a comment, but the woman did not translate it. I pressed her to tell me.

"Oh, it is just an old Hungarian joke. It does not sound the same in translation." I could see that she was embarrassed, so I insisted all the more. Reluctantly she said, "When you said you have no children, he said you must have—poor neighbors." Her eyes apologized, realizing that this was not the time or place for such crudities.

The major smiled with glee that she had decided to translate his great joke, then dismissed her. He sat staring at me with his repulsive grin and I stood to go, not waiting for his dismissal.

"*Viszontlátásra*," he said, rising also.

I nodded and turned away.

"*Viszontlátásra!*" he said more emphatically, stepping toward me.

He wants to hear you say goodby to him, Janet. For your own good, say it.

"*Viszontlátásra!*" he repeated a third time.

A faint, forced smile was the best I could manage, and I left his office.

As the girls in the cell squealed with delight over the two packages of cigarettes from the major, I envied them, wishing I too could be contented for the moment with so little.

Late in the afternoon, I was again called from the cell. I was told to wait, hands behind my back, at the threshold of the *nevelőnő*'s office. It was always a treat to be outside my cell, and I looked around to study the activity of the prison. Across the aisle I noticed a cell, number sixteen, with the door open. Inside was a very low bed—the mattress lay directly on the floor, in fact. I could see no window, and the walls were painted black. As I watched, a woman rounded the corner, followed by the *Vipera*, and entered the blackened cell. At first I thought it was a man, because she wore long pants, a T-shirt, and very short cropped hair. Poor creature, to stay in that cell even a minute, I thought.

"Jeanette!" the *Vipera* and another guard scolded me for looking around.

When the *nevelőnő* ushered me into the office, I stood before a husky, middle aged man with graying hair and large round glasses who sat behind a desk. On his shoulders were a few large gold stars. He was the warden of the Markó.

"*Guten Tag*," he said.

"*Guten Tag.*"

He spoke German well, though slowly and with exaggerated enunciation as if in a comedy. "You have problems?" That he came to the point was refreshing.

"Yes, several. First of all, my sister-in-law and brother-in-law were arrested with me, and I have no news as to their welfare."

"Ah yes. They were East Germans, were they not?" He adjusted his great, round spectacles in order to scrutinize me more closely.

"Yes."

"Well, they have naturally been deported back to their home country."

I knew it. I had known it for a long time, but this was the first time anyone had actually said it. "But I was promised I could see them before they left. The investigator *promised* me!"

"That is another department. I have nothing to say about it," he said flatly. "Tell me, why did you do this thing? Why did you violate our border laws? You knew the penalty." His voice had more the tormented quality of a father trying to understand his delinquent child than that of an accuser. The inflection was not upon why I had fostered an attempted escape, but why I was so reckless as to buck the Communist law.

I wanted to make him understand. Somehow I wanted this man, the only communicative human being I had seen in weeks, this bespectacled soldier with the important gold stars, this warden with the key to my freedom, to know that I was not just a *hooligan* without respect for law or law enforcers. But how? We each seemed to gravitate toward ideological poles too opposite for understanding.

"Because there was no other choice. Because my people could not exit legally. You, your government offers no alternative within the law. I wanted them to visit my home. Is that asking so much? Is that *criminal?* If we had had any other choice, a waiting list, a payment of money, any other way, we would have taken it."

The man was looking at his desk. He adjusted his glasses, grunted, cleared his throat, "Yes, well, what do you lack in your cell? Do you have enough to eat?"

"Plenty, thank you." Food again! They were always concerned about the quantity and never the quality. "But I would like to have something to read. I was given two small books last Saturday. Now I need new ones."

He spoke to the *nevelőnő* who had entered to observe me.

The harsh lines in her rigid face now softened in the privacy of her own office.

"Also, I would like to have someone to talk with. It is very confusing to me when the guards come to tell us something, and I cannot understand. The other day this lady came to the cell and became very angry. I have no idea why." I tried to look innocent. "If only I had someone who could explain things to me."

He again spoke to the women's director, listened to her reply in which she denoted the *kávé* incident, and said, "There is no one here at present who speaks German. When there is, you will be put with her."

Why did he lie? I had spoken to women on the stairs. Why did they keep me in seclusion? What about the "nun"?

"But there must be. I know there are women here who——"

"I told you there is no one," he said curtly, indicating I should leave.

I did not move. "Is there some means of getting supplies? I have my own soap and shampoo in my suitcase. May I have them?"

"No, but you may exchange dollars for forint and buy Hungarian supplies when the list comes around. Our products are just as good."

"Also, I need to write to my parents."

"You will be allowed to write later. Now," he said, placing a sheet of printed paper before me, "please sign this."

"What does it say?"

"Nothing, it just says you are staying here a little longer."

"How much longer? What difference does it make if I sign? I have to stay anyway."

"If you do not sign, it will merely delay your release that much longer." He narrowed his eyes to observe my predictable horror at such a possibility. How could I resist such a pleasant invitation?

Rózsi was in the cell when I returned. "*Négy*," she said, holding up four fingers. She must wait four weeks, then go to the *biróság* again. She was happy to remain in cell two until then.

That evening the hatch opened and the old wrinkled guard with the tired, concerned eyes called me to him. "Jeanette!" Carefully he tried to make himself clear. The girls picked out the words they knew were familiar to me and tried to explain, "*Holnap, biróság.*" Tomorrow I would learn what it was that Rózsi had been so terrified of.

21

IT WAS AUGUST FOURTH. My cellmates busied themselves excitedly over me. Vera insisted on combing my hair. Rózsi ran her perspiring hands over my unpressed dress to smooth the wrinkles. The collar lay limp and damp against my neck where the thick seams had not dried from washing the night before. Someone else rubbed my shoes with a discarded pair of underpants to shine them. And finally, Vera brought a precious bit of *baba puder* out from its hiding place. It was saved for special people and occasions, the only substitute for deodorant, to pat under my arms.

The guard and I walked through a maze of corridors and doors, up and down stairs, around corners, and through several rooms. In one small chamber, a room that served as a bridge between two buildings, my police escort strapped on a holster and checked to see that the gun was loaded. In the second building I arrived at my destination.

"Ah! *Grüss Gott! Grüss Gott!*" exclaimed beaming Dr. Nagy. He jumped up and squeezed my hand. "Do you know where you are, ha ha ha?" His effervescence seemed even more artificial than I had remembered.

"No. Where have you been?"

"You are at the office of the *Staatsanwalt*. Do you understand?"

"No, what does *Staatsanwalt* mean?" I could conjecture, but this seemed no time for approximations.

"Well, don't worry. This gentleman here speaks a little English." He introduced the man beside him.

The man stood, bowed briefly, and said in English, "How do you do? Please sit down. *Staatsanwalt* means 'prosecutor.'" Then in German, "Do you know what that means?"

"Yes, thank you."

"Fine, fine," he continued in German. "We will speak German except when you don't understand some word, understand?"

"Yes." I turned to Dr. Nagy. "Why haven't you been to see me? You said you would come often."

"Yes, yes, *mein Goldiges*," he patted my hand and grinned so that his only tooth and all his gums glistened. "And I shall, I shall. But I have not been able to get permission yet. Now be calm. I will stay for an hour when the prosecutor is finished. Do you understand? We can discuss everything at leisure afterwards, good?"

"Good," I agreed.

It seemed so strange, so pleasant to be *talking* with people at last.

Dr. Nagy said, "Now my dear, I must be quiet. I am not allowed to speak to you while the prosecutor is questioning you. But do not be afraid. I'll be listening to everything she says."

It was then that I realized that the woman who sat opposite me at a long desk was the prosecutor. Wincing inwardly, I remembered Gretchen's judgment about women law enforcers. But this woman did not look particularly ominous. She was short, plump but well-built, in her late thirties. Before speaking, she had the habit of compressing her lips in thought. She directed all her questions in Hungarian to the interpreter, and he translated them into German. When I paused too long before answering, he asked what I did not understand. He translated two or three words into English, but more often he did not know the English counterpart, so he used a different German phrase. He seemed to be trying, and I answered as best I could in German, generally in phrases rather than sentences. He translated back into Hungarian for the prosecutor. She then worded my answer for a typist who sat to my right, in front of a large window.

Two young men sat across the room on a couch. They seemed to be studying how the prosecutor handled me. Occasionally they whispered and smiled at each other in secret. They made me more nervous and I resented the snickering audience.

I was asked to again repeat the story of how I had met my sister-in-law and how we planned the escape.

"When did you and your husband first come to visit his family?"

"In December, 1964." I wondered if Busso could remember all the dates they asked. No, he would not. Our dates will conflict, I thought, and they will conclude we are lying and covering up something.

"And when did you leave East Germany?"

"The first time? January 10, 1965."

"It was during that period that you planned the escape, wasn't it?"

I was surprised that the prosecutor (or translator) had used the word "escape." "No, not at all. It hadn't occurred to us then." She was trying to trap me, to make it worse. "At that time my sister and brother-in-law had a wonderful baby girl. They were happy." It was hard to swallow the lump that grew on remembering little Susann.

The questions went on, covering the history of our two meetings with Busso's family. I wondered if my mother-in-law knew by now.

"Why did you choose this country, Hungary, as the crossing point? Did you think we are 'easier' than some other countries?"

They were on the defensive. I shook my head, "We didn't choose Hungary. The East Germans did it for us. If we had had a choice, we would not have chosen Hungary." I thought of Yugoslavia and the fifteen-day detentions.

"What do you mean, the East Germans chose Hungary?" A belligerence tinged the interpreter's voice as well as the prosecutor's.

"I mean my sister-in-law wrote that they were planning a vacation trip to some Eastern Bloc country, but that the authorities had not yet assigned them the country to which they could travel. Neither we nor they had a lot to say about it." I looked directly at the prosecutor. It was an honest answer.

The woman looked exasperated, as though I had been deliberately impudent. The interrogation was not taking a good turn. From there on, the questions were more pointed, with the prosecutor compressing her lips frequently.

The question was asked, "At what exact time did you decide to carry out this plan of yours? In June when you saw your relatives for the second time? Just before you left their home?"

"No, not exactly. It was only an idea then, a dream."

"When was it made definite?"

"After Christmas last year. January of this year. But in March, Birke had her heart attack, and we dropped the whole idea. She was in the hospital for six weeks. It wasn't until a few weeks after that that she wrote and said nothing had changed. She was well enough to travel, and they still planned their vacation, but didn't know where even then. It was not until May that they were told they could go to Hungary. We had a very tight time schedule, only a few weeks to get ready."

Then came *the* question: "Tell me exactly. Who placed the false stamps in the passports?"

Dr. Nagy interrupted by standing. He spoke to the prosecutor, evidently asking permission to speak to me. "Now, this question is very important, my dear. Be sure you answer very carefully. If you did not place the stamps in the passports, it will make a great difference."

"But it will make someone else look worse if I say that."

"You will not make it worse for your husband. He has a lawyer. He will have a good defense. You cannot help him." He seemed to be earnest, but always with that chuckle in his voice. "Why do you feel you must protect your husband?"

"Because his punishment will be worse if I say he did everything and I did nothing, which isn't true anyway."

"My dear, you are no naive, so naive. His punishment will not be worse if you did *not* do something. Don't you see that?"

It sounded logical, but from what I had seen, my logic and their logic had few similarities. If they were really interested in my right to protect my own interests, why had I not seen an American representative of some sort? Why was I kept in isolation?

The prosecutor had waited several minutes and was losing patience. The interpreter repeated, "Whose hands actually placed the stamp in the passports? Did you or your husband? Who?"

"I did not place the stamp in the passports."

"Your husband did then, didn't he? Or was there another man involved?"

They had intimidated me enough. "I did not see it." Let them find some "other man" if they wished.

"Weren't you with your husband?"

"Not every single second." I don't want to lie: the air is foul enough. If only someone were here to advise me. How important is this question? They are trying to force me to testify against Busso and clinch his conviction.

"Well then, did you *know* that your husband *intended* to stamp the passports?"

"Yes." Dr. Nagy squirmed and would not look at me. I dug my nails into my palms. The prosecutor dictated short sentences to the typist. She was ending the interrogation.

A woman entered the chamber. She was well-dressed in a tailored blue wool suit with blue shadow on her eyelids. I guessed that she must be Busso's lawyer. She left again shortly. The secretary inserted a new sheet of paper in the typewriter, initiating the only sound in the room for a minute; then the prosecutor held a notebook toward me. I was not allowed to touch it, just look. Two passport stamps were displayed like the one we had reproduced.

"Do you recognize the stamps?"

"Yes."

"Tell me which is authentic and which is not."

Dr. Nagy was standing near me, looking at the stamps and chuckling. "You see my dear, it is obvious. You were very naive, ha ha, very naive."

I could see no difference. On close inspection the name of the border, Hegyeshalom, was an umpteenth of an inch smaller in one than the other, that's all, but I could not remember which was which.

Dr. Nagy continued chuckling. "Just look at the pictures of the cars," he pointed out evidence of my blindness. "This is a Wartburg or maybe a Wolga, while the other"—he tapped the page, "this is obviously a western make, a Volkswagen!"

It wasn't true. I could see. There was no possible way to tell the make of the car by the sketches. The outlines were only a half an inch wide, and the ink was blurry. The car was the best part of the fake stamp.

"I see no difference," I said emphatically. "I do not know which is which."

The next time the door opened, Busso entered the room. By now my head was spinning, and all I did was stare at the tall, hollow-eyed, handcuffed man who had not yet seen me. The moment he did see me, he took one great stride toward me before the guard stopped him. Everybody began talking at once, evidently arguing over whether or not to remove the handcuffs. The cuffs were unlocked, and there was no stopping Busso then. He reached my chair and put his arms around me. I was half sitting, half standing, a little stunned.

Dr. Nagy interrupted us to say, "You may talk for a few minutes now; the prosecutor permits it. I'm afraid I must go. You probably do not remember me, Mr. Lemmé. I am Dr. Nagy, your wife's attorney. Very pleased to see you. Now, if you two will excuse me, I must go. *Auf Wiedersehen!*"

"*Auf Wiedersehen,*" I replied automatically. Then turning to Busso, "Well, that's my lawyer. What do you think of him?"

"Ah! they're all alike here. They all work for the State, not for us. I've got to get you out of here."

"I'm for that, but I don't think you'll have a very strong say about it here," I said lightly.

"I am going to tell them that I planned the whole thing. That's the truth anyway. And I'm going to tell them you didn't know a thing about it."

"You can't do that. I've already said I knew. It's too late."

"But you didn't do anything. It's not fair that you should stay here."

"Just tell them the truth. That's the only way to get through this thing."

"The truth! I've been telling the truth, and what good has it done? We have committed a felony just by believing in capitalism. What questions did they ask you just now? Was it bad?"

"Not so bad. They did not appreciate my explanation as to why we used Hungary."

"I hope you told them we would have selected Austria if we had a choice."

The interpreter interrupted us then. "You must go back now, Mrs. Lemmé." I stole an instant of warmth and did not put my hands behind my back in prison posture until I was out of the room—my husband need not see me in that subservient position. Walking back to my cell, I was filled with resentment. This was the third time I had cooperated with them, answered their foolish questions, and still I had nothing for it. What happened to my damned lawyer? He said he would stay an hour. How much of my life did I have to forfeit to them?

That night the hatch was again opened on my account. "Jeanette!" The guards apparently enjoyed calling my name.

"Igen!" I hurried to bend and see his face through the opening. It was the guppy-lipped guard, *Harcsa,* meaning a kind of fish.

"Jeanette! *Holnap biróság.*" He spoke slowly and raised his voice so that I would understand better. "*Holnap, érted?*"

"*Igen. Holnap, biróság.* Tomorrow again. *Now* what do they want? More testimony for the prosecution? When does the defense get a chance? I straightened and turned away.

"Jeanette!" The fish-face smiled disarmingly, his guppy lips moist. "Jeanette, *holnap biróság a Konzul! Tizenegy órakor!*"

"*Konzul?*" I smiled too; no, I grinned. The consul was coming. I would see an American. Maybe he had news from home. Tomorrow at eleven o'clock. *Köszönöm, köszönöm.* I had learned the word for thank you long before, but this was the best reason I had ever had to say it.

22

THE NEXT MORNING I thought eleven o'clock would never come. The inmates had no watches, of course, but I was sure the guards were late in summoning me. I made my bed neatly, re-folded my two underslips and dress and the other girls' clothing, and cleaned the toilet. I washed, dressed, and combed my hair. Since we had no mirror, I went behind the back bunk while Rózsi watched the door, and I stood tall to see my reflection in the lower part of the window. Then I waited.

At last I was called. The guard took me through the same chain of rooms in which I had been the previous day, but the last turn was different. It was a different prosecutor's office. A tall man with courtly manners and curly brown hair introduced himself in German as a prosecuter, bowed slightly as he welcomed me, and asked me to be seated in a high-backed, flowered chaise longue across the room from his desk. It was a large, old room, and a few other men entered and talked with the prosecutor, but I could not hear. One carried two parcels under his arms. After giving the packages to the prosecutor, he came to me.

"Hello. I'm Clifford Gross, American Consul in Budapest." He was about five-eight, approaching forty, I guessed, reddish blond, well-built, and beautifully, beautifully American. My heart was in my throat—there were no words for my gratitude that he had come. "Hello."

"I brought a few things you might need. The prosecutor is having everything checked. Some things may not be allowed," he said, seating himself in an overstuffed chair to my left.

The prosecutor served us Hungarian coffee, and I felt like a human being again. The coffee was held in demitasse cups and was bitter like Arabian coffee. Four sugar lumps were on my saucer, and I added all of them. Mr. Gross casually laid a half dozen Hershey bars in front of me as if they were a common sight, and I felt like Pavlov's dog, the way my mouth watered. "These are for you. Eat all you want," he offered. The prosecutor went to his desk across the room, and a third man sat down near me to my right. He spoke to Mr. Gross in Hungarian.

Mr. Gross said to me, "Don't let him bother you; he just wants to rest there." I liked his easy smile, held in reserve for just such *bons mots*. He opened his briefcase, "I have a letter here for you from your parents."

"How are they?"

"They had a bit of a shock, but they're holding up remarkably. Read for yourself."

The letter was mostly from my father. He reassured me that he and Mom would do everything they could to help us, especially by taking care of our affairs at home. They were paying necessary bills, and Thor, a friend, helped too. John, a business associate, was taking care of the landscape business as best he could, but we were losing our biggest contract. Dad said news of us was "meager" and that I should write whenever I could. He sent his love.

Mom also asked me to write. "The news (radio reports) this morning told us that you have been formally charged and will have a trial," she wrote. "I hope they let you have someone from our Legation to defend you." She expressed concern about my health, again asked me to write, and said not to worry about them. "Remember your code or behavior," she concluded. "It has done well for you in the past. Let this harrowing experience make you stronger spiritually—turn it into an asset. Remember the book by Frankl? Shall I send you a copy? What else?"

"They are good parents," I said to Mr. Gross. "I wish——"

"They'll be all right." He eased my mind. "Haven't you been allowed to write?"

"No. Do you know of my lawyer? His name is Dr. Nagy, János Nagy." I told him about my brief association with the man.

"They don't operate here quite the way they do back home."

"I've noticed." Mr. Gross offered to write home for me and take care of all he could, and I was thankful to have someone to count on at last. "My mother writes that I was formally charged and will have a regular trial. That's the first I've heard about what they plan to do with me. Do you have any idea how much my sentence might be?"

"No, not really. They vary quite a bit here. It depends a lot on the judge, of course, and on the day and the climate."

"But any idea at all——"

"If they dismissed the charge, you would go right now, but I'm sure they won't do that. And if they find you not guilty, you will leave right after the trial."

"And *I'm* sure they won't do that. What then?"

"The shortest sentence is three months. It goes up from there."

"What about the time I have spent here already?"

"That generally counts toward your sentence; that is, you have six weeks' time in already, don't you? What day were you arrested?"

"June twenty-ninth. When did you hear about it?"

"There was a small article in the paper the *Magyar Nemzet* on July tenth. I have clipped it out and will save it for you. I asked to see you immediately but was not permitted."

"The tenth!"

"Yes, and we wired it back to the States that day, but it was still twelve days after your arrest. There was some confusion, because Budapest reported that you are from Washington, D.C. so that's what our wire service picked up."

Somehow that came as no surprise to me. I did not know what a Consul actually does, but I knew he didn't have to wait for me to come along in order to keep busy. I apologized for the inconvenience.

"It's my job." He once again encouraged me to relax. "One of my major functions is visiting Americans who have gotten themselves in a jam here."

"You mean there are other Americans here in the Markó?"

"Yes, as a matter of fact, I just visited two brothers. From Oregon."

"Did they commit a real crime?"

"They wrote on a small poster. It had a picture of an airplane bombing a Viet Nam village or something. Printed on the plane were the letters 'U.S.' and they changed it to 'U.S.S.R.' "

"Maybe they are confined with my husband. I hope so. It's awful not to have anyone to talk to."

"Can't you talk to anyone? You speak German, don't you?"

"Yes, some, but nobody in my cell does. Sometimes, when they begin fighting, or when the *nevelönö* shrieks at them, I think I'm going crazy. It's lonely too."

Mr. Gross spoke to the prosecutor. The prosecutor stood immediately, saying, "*Igen, Igen,*" and went to the door to speak to a secretary in the next room, then came back to make a telephone call.

"I think he'll arrange something for you," the Consul told me. I had never managed to stir the dust, but I had the feeling my friend had just moved a mountain. He named the items he had brought for me: several pounds of foodstuffs, soap, toothpaste, letter-paper and stamps, "And cigarettes— do you smoke?"

"No, but I would like to have them. Maybe I can get some to Busso. Would it be possible for you to see him?"

"No, I tried, but he's Canadian."

"Is there a Canadian Legation here?"

"No, the nearest one is in Prague. I'll see what I can do about getting one of them over here. Incidentally—well, maybe I should not tell you this," he hesitated, "but I'm trying to arrange a visit between you and your husband." I could hardly believe it. "But don't count on it. It is against general policy to let two defendants on the same charge see each other."

"I won't count on it," I promised. "I'm learning better than to expect too much action all at once. Tell me, Mr. Gross, how shall I act at the trial? What shall I say?"

"I don't know much about your case, you know—just what I read in the *Magyar Nemzet*—and there is not much time to discuss it. Be natural and tell the same story you have already told. That's all you can do. The important thing now is to have the trial as soon as possible."

In about three sentences I told him the main facts, then asked what he thought our chances were.

"I think you stand a good chance of going home earlier than your husband does. You say you have seen your lawyer?"

"Yes, but he has never talked to me to any extent. He doesn't speak English, only German."

"I brought you a list of lawyers in case you want to change. They all speak English. Look it over. If you want to change, you had better do it soon. You're not eating. Come, have another chocolate bar."

For a few brief moments, I almost forgot where I was, where I had to return to. I asked about the Consul's job and family and was interested in his description of life in Budapest. He commented on the heat and asked if my cell was cooler.

"Not a lot. The girls don't wear or do much when it's sultry like today. There's nothing to do."

"Don't you have books?"

"The others don't read much. I was given two, but that was a week ago, and I have finished them long since. Could you bring me a Hungarian-English dictionary?"

"I'll try to get it through. I brought you some magazines today, a whole stack. They are not all this month's, but——"

"Who cares? I only hope they let me have them."

"I think they will."

Before I knew it, our allotted hour was up. My heart was too full of thanks for his coming to regret the brevity of the visit now.

That came later as I gazed through the bars, wondering, What next?

23

WHEN THE DOOR OPENED not long after my return, a tall, dark-haired girl entered. I did nothing but stare. She was beautiful. Her creamy complexion contrasted sharply with her auburn shoulder-length hair. Her eyes were hazel-brown, framed by dark lashes. She was long-legged and slender, and she moved with a cat's grace. While the other women gathered round her, introducing themselves boisterously and asking questions, I stayed in the background.

"Julia, Julia." They called for her attention. She seemed to be well known. Her blue suit, yellow blouse, sheer stockings, and high-heeled blue leather shoes set her apart from the rest of us. If I had not been in a prison cell, I would have thought she came to model.

When a break in the chatter came, I asked, as I did to each new comer, but without expectation now," "*Sprechen Sie*

Deutsch?"

"*Ja gewiss,*" she answered in accented but well-spoken German, "I do. I believe they transfered me here so that I could explain some of the regulations to you. Are you from Austria?"

I was overjoyed with my new acquaintance and told her about myself. With Julia, I forgave the Hungarian authorities for loneliness I had suffered, at the same time fearing them more in their power to whisk her from me again. "How long can you stay?"

"Only until tomorrow noon, I'm afraid. Then I go back to the other prison, Gyüta. The only reason I am in the Markó at all is that I go to trial tomorrow morning."

"Would you like to talk about your trial, or shall we avoid the subject?"

"I don't mind," she sighed. Julia was not one to jabber and giggle like the others. She was reserved, unimposing, as happy to listen as to talk, a bit of a dreamer. I liked her. "But first let me answer whatever questions you have about the 'Hotel Markó.' "

"Where shall I start? Why do you have such nice clothes?"

"Because my mother brought them to the prison for me. Your family is allowed to bring you clothes once a month, two changes, especially one for your trial. I have this suit and a jersey dress. I would ask my lawyer to bring whatever I needed, if I were you."

"I don't have much with me because we were only planning to stay overnight in Hungary; but the others, these women, all live here, and some don't even have one change. Rózsi wears pants and a sweater no matter how hot it gets."

"Some don't have anything at home. Some families are too poor to come to Budapest if they live in the country or far away. In Rózsi's case, her folks are angry with her and refuse to come."

"But the prison must issue clothing for those who don't have much."

"Sure, stripes. Nobody likes to wear stripes if they don't have to. Only after one is actually convicted is it mandatory that he don prison garb. Those you see in the courtyard have been sentenced and work in the prison. Most are kept here because they had only a month or so left to serve by the time they came to trial. Those who get months or years are sent out to other prisons. Almost every city in Hungary has a prison."

I complained about the police not allowing me to say farewell to Kurt or Birke, and Julia replied, "It's not just you they treat like that. It's everybody, the Hungarians too. The army, the police are the masters. I know in the West it is different."

The opposite extreme, I thought, but didn't say it. "It's hard to compare treatment. In the first place, I've never been in jail in the States. In the second place, we don't have this crime. We have so many people wanting to come to the States that we are glad when the dissatisfied ones leave."

I was called then to the guards' desk to be issued my food parcel from the Legation. The *Vipera* unwrapped each item and inspected it. Everything had been produced in Hungary: cheese, *kolbász* (coarsely ground sausage with a spicy paprika flavor), some sugar lumps in a small brown bag, and a chunk of fine sausage. The food was a surprising pleasure, rather symbolic, like Linus's blanket. There were also two rolls of toilet paper, but she only let me have one roll, and two cartons of Kent cigarettes. The letter paper was not visible, nor were the magazines.

"Cigarettes," I said, holding up one carton, "*egy,* . . . *férjem?*" I wanted to give at least one carton to Busso. "*Férjed?*" She seemed to get the message, took the carton and said nothing.

When I returned to the cell, the women had eyes only for the carton of cigarettes under my arm. A cheer went up, and I was showered with kisses. I opened the carton ceremoniously and handed each girl a package.

"You are exceptionally generous, Janet," Julia said as I handed her two packages.

"Why?" I answered, knowing myself unworthy of the compliment. "I have two packages left, and I don't even smoke."

At dinner it was fun to cut half the *kolbász* into chunks and pass it around. Julia would not accept any.

"When I left the Gyüta they gave me a large chunk of bacon," she explained. "That's plenty."

"But that's just raw fat," I protested.

"I'm used to it now," she countered.

"Of course, I'm used to it now too. But tonight we have something better. I want you to make me happy by accepting the *kolbász*. Do Hungarians outside really eat that raw bacon?"

"Only the poorest, and then they do not tell anyone. They must economize, and that is the cheapest food. But they are ashamed to admit they eat it." She still refused to eat the small piece of *kolbász* in front of her. At the end of the meal, Mauri asked Julia if she didn't want the meat. Julia said no, it belonged to "Jeanette," so Mauri helped herself to it.

Julia translated for everybody. They all wanted to know exactly what I had done. "With passports," Julia explained. She need say no more. It was a familiar story to them.

"What about the others?" I asked. "I think I understood Rózsi's story, but not completely. She tried to get into Rumania with false papers, didn't she?"

Julia asked Rózsi, then told me, "Yes, she and some boyfriends decided suddenly to go to Rumania for the weekend. Something different, you know? Rózsi didn't happen to have her passport with her, so she borrowed that of her boyfriend's sister."

"Sounds crazy. Just for a lark?"

"For Rózsi it was, but for one of the men, the one she loves, it was more than that. He had anticommunist leaflets with him."

"Is he in the Markó too?"

"She said yes, he's downstairs, on the fifth floor. He is expected to get not less than five years."

"Five years. Just for carrying literature with him." There was a moment's silence, as if by request. "Rózsi keeps trying to tell me something about sleeping or dying. What does she mean?"

"At the border when they were caught, she was so scared,

she slipped away from the guards on the pretense that she had to go to the bathroom, and she ate twenty-two sleeping pills. That was stupid, because they don't take their eyes off you for more than an instant. They caught her, and all she got for it was her stomach pumped, which isn't very comfortable."

"And what did Vera do?"

"She says she was in a gang with four men. She and one of the men were caught stealing."

Vera enjoyed our talking about her. Her black eyes sparkled with glee and she began demonstrating with pride how she had stolen money. Her pantomime seemed to show that she reached right into a man's front inside jacket pocket, and I asked if she were a trained pickpocket.

"No, she's not that bright. The man was sleeping. For that reason, her sentence will undoubtedly be quite severe, because a sleeping man is helpless, like a baby."

"What about Mauri?"

Julia asked Mauri, but the young girl with the long, thick brown hair said little. Rózsi and Vera filled in the details. "She stole things," said Julia. "She stole sweaters and other clothing from stores, and her big mistake was that she stole money from her mother. Her mother turned her in."

"But she is so young."

"Only seventeen."

"I'm surprised she isn't in some kind of juvenile home."

"She would be, but they are so crowded. She stole a terrific amount of apparel, thousands of forint worth, which puts her above the range of juvenile crime, I guess. She would be separated from the older women here, but there is no space. The only thing they could do is put her in a cell by herself, but that's against all prison regulations."

"Not the regulations for foreigners, it seems. I was in solitary for a week."

"But it is strictly against the rules," Julia objected. "Where? It must have been at the A.V.H., the *Belugyministerium,* called

Allamvédelmi Hatosag. The A.V.H. and the A.V.O. are external and internal police and are greatly feared here."

"Well, they know it pays not to let the foreigners know about the rules." I asked about others in the cell, or those who had been transferred out. They had committed various acts: embezzling funds from the State, beating and neglecting children, black marketing. Anything to do with money was labeled a crime against the State.

"And may I ask what you are here for, Julia?"

"*Valuta. Divisen.*"

"*Divisen?*"

"Currency. Black-market exchange. Foreign money, from tourists and traveling salesmen from other countries, can be exchanged on the black market for almost twice what the bank will give you."

"You seem to know a lot about the West. How?"

"My fiancé is from Belgium. He tells me all about it. That is, he was my fiancé until six months ago when this"—she pointed to the cell—"this happened. Now I'm not sure he will want me. He told me not to—to fool around with the black market." Her large eyes were dark with regret. I consoled her by saying that he must be a good man or she would not love him, and if he is a good man, he would stick. "Yes," she agreed, raising her arched eyebrows, "he is a good man. But even so, it will be years before we can marry. It would have been next year, but now I will not be able to get permission from the government to marry a foreigner for at least two or three years, if at all." I wondered if the United States government approved of my marriage and travel with a Canadian and former East German! Julia looked so forlorn I could not think of any solace. "But never mind me. What's done is done. You asked me how long you might get, and I still have not answered. All I can tell you is of the cases I know about. One Austrian girl got three months, a German girl got eight months, and another Austrian got nine months. They all did something similar to your act."

"How did one manage to get off with the minimum?"

"She was pregnant, I think that's why they were lenient. They sent her home right after the trial. Also, perhaps the judge understood that she was being used by the others."

"Were the others caught?"

"Yes. It was a sad story. She was Austrian and took a vacation in Brazil. There she met a handsome young Hungarian-born Brazilian. She settled in Brazil for a time and hoped to marry her great boyfriend. Since she was rich, he got her to pay for a trip for the two of them back to Hungary. She was glad to do it, because she loved him, she liked Hungary, and she wanted to visit an old girlfriend here. Unfortunately, when the boyfriend and the girlfriend met, they fell in love. The Austrian girl was already two months pregnant, so the man agreed to stay with her, even marry her, on the condition that the Hungarian girl come back to Brazil with them. The Hungarian girl and the man had to serve most of a year, and the Hungarian girl is of course forbidden, when she is released from prison, to leave this country."

Julia asked if I had money, and I told her I was far from rich. "No," she laughed, "I mean do you have any money here at the Markó, any forint with you?"

"No forint, but I have about thirty dollars. That may have to get me home. My husband has most of our money and our tickets to return."

"They will let you exchange your money for forint in order to buy supplies like tooth powder and toilet paper. I'll help you. What else do you need?"

"Books. My husband. And my lawyer."

"In that order?" she teased.

"Do I have a choice?" I rejoined. "Under the circumstances you would think the lawyer would come first—but he doesn't come at all. What can I do?"

"Nothing. He'll come when he's ready."

"I have a list of English-speaking lawyers here," I told her, and showed it to her.

Looking them over she said, "You can change, but it won't make much difference."

I asked questions about the general rules governing the prisoners. "Why can't I write a few sentences home to say I'm all right?"

"Before the trial, prisoners may write once a month. After, once a week."

"Then I have one letter two weeks overdue and one due me two weeks hence."

"A prisoner has nothing 'due' him, Jeanette," she reminded me courteously.

I promised not to start a riot over it and asked her why other women were allowed to see their families and I was not. "I don't know," she answered. "Even when both parties are charged, they make arrangements to have a guard listen to be sure they don't discuss the case, but they are allowed to visit. We are allowed to see two visitors once a month for one hour before the trial, and for two hours each month after the trial. You can write out a request slip. It is up to the prosecutor and the warden to approve it."

We talked on, covering as much as we could in one precious evening. Such a beautiful girl, I kept thinking, kind and gentle, and so young; like Rózsi and Vera, Julia was just twenty. I wondered how she ever became mixed up in the black market, but didn't ask. We talked through the wash period until lights out, and then continued talking from our bunks. It disturbed no one because the others were chattering too. When footsteps were heard, there was a flustered "Shhhhh!", the light flicked on and off again, and we resumed our conversations.

"Listen Jeanette," Julia advised. "If they ever do let you see your husband and you want to see him more often, I'll tell you a trick. Tell him that when he goes for the exercise period, the *séta*, in the afternoon, he should walk for a short time, then tell the guard that he must go to the lavatory. He must make it sound urgent. The guard will take him into the building, and to do so they must cross from their courtyard through yours. In the morning the men on the fifth floor do not walk at the same time we do, but in the afternoon they do. Understand?"

"Yes, thanks. What makes you think it will work?"

"I know it will," she assured me. "The Austrian girl, the one that got nine months, her husband did it many times. I was in her cell for six weeks. It worked for them."

"Why did she get nine months? That's a lot compared to the others."

"Yes, she and her husband each received a sentence of nine months, and I've never seen two more innocent people. They provided the means for a Hungarian Jewess to flee who is now in the United States, I hear, but they did not realize the full impact of their actions. It was an Austrian businessman, the woman's boss, who planned and implemented the whole thing. The couple was duped into carrying the passport to the escapee with the assurance that no harm would come to them. I guess the judge didn't believe their story, but I know it's true. I lived with the girl for six weeks and I know."

At breakfast the next morning I passed around chunks of *kolbász* again, making the pieces smaller this time, for my supply was already low. The women seemed pleased. Julia translated their thanks. "Vera wants to know which you like best, the *szalámi* or the *kolbász*."

"The salami, I guess. Why?"

"I think she just likes to ask questions," Julia laughed. The guards came early to take my friend. "If it were up to me, I would stay with you, Jeanette. You know that," she kissed my cheek. I implored her to obtain consent for me to write home before she left. Five minutes later, a sheet of paper, an envelope and a pen were brought to me, and Julia was ushered back to tell me, through the hatch, "You may write thirty-two lines, on one side only. Write nothing about your case. They told me to tell you." She was taken away.

I wrote the letter quickly, trying to say as much as possible in the short space allowed. Passing it back through the hatch I urged the guard to send it airmail. He seemed to understand, saying *"Igen, igen."* (More than five weeks passed before my parents received the letter. It was not sent airmail.)

Rózsi did not talk or smile at me that morning. She was cross. Evidently because Julia and I had spent so much time together the night before and had ignored her, she was jealous. Crazy Mary was mad at me too, but I was glad that she pouted and did not speak to me.

I was told by a guard that morning to prepare to be called to the *bíróság*, and Rózsi used that period to get even with me for my neglect of her. As cell supervisor, she made use of her authority. I had done my part to clean the cell, then washed and changed into my other dress, the pink and white one, with the tenuous hope that I might see Busso. When I was ready, Rózsi decided that the *lavórs*, washpans, had to be cleaned, and that I was the one to do it. The day was already very hot at only about nine in the morning. The cell was humid and cleaning the *lavórs* was a dirty job. One had to rub toothpowder vigorously over the inside. The powder absorbed the dirt film from the metal and left it shiny. Rózsi not only told me to clean my own *lavór* as was the usual procedure; she said I must clean all of them. I did not argue, but followed instructions, glaring at the cell captain. Soon my hands were covered with gray metal-colored powder. I worked slowly, trying not to perspire and to keep my dress clean. Luckily I finished the job just in time to clean up before the guard came for me (you must come as you are; they don't wait), but only because a couple of the girls voluntarily helped me. Rózsi would not look at me as I left.

I was taken to the same room where Mr. Gross and I had met the day before, and Busso was there waiting for me. A little old white-haired man sat with us at the coffee table. He introduced himself in English as the interpreter, "But you need not fear me. I shall just listen a *little*," he said kindly in his faint, raspy voice. "Please though, do not talk about anything you are not supposed

to; you know, politics or your case." We were given one hour.
We did not squander it on politics.

We asked about one another's health, and I told my husband I
was concerned about my lawyer. "He hasn't been to see me, has
yours?"

"Are you kidding? Mine quit. I payed her two hundred dollars, so she decided to take a vacation to Vienna. They'll give me
someone else before the trial," he said bitterly. "Don't expect any
help from your lawyer, and don't you give him any money, no
matter what he says to you. They are paid by the State anyway.
I'm sorry I gave them the money now. It's such a racket here."

"I want to change my lawyer. I want one who can speak
English. It makes me nervous not understanding everything in
German."

"What difference does it make? Janet, honey, you still don't
understand. It is all a setup. It is just a performance they put on,
this hearing or trial or whatever it will be. Did the warden make
you sign something?"

"Yes, do you know what it said?"

"It said that we are being held here for one more month by
our own consent. Sure, like we sign every damn piece of paper
eagerly without being able to read it."

"Shhhh, not so loud. You're too vigorous. Please be careful,
honey."

"By the way," he said casually, "I managed to smuggle a letter
out to Mom and Dad, and one to Thor in Seattle too."

"Great! How? You certainly adapt well to this life."

He did not tell me how immediately. "Takes know-how, kid.
A man has to use a little finesse. You've either got it, or you
don't." He shrugged and blew on his knuckles.

"O.K., big-shot convict. Let's just not make a career of it, all
right?" It was a pleasure to see the old sparkle coming back into
his eyes.

"Hey now, I'm not a convict yet. There has been no conviction, you know." He told me he had sent the letters out by means

of a cellmate who was being released and who promised to mail them. It was a chance. If the man informed, Busso would pay; if the courier was honest, but was caught, both would pay. (The messages reached their destinations without trouble.) "Listen," Busso said excitedly, "I can see you once a week through a crack in the hatch, when you go to the shower room," he glanced at the interpreter who looked like he wasn't paying attention. "Don't ever walk too close to the railing. Men devise ways to look up at the women. You wouldn't believe how filthy they can be. Some even masturbate in front of the whole cell."

"Forget them. I know of a way we can both see each other." I related the plan Julia had outlined. "Will you do it?"

"Of course. It might work." (We also set up a code to cough a greeting to each other but later found that there was much interference and contact was uncertain.)

In this manner we talked of the things most important to us, the contacts we might make. We also reviewed the matters I should take care of if I were released sooner, problems which mounted as the days passed. "Try to take my film out with you. Do you realize I have seventy rolls of movies, three of which are of Hungary? The police haven't bothered with it yet, and there is no reason they should. I have no ill intention, but they have a way of creating one to suit their purpose. If you can't get the negatives, don't make an issue of it. I would like to help the Hungarians by limiting my visit as much as possible." And there were many other personal details to be attended to.

The time was suddenly up. "You must go back to your cells now," announced the tall prosecutor whose manners were so courtly. I kissed my husband good-by. "If I do go home early," I said, "it will be awful to leave you behind. I'd almost rather stay."

"You're a silly kitten, you know that?"

Maybe so, but it was hard for him to turn away from that "silly kitten" and walk back to prison.

It was hard for the kitten too.

24

LUNCH WAS JUST OVER when I got back to the cell, but the girls had saved my noodles for me. I ate as much of the dry, unflavored starch as I could, thinking it was thoughtful of them to have saved it for me, then I hungered for a piece of meat. Reaching into my box, I found it nearly empty. Where was my *kolbász?* I looked at the girls.

"Jeanette," began Vera. The others chimed in, repeating my name and saying that I liked salami best and they liked *kolbász* best.

"See?" Vera demonstrated, "we were quite fair. We left the bit of salami all for you!"

I spent the rest of the weekend thinking and reading. They had given me a new book at last—not my first choice in reading material for a prison cell, but a book nonetheless. Written in German, it was called *Nackt Unter Wölfen* (*Naked Among Wolves*) about the "Communists'" struggle under the Nazis at Buchenwald.

Sunday was a dark day. I stood on a *hocker* and leaned against the top, unoccupied bunk in front of the window to read, because that was the only way sufficient light could be shed on the book. After some time, I became aware of a strange stillness in the cell. The girls had been talking and giggling over a domino game, but now they whispered or talked not at all. It slowly dawned on me what was occurring. I waited another moment until I thought the time was right, then turned to face them. Sure enough—Vera and Rózsi both had their hands in the little brown bag of sugar lumps that I had placed in the table drawer. A fury grew inside me. They did not have to sneak them. I put them there for everybody; to share, not to sneak. As if stealing my *kolbász* was not enough—but maybe they had seen less sharing than sneaking and stealing. Maybe that was why they were here.

I tried to ignore it, but the fact was, the cigarettes were almost gone too. Within a day each girl had smoked most of her pack. There was no effort to save or ration. It seemed they were racing to finish them. Tomorrow they would be asking, no, begging for the rest of mine. Then they would want me to ask the major or Mr. Gross or anybody for more, and when they had no more, the fighting would intensify.

Monday morning brought a great surprise: Julia returned to cell two. Because it was very warm outside, she had done her hair up into an attractive upsweep on top of her head (hairpins were allowed at the *Gyüta* prison), and she looked stunning. Her beauty was unreal in a prison.

"Did you get to see your husband?" was her first question.

"For a whole, marvelous hour."

Julia was nervous that day, more than before. She did not have a lot to say. "There are fifteen defendants in my case," she told me, "and I am the major one. That is, I am charged with the greatest part in the money-handling, and the others are accomplices."

"Does that mean you will get the longest sentence?"

"Not necessarily," she explained. "Some of the others have second and third charges against them—charges in which I am not involved. I feel very sorry for them, and I wish I had never heard of the black market."

She was quiet the rest of the morning until she went to trial. I kissed her and wished her good luck. "Will you come back here before you leave again?"

"Yes, dear Jeanette, I think the trial will last several days. I will be allowed to stay with you until it's over, I hope."

Julia returned to the cell about twelve-thirty. "What happened? Tell us about it," she was asked in Hungarian and German alike. She first satisfied the curiosity of the majority, then

deal of fighting."

"Eight-year-old boys? How?"

"They could move faster than men and were harder to shoot, so they were the ones who darted in front of the tanks and planted hand grenades and homemade bombs in the armor. They put many tanks out of commission."

"You must have been terrified for your brother."

"Yes, he was lucky, though. A piece of schrapnel wounded his foot and put him in bed for several weeks. It may have saved his life."

At noon, on Wednesday, August tenth, I was called from the cell and taken through the main iron gate that separated me from the rest of the world and into a small, barren room with long tables and narrow benches, the conference room. There to greet me was smiling Dr. Nagy. *"Ah, mein Goldiges! Grüss Gott, grüss Gott! How are you?"*

We shook hands.

"Shaking hands is not allowed," admonished the guard.

"Fine, thank you, Dr. Nagy. I expected to see you sooner."

"Ah, my precious girl, you would not believe how very busy I am. I must rush from morning until night!"

"I wish I had your problems," I commented, not really for him to hear.

He must have thought I was joking, because he laughed. "Look now, we do not have much time," he chuckled as he spoke. "I have a letter here that Mr. Gross gave me from your parents. Do not touch the paper with your hands. I'll hold it and you may read it quickly. You are not allowed to keep it."

I read the letter and a tear managed to squeeze its way past the dam I thought I had erected against such mishaps. "Now, now, *mein Goldiges*, do you have a handkerchief with you? No? Take mine." He sounded worried that I would never stop crying, but I did. There was much to discuss.

"How long can you stay?" was my first question.

He looked at his watch, "Another eight minutes. I have to be in the courthouse at twelve-thirty. What do you need?"

"I would like to see Mr. Gross again as soon as possible."

"Again? What for?"

"There are many matters at home to be taken care of: our business, our car, and others," I explained. Mr. Gross knew of those things, in fact; more true was that I wanted to talk to him about changing to an English-speaking attorney. "Do you think he will come tomorrow?"

"I'll call him today, as soon as I leave here," he promised.

"Thank you very much. Dr. Nagy, how long do you think I will have to stay here?"

"Oh, now my dear," he chuckled cheerfully, "I cannot tell you that. That is for the judge to decide. But I will tell you one thing: I shall do my very best to see that you go home as soon as possible."

He sounded sincere. "I believe you," I said with equal sincerity, "but how long do you think the whole thing will be?"

"Well," he looked at me, then at the ceiling, then at me again, "maybe six months for you and more for your husband."

"Six months!" I almost jumped from my bench. "But I don't want more than the minimum. I cannot stand more than three months here!"

He smiled as though he had never seen such a dramatic display. "It is not so much. They could give you a lot more you know. Yes, I think I can get you off with six months."

"Won't you even try for less?" I protested. "Why not six weeks? It has been that long and I have been punished enough."

"I know how you feel, my dear. Naturally I'll try, but I know the judges. I have a feeling—" He seemed to flounder. For a moment I sympathized with Dr. Nagy. If he was on my side, it was not the most pleasant position to be in: a Hungarian lawyer defending a Westerner against the criminality of his own government. "I know it's not easy for you to defend me," I said, "and I will appreciate anything you can do."

"Well," he chuckled, "we will do our best, won't we?" He patted my hand while the guard wasn't looking and put my parents' letter back into his briefcase.

"Dr. Nagy," I said urgently, "Mr. Gross said that the sooner we have our trial, the better. Could you arrange that?"

"Let me see," he looked at the ceiling as he thought. "I will have to find out which judge has been assigned your case. It could be either of two judges. One is good, the other hard on foreigners, on everybody as a matter of fact. With him you will get six months."

"Dr. Nagy, will I know what the charge against me is?"

"Yes, the prosecutor will construct an indictment. I will read it to you."

"I want to read it myself. I want it translated into English."

"But you will have to pay for it."

"I don't care. My husband will pay. Please have it translated."

"Yes. Now I'm afraid I must rush. *Grüss Gott. Auf Wiedersehen, mein Kind.*"

Nothing much happened the rest of the week—little that was good, that is. Julia was a comfort to talk with, the only pleasure throughout the unending days, and I grew to be quite fond of her. Once some kind of warden's bulletin was given to her to read to the occupants of cell two as we all stood at attention before the *nevelőnő*. It was about four or five single-spaced, typewritten pages long, and a bore to stand through. "What was that all about?'

"You didn't miss anything," Julia replied. "It listed the prisoners who were bad, about fifty of them, and the ones who were good, about twenty-five, and named their penalties and rewards."

"Is that all?"

"It told about various departments, the laundry, the kitchen, and so forth. I think the reason they sent out the bulletin was to tell about two prisoners who tried to escape from the Markó a few months ago. They killed one guard and beat up another until they thought he was dead in order to steal the uniform and escape. This bulletin announced that they were hung this morning—just to keep the rest of us in line."

It was hot enough to bake us alive in the cell: a barred oven with no refuge. Everyone sat still, lazily sipping tepid water and trying to think of something besides the humidity.

Our number dropped at one point to six girls in cell two, with Julia, Vera, Rózsi, Mauri, Crazy Mary and me still together, and it was pleasantly roomier that way. But it didn't last long. Before the day ended, two more women came, one of whom was the old gypsy woman I had seen in the courtyard. She wore a multi-colored, flowered skirt, an unusual printed blouse and a tattered shawl, and she sat swaying in rhythm to her moaning and said little to anyone. "Watch out for that one," Julia cautioned me. The lonely old woman was such a sorry sight that I questioned her malevolence. "I was in another cell with her," Julia related. "She bragged in cell seven that she stole four hundred forint. Now she says she only stole a sweater to keep warm. I have seen her steal from her cell mates too."

The old woman wasn't with us long; the others saw to that. The sun had not set before they had galled her into an argument and called the guards. The colorful gypsy was transferred to quarters with gypsies only.

In her place came a woman about thirty-two years old, short and plump, with bleached golden hair. About two inches of her brown hair had grown out, making an ugly division of color.

"Julia!" the plump woman exclaimed, tears in her eyes.

"Marie!" Julia rushed to embrace her.

The two were old friends, Julia told me later. She introduced me to Marie, and the little woman put her short arms around me affectionately to show me that any friend of Julia's was a friend of hers, especially an American. "She likes Americans," Julia explained to me, "because she used to have an American boyfriend."

"What a coincidence that you two should meet here," I said. "Where do you know Marie from?"

"We used to work together."

"She seems like a nice person to work with. What did you do?" I asked idly.

"Oh, well, we didn't actually work together. We lived nearby and saw each other frequently."

It was not an answer to my question, but Julia was engrossed in discussion with Marie, and I was just making conversation anyway. Marie was miserable. She cried a lot and Julia tried to comfort her.

"What did she do?"

"She—she had too many boyfriends, if you know what I mean."

"It's legal in West Germany. Isn't it legal here?"

"No."

"Did the police catch her taking money from the men?"

"I don't know. Why?"

"I just thought that a girl could not be charged unless there was proof of a money exchange."

"It's more complicated than that in Marie's case. A girlfriend turned her in to the police and told them everything. Marie had to admit it."

"What kind of a friend would do that?"

"A no good one. She's here too. Her name is Kriszta. I'll point her out to you during the *séta*."

I wanted to ask more questions, but somehow I was always diverted. "It's terrible," Julia said, "because Marie has an eight-year-old daughter at home and she is worried sick about her." The two women spent a lot of time talking to each other. Though I was curious to know what they said, I contented myself with knowing that Julia was nearby in case I needed a voice.

After a couple of days they had talked themselves out, and there was more time for Julia to translate for all of us from Hungarian to German back to Hungarian. She didn't bother to translate some of the things the others said. When they laughed, I was particularly curious, because I wanted to laugh too. Often my interpreter would dismiss the remark with, "Oh, they are just being silly again, you know?" Yes, I knew how nonsensical they could be. Another standard reply was, "Oh, they are just talking about homos again."

"What about homos?" I tried to persist.

"Nothing. They are just speculating on who is and who isn't in the other cells." It seemed to me they spent an enormous amount of time discussing could-be homosexuals.

Vera left her position on the floor long enough to go and get the prison paper, a two- to four-page publication circulated once every couple of weeks inside the walls and strictly forbidden outside. There was a picture in this issue showing a couple of Americans with rifles aimed at a line of Vietnamese "civilians" along a wall. Without being able to read it, I knew it said that the "American Imperialists" were about to shoot innocent citizens.

"Why are the Americans trying to take over Viet Nam?" Vera asked. "It's such a small country, and so far away from you."

"We are not trying to take over the country. The government of Viet Nam asked us, and other countries, to help them. China and North Viet Nam are the aggressors. We are helping the South Vietnamese defend themselves. I think it's tragic that American boys are fighting and dying over there, and I wish the war would end today. But it is not so easy to pull out now." I felt more helpless than ever at that moment, knowing nothing I could say would change their judgment of us, not knowing the answers myself. Only my certainty that our purpose would be accomplished and the war would be over by the time we were all released gave me comfort.

"If you are helping the Vietnamese, why didn't you help us? Why didn't the Americans come in fifty-six when the Hungarians needed them?" Rózsi asked, and I remembered that her boyfriend was about to be sentenced to five years for being anti-Kadar and he had probably been involved in that revolution.

"What about the East German revolt of 1953?" someone else

asked. "Why didn't you come then?"

A guard came to check on us through the peephole. I had that "saved-by-the-bell" feeling, and the conversation was ended.

On another occasion, Vera asked, "Do you hate Negroes, Jeanette?"

"No, some Negroes I like very much, such as Harry Belafonte, Sidney Poitier, and 'Satchmo' Armstrong," I replied, naming people they knew of. "Some black people are attractive, nice people, and some aren't."

"Do you think gypsies are dirty and ugly?" Vera persisted.

"The dirty, ugly ones, yes. But there are clean, attractive ones too." Vera, although as pretty as a daisy, was sensitive about being a gypsy.

"Some people call gypsies 'the Negroes of Hungary,' " she blurted, eyeing me sharply for a reaction.

"I've never heard that, but what difference does it make if one has nothing against black people?" Only now did I learn that Hungarian gypsies have the same problems with prejudice in their country as American Negroes have in ours. Vera continued to study me for a time, then seemed to re-accept me.

Julia told of an experience she had once had with a Negro. It seemed that a black man had asked a friend of hers for a date after meeting in a dark bar, and the friend gave Julia's phone number. The man was nice, but Julia was engaged, and she had a devil of a time losing him. She got even with her friend, however, by giving her Ex-lax, unknown there, and telling her it was chocolate.

Crazy Mary related all sorts of stories, most of which Julia didn't bother to translate, about her experiences with Negroes and with policemen. The crazy one worked herself into such a state of excitement that she seemed to have a kind of fit, almost like an epileptic attack, but it was not from physical causes, and we had all seen her spasms before.

On that particular evening I cared less than I might have otherwise, because I was having stomach-ache problems. I had been having trouble for quite a while, but this time it was severe. I had not mentioned it or the absence of my period to the doctor because it frightened me to think of taking Hungarian medicine. The sleeping tablets were enough. Besides, I was told that the doctor was not a real doctor, but a prisoner who had had some medical training and who worked out his time in this way. My pain was intense. I could not walk straight and had to catch hold of the bedpost before doubling over. The girls became worried about me and rapped on the door. A guard came and ordered me to lie down, and eventually I felt better. "It must be gas," I diagnosed myself to Julia, but I began privately to worry about my health.

On Monday Dr. Nagy saw me for about ten minutes. "Bad news," he reported. "We didn't get the good judge. Your judge will be Dr. Stefanics. He is not popular. He is a cripple, and we have a saying in Hungarian about cripples. I can't translate exactly but——"

"Never mind, I can't understand exactly," I interjected.

"It says, 'watch out for a lame man. He always looks for opportunities to pass on his suffering to others.' "

"That's not a very kind saying." I was irritated.

"Now I shall tell you the good news," he said with delight. He gestured toward the other side of the room. "See that big box? I bought you a nice food parcel."

"Thank you. My appetite is beginning to wake up. The food will be a welcome sight, believe me."

"You must eat more, my dear. You are so thin. I brought you cheese, and sausage, and sugar. Oh my, I don't remember what all is in there."

"I thank you very much, Dr. Nagy."

"It's nothing. Glad to do what I can."

The food parcel had to go through a downstairs check, then an upstairs check; then I received it. There was about five pounds of food, maybe more. A general rule was supposed to limit parcels to two kilos, about four and a half pounds. As Dr. Nagy had said, there were cheese, sausage, sugar lumps—more than two pounds of them—and *kolbász*. There was also a half pound of real, fresh *butter*.

On the same day three other women in cell two received food parcels. They shared nothing. I couldn't be quite that miserly—after all, I had America to go back to—but I did learn to ration the giving so that the food would last a little longer. I gave the butter away freely, though, because it would soon go rancid in the heat. With good food in my box under the bed, I must admit that the world looked a lot better, even from a barred window.

That Monday was Julia's last day on trial. "I hope you don't have to serve another day," I wished her.

"I will have to, dear Jeanette," she said resignedly, "don't waste your hopes."

But she did not receive the verdict until the next morning. She had been a nice person, a good person to all of us in the Markó. Everyone quietly awaited her return with the final decision.

She entered the cell dry-eyed. *"Tizenhat hónap,"* she said. I understood the number: sixteen months.

Hungarians have a third of their penalty taken off when it is their first offense. "How long does that mean you have to remain, with the third removed?"

"Until the middle of January," she replied in a monotone. "I just can't imagine being in prison for a whole year of my life," she said half to herself. "And on the other hand, I find it hard to imagine getting out now." I knew the feeling.

We had been memorizing each other's addresses all week and now repeated them once more before the guards came to take Julia to a new prison. "Don't forget to write," she reminded me.

"I won't. I'll send you *San Francisco*." I referred to the music I had taught her.

"I'll visit you there some day."

Dr. Nagy came briefly the next day, August seventeenth, again at noon. I think he had orders to come at noon because there was less traffic in the prison, and fewer prisoners had the opportunity to try to talk to me then.

"Just one item of news today," the lawyer announced. "Your trial is scheduled for September sixteenth."

"But that's a whole month from now!" I complained. "I thought you said you would try to make it soon."

"It is the closest date we could get. The judge is on vacation until that week, so we have to wait."

"Isn't that a good reason to get another judge then?"

"*Mein Goldiges*, it doesn't work that way here."

"Is there any chance that I could go out on bail then, until the trial?"

He was chuckling as usual, "No, ha ha ha, I'm afraid that is not possible."

"I could go out in your custody, or the American Legation's, or in the police chief's custody, or——"

"No."

"I would sign a paper, sign anything."

"No, my dear, impossible."

I felt like throwing a tantrum. Instead, I slowly preceded the guard back to my cell. Many weeks already wasted, and now another month.

25

ON AUGUST eighteenth I was allowed to spend one hour in the prosecutor's office with Mr. Gross.

"I was hoping you could come sooner," I said. "Did Dr. Nagy give you my message?"

"Message? I tried to come. I applied right after our last visit, but this is the earliest they would grant permission. Do you know that your trial date is set for September sixteenth?"

"Yes. Will I be able to see you again before then?" Already I was concerned about losing him, my sole link with the sane world.

"Sure, they should permit me to come at least once again in the next month." He placed a bundle in front of me. "Here are some sandwiches for you, and pastry too." There was a thick tuna fish sandwich, my favorite, and ham and cheese, both on white rye. "I brought a thermos of American coffee, since you prefer it to Hungarian."

It was a banquet.

"How are things going?" I could have listened to him speak for the entire hour. When you haven't heard your own language for a long time, such common inquiries are music with new meaning.

"Better since the last time I saw you. After you put in the good word, they gave me someone to talk to for ten days. Her name is Julia. Her case, *divisen* exchange, has been in the papers. Have you read about it?"

"Black marketing foreign currency? Yes—I think I know the one you mean. Did you receive the magazines?"

"No, not a page. Maybe a guard 'borrowed' them. He will probably defect to the West next month to get the following issues.—Mr. Gross, I want to change lawyers. Will you help me?"

"I will if you're sure. Why?"

"Because Dr. Nagy's German confuses me. We don't seem to talk about anything important. He doesn't *do* anything, and I don't have confidence in him as an attorney. He brought me a parcel, but——"

"Good, then you got our food parcel."

"You mean *you* gave it to Dr. Nagy?"

"Yes."

"He didn't tell me that it was from you."

"Well, it doesn't matter, as long as you received it. I brought toilet articles for you today, and more food." A mere "thank you" seemed inadequate for such luxuries.

"I don't like Dr. Nagy. I don't trust him. He should have told me, not led me to think—" Mr. Gross was pursing his lips. "What's the matter?" I asked. "You think I'm unfair, don't you?"

"Not unfair. It should be your prerogative to choose the lawyer you want, but you have to consider where you are."

"What are you saying?"

"I did not realize that it would take this long to see you again when I gave you that list, and I don't know how changing lawyers at this late date would work, but I'm sure it would not be rapid."

"You think it might delay my trial even longer? You think I should not change?"

"I don't think it makes much difference who defends you. These things are generally pretty well pre-determined."

"All right," I said, resigning myself, "I'll stick with smiling Dr. Nagy. Have you heard from home?"

"Yes, there are lots of people who would like to help you. Your parents want to come to the trial."

"Oh no, they shouldn't. The trip is too expensive. They can't afford it, and it won't do any good anyway. I may not even be allowed to see them. Please tell them I love them but they must not come."

"I think you are right. Here is a letter from your parents."

In the letter, Mom listed numerous people who wished to help us. "This goes to show how wrong you can be about people," I admitted. "I thought most of them would forget they knew us."

"No, people are very concerned. The newspaper reporters will be waiting for you when you are released."

"Papers?" I was dumbfounded. Feeling desolate, I had thought only vaguely about publicity; to be in the news now was embarrassing. "I wanted to go home in the worst way, but now it scares me. I don't want people to know I've been in prison. What will they do to me?"

"They?"

"Our government, I mean."

"Don't worry about it. You've got lots of friends." He smiled, and that one winsome smile dispersed the butterflies in my stomach. I relaxed and began to eat the delicious food. We talked about the Hungarian judicial system. "A case like yours depends a lot on the political climate and foreign relations for its outcome," Mr. Gross told me.

"Have the two other Americans been sentenced yet?" I asked between sips of hot coffee.

"Yes, they received four months each. It won't be long until they fly to Vienna, then home. Oh, that reminds me, the luggage you stored at the hotel in Vienna is being held for you at the Embassy there."

"Thank you very much," I said with my mouth full of tuna fish.

"The airline tickets may be cashed in when you are free."

"What about our car?"

"The agency should send a man to pick it up. I'm working on that now." The Consul had taken care of a host of other problems for me too, such as assuring that our quarterly business taxes were paid, our mail picked up, the airline notified so that we would not lose the five hundred dollars paid on unused tickets. He had even written my apology to Ray, my now-former boss.

"What's happening outside? What about the war? Is it over?" Surely the world outside must be progressing toward peace; they must realize how valuable time is.

"No, I'm afraid there's no end in sight."

"I'll bet the Hungarians hold you personally responsible here."

"Ours has been luckier than some of the Embassies, but unfortunately, there have been anti-American demonstrations in the streets here lately. These things tend also to influence court decisions. It isn't going to do your case any good."

Mr. Gross asked if there were anything else he could help me with and I asked for a pair of nylon stockings to wear to the trial. "Thank you for all your help," I said as our time was up, wishing there was something I could do to prolong the brief respite.

Before I re-entered my cell, a guard led me to the warden's office. The prison director sat staunchly behind his desk, looking quizzically at me through his round glasses and toying with a parcel before him. I had the impression he called me only to practice his German. "This package was sent to you from the Americans, but I'm afraid such things are not permitted."

"None of it?"

"Some of it, of course, but not everything; do you understand?"

"Yes."

"How are you getting along? Do you need anything? Did you get a book?"

"Yes, thank you, but I'm finished. May I have a new one?"

"Yes, whenever you need one, tell the cell captain. She is in charge, do you understand?"

"Yes, thank you."

"Do you need anything else?"

"I would like to wear nylon stockings to my trial. The Consul will bring stockings for me, but I also need my garter belt from my suitcase."

"You may fill out a request slip for it. List all the things you need. I saw your husband today and told him you are receiving this parcel and that you are very well."

"How is he?"

"He is getting a parcel also, from the Canadians. They visited him. I told your husband that you have plenty of cigarettes." I bit my lip and waited while he took his time to continue. "He insists you do not smoke."

I took a breath. "Well—he doesn't know. You see— I've never smoked in front of him at home." What could be more true?

Since I don't smoke, I have never smoked in front of Busso. The warden was accustomed to deceits, I guess, because he accepted the explanation.

"How many cigarettes are in this carton?"

"Twenty per package, ten packages. That's two hundred."

He handed me both cartons. "You may have these, but no more for a month. Do not pass them out to the others. Do you understand? Do not order more cigarettes from the supplies list. There is a limit of four hundred per month and you have already had your quota. And this," he held up a bottle of green liquid, "what is it?" He opened it, sniffed, and put a drop on his finger to taste, even thought I told him it was shampoo.

"I would like to have it. Soap is not good for my hair."

"It is not permitted. You may buy Hungarian shampoo from the supplies list."

It seemed incongruous to me. "But why should I spend my money when I have shampoo right here?"

"Foreign shampoo is not permitted. It is the rule! And neither is this!" He held up two rolls of toilet tissue.

"Why not? It is a necessary item. I was permitted a roll before, why not now?"

"You will be permitted one roll, and that's all. No more, ever. You must buy the Hungarian paper. It is very good." He picked up two pencils with eraser tips, some paper and envelopes, and said, "This will be kept here in the office for you."

"May I write a letter today? I have only written one in all my time here."

"No, you may write when the others write. He opened a tube of Hungarian toothpaste and four bars of Dial soap, inspected them, then handed them to me. I was given the food without much inspection, the same tasty variety as before, plus some apricot jam which was transferred out of its glass container into a pan, all without much inspection, for none of it was wrapped, having been purchased at a Budapest market.

The warden commented that with such a generous parcel, I

could hardly need anything else. "My magazines," I contradicted, trying to gauge his reaction to the words to determine whether or not he had seen them.

"Magazines are not permitted." There was no room for discussion.

I hesitated to leave, thinking of the cigarettes. I didn't need them and wanted Busso to have them. The women wouldn't appreciate them and I dreaded the fighting. "Could I please give these to my husband?"

"No. He can buy some from supplies. He has enough anyway."

"But he isn't used to Hungarian cigarettes. He likes American."

"I told you it is impossible! No!" His voice changed from a commanding to a curious tone. "But why don't you want them?"

"I've decided to stop smoking."

"You have? Here? Don't you think you'll need them—under the circumstances?"

"Smoking isn't good for me. I have strong will power and self-control. I shall quit," I said, delighted with my fib.

"All right. The cigarettes will be put with your belongings in storage." I objected, but I had stretched his patience as far as it would go, and all I could do was return to the cell, feeling both guilty and glad.

While I had been gone, the women had all but engaged in major combat. No one greeted me, not even to vie for possible cigarettes. They were sullen and unspeaking, except for an occasional biting remark tossed in the air. I didn't know what it was all about, and didn't care. Without disappointment, I noticed that Crazy Mary was gone.

Unfortunately, she returned to the cell a few minutes later, and Rózsi was called. When she came back, Vera was taken. Then Marie. Then Mauri. Then Crazy Mary again. This time she packed her blankets and utensils into her *lavór* and left for good.

No one said good-by.

After she was gone, Marie, Rózsi and Vera tried to tell me what had happened: Mary had had one of her crazy fits, only worse than usual. The girls seemed to think it was very important that I understand.

The door opened again. "Jeanette!"

The warden looked even less cheerful than usual. He was upset, the poor man. "Did you look out of the window?" he came immediately to the point.

"Pardon me?" I needed a second to think, to determine how serious this was.

"Did you *look out the window at your husband?*"

"Yes."

"How many times?"

"Several."

He was breathing hard, "But you were told that that is strictly against prison regulations, were you not?"

"Nobody told me exactly—but I sort of guessed it."

"You surmised that it was not permitted, did you not?" His voice fairly smoked, and he did not wait for my answer. "Do you know that you will be severely punished for this?"

"But I——"

"Most severely punished! Have you seen our solitary cell, cell number twenty-five? Have you seen our dark cell, number six-teen? You may not be pleased with the food now, but how would you like half rations every other day?"

I thought he was going to spring across the desk at me. He was silent for a moment, giving me time to shrink from the thought of being alone again. "But I am going to be lenient with you," he said in a suddenly calm voice.

"Who told on me?"

"What makes you think somebody told?"

"Never mind. I know who did it. It was that crazy Mary, wasn't it? That lunatic."

"Are you unhappy in cell two?" the warden could sound

very paternal.

"I'd be unhappy in any cell. I want someone to talk to."

"I told you before, there is no one. You had Julia as long as she was on trial. When there is someone else, you will be put together."

"Thanks," I said dully, realizing he probably knew I knew he lied and he didn't care.

"Do you know your trial date yet?"

"September sixteenth. I can hardly wait. At least then I'll know when I can go home."

"What do you mean? Don't we treat you fairly here? Why should you be unhappy? Don't you have plenty of food—you said yourself you did—and we let you have two food parcels." He was honestly offended, as if I were criticizing the hospitality of his home.

"It's not the conditions here, it's the whole system," I tried to explain, but I could see by his expression that my few words were inadequate to bridge the void between us. For one thing, he was obviously not used to conversing with a prisoner in this manner. That alone perplexed him beyond words, yet he was fascinated.

"The fact is, you broke the law, and the law states——"

"The fact is, some laws should not exist."

"That has nothing to do with it! It is neither your place nor my place to challenge the law." He was a military man, not a philosopher.

"I do not agree."

"Nonetheless, you are a prisoner. You must follow the prison rules. This is not America!"

"Yes sir, that is true." I had treaded one step too many perhaps, but at least we had agreed on something.

"Dismissed!"

Ten minutes later the cell door opened. "Jeanette! Hurry. Hurry!"

"I quickly piled my possessions into my *lavór* as directed, now regretting my impudence and dreading the punishment I faced. Mauri ignored me, but Vera, Rózsi and Marie had tears in their eyes as they kissed me goodby, and the guard led me toward number sixteen, the black cell.

Part Four

26

FIVE MINUTES LATER, instead of finding myself in number sixteen as expected, I found myself in twenty-two, a cell next to the warden and *nevelőnő*'s office. There was a sink, a toilet, two double bunks and four *hockers*. It was a dingy, cramped cell. The only window, on the east side, let little light in. Three women faced me. "*Guten Tag*," greeted the youngest, a girl my age.

"Don't tell me you speak German," I exclaimed.

"Of course I do. It's good for business," she chuckled easily, took a long drag on a cigarette, and carefully appraised me from head to foot.

"My name is Janet."

"Jeanette, I know, the American. My name is Kriszta."

"I know. Marie told me."

"Oh yes. You come from her room. What did she tell you about me? That I am bad? That I got her in trouble?"

"She didn't say much. She doesn't speak much German, you know, only a few words." So this was the "evil Kriszta" Julia had pointed out to me. She was attractive; not pretty, but handsome. There was a masculinity about her, an independence, a shrewdness that put me on my guard. It was best to say as little as possible, let her do the talking. "How did you know I'm American?"

"The telephone," she thumbed in the direction of the water pipes.

"Then you must know all about me. Tell me about you. Why are you here?"

"Didn't Julia tell you? The same reason she and Marie are here. I'm a whore." She caught me off guard and it must have been evident. "No, I can see that *sweet Julia* didn't tell you. Cigarette?" she offered.

"No, thanks," I said, glad to find something to reply to her.

"She didn't tell you, did she? What did she say she's in for, stealing apples?"

"She told me," I didn't like the sneer in her voice. I didn't like her insinuation that Julia was a liar. "She didn't put it quite so crudely, that's all."

"Why not? I can't think of a better word for it myself." She continued talking, but I wasn't listening. Julia had lied to me, she had deliberately avoided the truth. Why? It was one thing for Gretchen to fabricate, but Julia was different. I trusted her. She was my friend. The things she had said suddenly began to form a pattern in my mind: Marie had boyfriends and she and Marie had "worked together—well, not exactly together." At what? Her girlfriend had given her telephone number to a man in a bar. She got her *divisen* "from tourists and salesmen." Mr. Gross had hesitated when I told him about her. "I'm not good," she had said, but I never considered the motive for such modesty. She should have told me. She should have known that I did not care what she had done. What was our friendship now that she had not told me? But maybe I never gave her a real opportunity. She was no common gamin, of that I was sure.

Kriszta was an altogether different breed. She was straightforward enough, but she enjoyed using the truth in a cruel way. I would have to beware.

"Why were you transferred out of two?" she asked.

"For looking out the window at my husband."

"What room is he in?"

"Fifth floor, twenty."

"You watch the door." She went to the window, whistled, talked, listened, and reported back, "Too bad, he was transferred today too, otherwise we would be neighbors."

"Where is he now?"

"They don't know."

I asked about the other women in the cell. One, Anna, had stolen linen from the factory where she worked. She was a plump, inconspicuous little middle-aged woman, ashamed of her crime, afraid of her penalty, who sat in the corner praying for atonement and crying. "I keep telling her to cut the bawling, it won't do any good, but she's too stupid to listen," Kriszta told me. "She's so dumb she thinks there will be an amnesty Saturday."

"I've heard talk of it."

"Well there won't be an amnesty, so don't hope."

The other woman was named Julika, meaning little Julia, and she had a quick, toothless smile. She looked like a hybrid of a monkey and a prune, one of the homeliest people I have ever seen, yet she was a delightful companion. Julika had an amiable Red Skelton kind of humor, the soul of a baby, and Marcel Marceau's unique ability to communicate. She wore a pair of cotton fleece navy blue sweat pants and a tattered brown shirt—her only clothing inside or outside the prison. I judged her to be at least forty-five, but Kriszta told me she was thirty-one. "She's a drinker," Kriszta explained. "Her only complaint here is that there is no wine."

Julika's favorite place was the toilet seat. She moved herself only when somebody had to go or when she wanted to take her *pohár*, her tin cup, from the shelf. Each time, she held the beaker of water in her hand and, after resuming her position Indian style on the toilet, she would stare forlornly at the cup and repeat the word, "*Szomorú, szomorú.*"

"*Szomorú* means 'sad,' " Kriszta translated. "Julika is lamenting how sad it is that they do not have wine in the tap instead of water." I asked why she was here. "She stole a raincoat. One of those nylon raincoats that are so popular in the West, you know?"

"Yes, I bought one for eight dollars in Vienna."

"She didn't steal it for herself. She wanted to sell it on the black market to get money for wine."

"She's such a lovable little thing," I said. "What kind of life does she have?"

"Drinking is her life. She has never been married. She'll never have children, her insides are ruined. I think she is still a virgin, for that matter." Kriszta shuddered at the thought. "Her body is wasted."

Virgin, wino, whatever—Julika was a dear cellmate. Each morning and each evening she gingerly held her *pohár* against mine and we drank a toast to each other, sometimes to Hungary and America, to Kadar and Johnson, to the whole nonsensical world. When she left our cell a week later—after her trial, where she was sentenced to four months of cleaning duty in the Markó, she wished me luck with a smile of optimism that banished self-pity, and left me with a story: A judge heard a funny joke in court and was still laughing after adjournment. His friend met him in the corridor and asked what was so amusing. "I can't tell you," replied the judge, "I just sentenced the man who told it to five years."

Cell twenty-two was quite a change from two. It was dark even during the middle of the day, because the window faced a small courtyard where coal was stored. It was quieter, less hectic; and cooler, since the sun never hit directly. At first I thought it was a change for the better, because I had someone to talk to. Kriszta was twenty-four, a year younger than I, and she had little good to say about anybody, but she was an intelligent young woman, well educated in the arts, and interesting. Her German was poor—something worse than José Jimenez's English and often as laughable. She asked me to help her but was irritated when I corrected her. I made profuse errors, but she was not proficient enough to recognize them. When she did spot an error in my grammar, she jumped at the chance to point it out. In one case, it was not my grammar but my choice of words that disturbed her.

"*Ich bin so heiss*," I said, which means, literally, "I am so hot."

"Don't say that!" Kriszta commanded. "That is wrong. It sounds awful."

"All right, I'm *warm*."

"No!" she cried, "that's worse."

"Why? I really am hot," I insisted, knowing what bothered her but pursuing it all the more.

"It is hot outside, you can say, or it is warm to me today, but not I am hot. That's dirty."

"Phooey, that's childish. If the weather is hot, I'm hot."

"Don't say that! I'm warning you, Jeanette. If you get in with the wrong company—" She let the sentence dangle ominously in the air, even more vexed because I smiled in rebuttal.

If I irritated Kriszta, the irritation became mutual. She blocked every attempt I made to learn Hungarian. "What did the guard say, Kriszta?" I often asked. "What does that word mean?" I always received answers just a little short of what I needed to know. "Kriszta, I want to learn Hungarian. Help me!"

"Hungarian? What the devil for? Who in this world will you talk to when you get out? Don't waste your time." She constantly refused.

There was a chess board in our cell and I asked Kriszta to teach me to play.

"It is not an easy game to learn," was her uninterested reply.

"Kriszta, it would be something for both of us to do. It's better than sitting. Teach me!"

"All right." She showed me how to set the board up. "I'm not sure whether the queen stands to the right or to the left of the king, but it doesn't matter." She named each figure and told how they were permitted to move. We began to play. It was confusing, not at all like checkers, at which I am a consistent loser, anyway. Kriszta made her moves, explaining which of my men were in danger and pointing out counter moves for me. As the figures were eliminated from the board one by one, I began to catch on. I even made a couple of decent moves on my own that made Kriszta think a little more than she had anticipated. With her help and beginner's luck, I won the game.

"Let's play another," I suggested. It was fun, the first thing I had done with enthusiasm in prison. "Or should we wait until after the *séta?* We only have about a half an hour."

"Don't worry, there is time," Kriszta replied levelly. She was right. There was no reason to worry about being interrupted by the walking because the second game lasted only minutes. Kriszta would not help me with a single move. I got mixed up and forgot which man could move in what direction. Kriszta said only, "You can't do that. That's wrong." To the other two women who were watching us Kriszta commented each time she took easy victory over me. When she called out, "Checkmate!" I was glad. She made me furious. I decided to learn the game in spite of her, or just to spite her. From then on, it was war on the chessboard.

Saturday, August twentieth, 1966, marked the tenth anniversary of the last amnesty granted prisoners in Hungary, the amnesty of the revolution. Mention of it in the prison paper had promoted the rumor that there would be a similar release of prisoners this year and many women, like Anna, clung to the hope and prayed for the miracle.

Some dreamed vaguely, like me, "Wouldn't that be great? I would be home in time for the hydroplane races."

And some scoffed at the rest of us for our delirium, like Kriszta. "You're as stupid as Anna, Jeanette."

The twentieth began with a current of electric anticipation at the morning *séta;* then the day passed like any other Saturday, and ended with distraught abandonment of vain hope. The wailing of some was louder than usual that night.

Even though I now had a translator, the daily problems still remained. "Please ask for a book for me, Kriszta," I requested at least fifty times.

"You do not just ask for a book here. This is not a library, and those bulls out there are not your errand-boys. You will get your book when *they* are ready to come around and give you one."

"But the warden told me I could have one any time I asked."

"Why should you be treated any differently from the rest of us?"

"But Kriszta, I'm not asking that. You like to read. You said yourself a couple of days ago that you wished you had a new book too. Why can't you ask for both of us?"

"Can't you get it through your head that I cannot make demands, not for a book, not for anything, until they give me permission to make a request? Besides, the less I talk to those pigs, the better I like it. I'm the cell captain. I have to follow the rules even if you don't. I speak only when spoken to."

"If you won't help me, I'll help myself."

"It's your neck," she warned me. "Why don't you just relax and have a smoke. It helps the time go by."

"No, thanks." She made me boil. She was in a position to help me and she wouldn't. And, what angered me more, for a week Kriszta had repeatedly won at chess. I wanted a book to distract me, and I determined to get one. The next time a guard passed our door on his rounds, I tapped lightly on it with my knuckle, not a spoon, to draw his attention. He looked through the *spy*.

"*Mi van*, Jeanette?"

I held up a book. "*Buch. Könyv, kérem*." It was no sentence, but it was polite. Two hours later I had a new book to read—and a cell captain who spit fire.

Another problem was less easy for me to solve by myself. The supplies that Julia had helped me order, shampoo, toilet paper, soap, *baba púder* and baby cream, were supposed to be delivered to me within a few days. Two weeks later they were still not there. "Kriszta, please ask the *nevelőnő* what happened to my order. I need the shampoo. This soap is ruining my hair."

"I'll ask her when she's in a good mood and not in a hurry." But that time never came. I badgered Kriszta about it until finally she asked. "The *nevelőnő* says it should have been here by now. It must be lost, so you will have to fill out a new order." For once Kriszta helped with a minimum of argument. "When you get your baby cream, I'll show you how I used to get a facial massage every day. I'm very good at giving them too."

When the supplies finally came a week later, she had me lie across three *hockers* while she gave me a facial. The cream was a dark-yellow color, like mustard, but the massage was fun. The only problem was getting the "mustard" off my face again with slick toilet tissue and cold water.

The first Monday after the shampoo came, I put it with my towel and soap to take to the shower. "You can't take that shampoo with you to the shower," Kriszta commanded.

"Why not?"

"Only soap and a towel are allowed."

"But I want to wash my hair."

"You're not supposed to wash your hair in the shower."

"When am I supposed to wash it then?"

"On Thursday when we get warm water in the *Kana*."

"Are you kidding? One pitcher of water for four women?" I flared. "That's ridiculous."

"It's the rule. I forbid you to take your shampoo to the shower, and I forbid you to wash your hair there. It's for your own good. Shampoo is not allowed in the shower."

"Other girls wash their hair. Why shouldn't I?"

"Other girls get in trouble. I'm warning you."

"All right, I won't take the shampoo." I knew Kriszta was overexercising her power, so, before we left the cell, I rubbed shampoo around the base of my scalp and then lathered it under the shower. It worked out well. I didn't get in trouble, and Kriszta didn't say a word to me the rest of the morning.

During that same week I tried also to coax Kriszta to write out a request slip for me to obtain my garter belt, high heels, and deodorant.

"You'll never get the deodorant," she predicted.

"Just write it down anyway. Please!"

"I will in due time. But your trial isn't for weeks yet." And that's how she left it.

We argued about the guards, she insisting that they were all sub-human and I maintaining, though I had little adoration for them myself, that they couldn't all be evil. She retorted as usual, "You're a foreigner. You don't understand."

It seemed that Providence was on Kriszta's side this time, and I was to learn to understand through one explicit example:

Kriszta preferred blond men. One of the guards was blond and good-looking. One day after the *séta* where he was on duty I said, "I think that one has his eye on you, Kriszta."

"He would be my type, if he weren't a guard." She was definite about it. "I like men; guards aren't men."

"A man has to earn a living, you know."

"Not this way, he doesn't. He can dig ditches or wash dishes, something more respectable."

"Well, whatever he is, he sure likes to look at you."

"Let him," she replied without interest. "I don't charge for looks."

It was Kriszta's habit to take her time about bathing in the evening. She didn't put her washpan on the floor and squat over it as the others did. She placed it on a stool, then spread her legs and sat around the rim. It took a certain amount of balancing to avoid tipping the water out, but it was, in a way, more stately than squatting on the floor.

"Shouldn't you turn your back toward the door when you sit like that, Kriszta? Or are you on exhibition for some peeping bulldog?"

"Watch your mouth, Jeanette," she threatened coolly. "You know I'd sooner spit in their dirty faces. The guards can't look in during wash hour. It's strictly forbidden."

"Do you think they follow the rules any more than the prisoners do?"

She didn't answer, but for the next couple of days, she turned her back to the door.

Eventually, however, the conversation was forgotten, and Kriszta sat as she pleased on her wash pan. I was startled one evening by a ribbon of smoke which slithered into our cell through the *spy*. "Hey look. Something's burning." But immediately I knew that such a trickle of smoke comes only from a cigarette. "Someone is watching."

Kriszta was furious. "It was that ugly blond rat," she said, "I know it was. I'm going to report him if it's the last thing I do."

I knew how difficult it was for Kriszta to speak up in front of the *nevelőnő*, and informing was strictly against her code of ethics, but this time she made an exception. I was there when she reported the guard. She said it quietly and did not waste words.

Never before had I seen the *nevelőnő* verbally assault anyone the way she did Kriszta. She swore, she shrieked, she slammed the door so that the bolts nearly flew off.

"What happened?" I forced my gaping mouth to close.

"She called me a liar and a dirty, stinking slut, and if that wasn't enough, she called my name so that the whole building knew who she was screaming at and called me a filthy cocksucker. Now do you understand why I hate to talk to these pigs? Don't get the impression that the *nevelőnő* is the worst there is," Kriszta pressed me to understand. "She's mild compared to the *Vipera*. That one is out for real blood. She took this job originally to avenge her husband's death. He was transporting a prisoner years ago from Budapest to another prison out of the city. The handcuffed man broke loose and pushed the guard off the train. His body was crushed by the train. The killer was hung, but that wasn't enough for the widow. She worked into her husband's job and has been torturing cons ever since." My roommate stalked the cell as her vehemence poured forth. "Then in fifty-six when some of the prisoners broke out, they cornered the *Vipera* and the *nevelőnő* in a cell and beat them so badly that the *Vipera* was in the hospital for over two years and the *nevelőnő* for at least half that. Both are bitter, which is understandable, but they are evil besides. Don't think the men are any better," she added, "they want it from every girl. Watch out for that *civil major*." I could still feel his quickened breath on my neck. "I think you would title him the Political Prisoner Overseer, or something like that. He's married to the fat one downstairs who searches you." I recalled the one who brushed off the sleeve I had touched. "With a wife like that you can hardly blame the slob for taking what he can get. He's a coward, so keep your distance, and he is easy to handle." She waited for her tutelage to sink in, then repeated her question with greater urgency, "Now do you understand?"

"I am beginning to," and with greater understanding, hostilities are magically diminished.

27

Two WEEKS ELAPSED before Dr. Nagy came to see me again. He did not bring a letter from my parents. "They must not have written," he offered.

I did not believe that my parents had not written, and I did not believe that he had even talked with Mr. Gross as he claimed he had. He asked how I was, and when I automatically replied "fine," he responded, "Of course you are. You're looking very well," which I did not believe either, and which was just enough to bring me to say what was on my mind.

"Dr. Nagy, what do you propose to do for me at the trial?"

"Why my dear, defend you of course. You need have no worry there."

"But what will you *say?*" I persisted.

There was a pause as he looked at me rather blankly. "What are you getting at?" he asked with a note of suspicion. The absence of "My dear" was noticeable.

"You always seem so rushed for time. You haven't been here

five minutes, and already you've looked at your watch three times."

He chuckled, "*Aber, mein Goldiges*, I am very busy. All attorneys are. I have appointments to keep, other clients to defend. Do you realize that I have at least forty people to defend? I would like to stay with you and talk, but——"

"If you don't have time to talk to me, how will you have time to study my case?"

"The reports are available to me. I told you, I already read them." He seemed satisfied with that explanation.

The Hungarian reports. What did they say? I gave up. "Dr. Nagy, I understand that you are very busy. Perhaps we would both be better off if I find another lawyer."

"In addition to me? But you would have to pay him. The State does not——"

"Instead of you. The State would pay him instead of you."

His injured expression surprised me. I hadn't thought that it mattered to him one way or the other. "Aren't you satisfied with me?"

"It's not that exactly," I hedged, "it's just that I would feel more comfortable with an attorney who speaks my language, English."

"But we understand one another."

"We understand the small talk like 'how are you,' but we don't seem to get down to business, to say anything of importance. I didn't even know the word for *prosecutor* until that other man told me."

He lit a cigarette. "All right," he said, blowing the smoke out slowly, "but you don't know any Hungarian lawyers, do you?"

"Mr. Gross gave me a list of English-speaking Hungarian lawyers. Please call him. I would like number two or number seven on that list. He will arrange it for me. Will you call him?"

He smoked in silence for a moment, then replied, "Yes, I will do that for you, Mrs. Lemmé."

"Thank you. It will be appreciated. Please believe it is nothing personal, you understand."

"Of course. Of course."

I returned to my cell, wishing I had never mentioned the subject. Mr. Gross and Busso both had told me it didn't matter, and Julia too. I told Kriszta what I had done. "Jeanette, you are so naive," she reacted with a sigh of pity.

"Thanks, but I've been informed already." I was more irritated at myself than with her.

"But you are. Your Mr. Gross is right. It won't make any difference who you have, or if you have one at all. You'll be sentenced to whatever the judge decides. In fact, it's probably already decided, and your lawyer knows it."

It was so frustrating I could have clawed the walls down. "But what am I supposed to do? Sit by and do nothing, resign myself to whatever whimsical fate the judge chooses to impose on me? At least now I'm making an attempt to help myself. The lawyer must do something at the trial. He must say something. Dr. Nagy is a nice old uncle, but who would ever listen to him even if he could choose succinct, impressive words? I want someone dynamic."

"There's no such thing as a dynamic lawyer. There are just money-hungry ones."

"Dr. Nagy has never asked for money. That's one good thing I can say for him."

"He will, don't worry. Look, I know what I'm saying. I went that route once myself and learned the hard way."

"What route?"

"I was in jail before, in a children's jail, you know what I mean?"

"Yes, we call them reformatories. Why were you there?"

"Same thing, whoring. I hired a lawyer. I was really scared then and I wanted him to save me from the year in jail I faced."

"Didn't he help?"

"Are you kidding? I paid him the five thousand forint he demanded before the trial. He swore I would not get more than six months. I got fourteen. No thanks, I don't need any more law-yers."

"Not even now?"

"When I get to court, they will have one there waiting for me, but he can go to hell for all I care."

A week later I was called to the counseling room. It was good to be out of the cell, but I felt apprehensive. Who would my new lawyer be? Could he speak English? What if he was even worse than Dr. Nagy?

"*Grüss Gott, mein Goldiges!*" A familiar voice flourished its overabundant cheer on me. I returned the greeting with more en-thusiasm than usual, genuinely relieved to see Dr. Nagy.

"*Nun mein liebes Kind,*" he began immediately without wait-ing for my questions, "I tried everything, absolutely everything to find another lawyer for you." I listened quietly. He had pre-pared his speech; let him carry on. "I called both the lawyers you asked for. The first one was out of town." I nodded and he con-tinued with an urgency I had never guessed was in him, "There is no way of reaching him, and he will not be back until after your trial."

I pondered as to whether or not to ask him why he had not called and asked Mr. Gross to handle it as I had requested, but decided it would only antagonize him unnecessarily. "I see. That's fine, I don't care," I assured him. Dr. Nagy seemed so con-cerned that I felt guilty for having bothered him, but he would not be stilled.

"And I tried repeatedly to contact the other one, what was his name?"

"I don't remember. It does not matter." I was tired, so tired of trying to get somewhere; it made me even wearier listening to stories, true or not, of how other people got nowhere too.

"Well, anyway, whatever his name is, I couldn't reach him at all. He was never in, never! You know how busy we lawyers are here." He continued his monologue, and I let him run himself out. It was the most he had ever said to me. "Oh yes, before I forget, here is a letter from your folks."

He held the letter and turned the pages for me. Dad was the best tonic to revive my wilted spirits. He wrote, "I took Joli (the dog) to have a coke with me the other day and the waitress, a real dumb blonde, was surprised I ordered a soda for him. I had to explain to her that he's too young to drink beer." I laughed right out loud. It seemed to me the funniest joke I had ever heard. Mom wrote, "I was sorry to hear from Mr. Gross that it's not possible for an attorney from the Legation to defend you," and I laughed again. If Dr. Nagy could read English, I believed he would have answered the letter to tell Mom how "naive" she was.

Before he left, I said, "Dr. Nagy, I hope you will excuse me for putting you to the trouble of looking for a different lawyer. I'm sure you will do all that is in your power."

For the first time, the artificial smile, the theatrical cheer left Dr. Nagy's face, and he said, "You can trust me. I am on your side. Nobody could wish your release more than I, believe me." His voice was serious and he leaned across the table closer to my face. "Listen carefully," he whispered. "My son is in the West. He left this country not long before you entered."

"You mean he escaped?" I was dumbfounded.

He nodded but would not use the word. "That's all I can tell you. He was a law student, planned to be a lawyer like his dad," his eyes glistened like a father's, with moisture and pride. "I'll tell you about it some day." Immediately his gay façade returned and the subject was dropped, but a new fondness for the red-faced old lawyer eased its way into my heart.

Later that same afternoon I went to the doctor's office. Next to me in the waiting room sat a woman who spoke both German and English. I told her why I was in the Markó and asked about her.

"I tried to escape," she whispered. "My husband is sick—it's a long story—and I tried to get him to Italy where a doctor I've heard of might be able to help him."

"Might? You mean you're not sure?"

"No, but it was worth the chance. He'll die without special treatment, that much we know. He can only get that treatment in the West."

"What's wrong with him?"

"He has radiation poisoning. He was in a concentration camp for nine years. He was sentenced to twelve years, but was released early, in 1962."

I could not find words to express my horror.

"It's worse now. This is our second attempt to escape. If we don't find a good lawyer and have our trial soon, he'll die in prison."

"I have Dr. Nagy. Have you heard of him?"

"Nagy? János Nagy? I know him personally. He lives not far from me."

"What do you think of him?"

"Do you want the truth?"

"Of course."

"He is a failure as a lawyer and as a man. He forces a laugh all the time to cover up the fact that he drinks too much. He's a lush. Nobody can stand him. Even his son ran away to the West just a few months ago to escape him. He's no lawyer. He's a bum."

Before I could ask why, if he was such a loss, he was allowed to practice law, the *Vipera* came into the room, scowled at both of us, and took the woman away. I returned to my cell, feeling sorry I had asked and wishing I could have asked a lot more.

I tried to tell myself that soon after the sixteenth my interment would end, and that I should look on the experience as a test of endurance that would "make me stronger spiritually," as Mom had written. But my nerves would hear none of it. I did not feel, as one might in fear, that I stood at a precipice with the rock slowly falling away from under my feet. I felt I *was* that rock. I felt that day by day a chunk of my strength, of my sanity, of my life crumbled into dust. There was no such thing as my "adjusting to the environment," I thought. Nothing short of freedom could remedy my quasi-claustrophobia.

It was probably a combination of causes rather than just the food that brought on my diarrhea. The food, to be sure, was reason enough to become ill, but if it had been the sole cause, I think I would have succumbed to it much earlier. True, I had had only a couple of eggs at the *Stasi* and none since. Next to no meat at all was served, just a few pig's knuckles every week or so. Occasionally a few yellow Hungarian paprika were allotted each prisoner, and even less often, a mini-pear or apple. My favorite dish, other than mashed potatoes, was cabbage in tomato paste, but the general fare was noodles: *tészta, tarhonya, csigatészta*—each shape had a different name.

I think it was more an emotional reaction, mostly to Kriszta, that caused my stomach-ache. Until I entered twenty-two, I had been in a state of shocked, solemn depression. Because she angered me so thoroughly and so often, Kriszta rekindled the fight in me. I became so nervous that, particularly during our daily chess game, while I was losing, I had to use the toilet repeatedly. Having diarrhea in confinement and without privacy is one thing I shall not attempt to describe for the reader.

I asked the doctor to give me something for it. He mashed some charcoal squares in water and gave it to me to swallow twice a day. After three days of charcoal and no results, I decided the affliction was easier to bear than the treatment, and that I would cure myself with discipline. My throat was sore most of the time, but it was a good excuse to go to the doctor often to have it swabbed. The thing that bothered me most was the pain in my stomach. It came irregularly. I did not want to tell the doctor: I did not want him and his assistants to examine me, and I did not want any foreign medication for it. I had not menstruated since early June and visions of bearing a child in prison haunted me.

Everything rested on the trial. If only it would be today. If only I could know how much longer I had to remain in this iniquitous hole. At night I took sleeping pills while the aide who brought them watched to be sure I swallowed them. Even so, I learned to fool him by slipping the tablet under my tongue, faking consumption, and removing it after the guard moved on. One pill was not strong enough to assure sleep. By saving one every second evening, I was sure to sleep on alternate nights. Sometimes I slept in between, without the drug; perhaps because the fear of insomnia was relieved.

Part of my problem in sleeping was the noise of the dogs outside in the coal yard. I had heard them often from cell two, but it had been distant and not so disturbing. Now three dogs entertained themselves nightly directly outside my window. I asked why they were there. "To torment us?"

"They are hungry," Kriszta explained. "They are here to catch rats."

"I thought cats are supposed to catch rats."

"Not these rats. The dogs are specially trained."

"What rats? Where?"

"Rats in the sewer pipes. I've heard tell that the rats have climbed right up to the sixth floor. It's true, I'm sure it is." She watched me turn green. "Have you ever seen rats as big as a cat? Shall we leave some bread in the toilet tonight?"

"Let's not—unless you want me to scream your eardrums numb."

When it seemed to me that I had hit bottom and things had to get better, Erszi came to our cell and proved how wrong I could be. She was about five feet six, my age, with a pleasant, freckled face, and weighed at least two hundred pounds. Julika was already gone, and Anna was transferred to another cell that same day, so there were just the three of us, but the cell still seemed overcrowded with Erszi's obese figure occupying enough space for two.

Kriszta was delighted to have someone to talk to instead of

weepy Anna. The two Hungarian girls spent the first couple of days in constant dialogue and left me to read a thick book in German about a young woman's love affair with communism. Kriszta did not entirely ignore me, but I sometimes wished she would. Whenever she talked to me, it was either to argue or to play chess, and playing chess was the same as arguing. During the games, Kriszta continued to talk, make jokes, and laugh with Erszi. I knew it was a deliberate attempt to show me she was so sure of victory that she didn't have to give the match her full attention, and I concentrated on every move. At last, convoking all the lessons I had learned, I won a game. Kriszta was amazed, and so was I. She concentrated a little more for the next round and won. Then, in order to distract me, she began singing during the games. That took the cake: I blew up and refused to play anymore.

"Suits me. I thought you wanted to learn," she shrugged. "It's your loss."

She was right, it was my loss. She and Erszi could amuse themselves talking together or playing a simple game of dominoes. Erszi's favorite pastime was to post Kriszta at the door, climb up on the radiator to look out the window, and talk to the men on the fifth floor. Since our cell was on an inside corner of the building, we could see the barred windows of the cells adjacent to us. It was dangerous to stand at the window during the day, however, because of the *nevelőnő's* office next door, so Erszi tried to contain herself until after six. At night she did not need the radiator, because she stood on her bunk, the one above Kriszta's and could talk from there. Usually she talked at wash time, neglecting to bathe herself, bouncing on the mattress with her skimpy underslip hiked up on massive rolls of fat and her not-so-large breasts jiggling up and down on a gargantuan abdomen. She often coaxed Kriszta to the window too. Kriszta appeared to enjoy herself almost as much as Erszi, but she told me candidly, "Those grubby men are not good enough for me. They are thieves and liars. They all say they are innocent. I like a man who does what he believes in, like I do, and admits it when he's caught."

Women could have come to their windows across from ours too, to talk to Erzsi, but it wasn't worth the risk. Except for one, that is, one who called out in a brazen voice so that the whole cell block could hear—but then Erzsi dropped back from the window in fear of exposing herself. I asked Kriszta who it was that flaunted the rules so blatantly.

"That's Bertha. She has been in prison and in the dark cell so many times that the guards know it's no deterrent." I asked why she was here and what she was shouting. "She's a lesbian. I don't know why she is in this time, but she is hollering out the window that the guards are a bunch of pigs. She says they have no understanding or feeling for people in love."

"She's in love?"

"Ja, she has a girlfriend here in the Markó. I don't know who it is. Probably your dear friend Julia."

"Julia isn't in the Markó." I refused to take the bait for another quarrel. "You mean she actually admits she's a lesbian?"

"Sure. She's not ashamed of it. And you'll never find a more faithful lover, either. A few weeks ago she was in the same cell with her girlfriend—maybe that's when this great love was born. She thought someone else was trying to steal her sweetheart and tore into the girl like a mad dog. All three women had to be separated."

"I remember some commotion. I thought it was a break-out by the men on the fifth. Is she really jealous, like a man, over another female?"

"That's putting it mildly. You should see her fight. Just like a male." Kriszta described her to me, and I recognized the description as that of the woman I had seen entering the dark cell once. "We were in the same cell for two days," Kriszta told me, "and I think she was developing a crush on me." I commented to the effect that people seek out their own kind, and Kriszta took it lightly, as intended. "She was sent to the black cell for spitting on a guard, so I never had a chance to set her straight. She didn't mean any harm, not to me, I mean."

I found Berta one of the few seemingly normal things about the Markó. "In a place like this, you can see why people get confused."

"*Ja*, well, Berta has been confused this way all her life, long before she came to prison. She has been in at least a dozen times just for homosexual activities in Budapest. You better let this be a lesson to you, Jeanette. Watch who you sympathize with in here. Watch who you smile at—and don't say 'I'm hot'!"

I was not as worried about Berta as Kriszta would wish; I was just curious. I coaxed Kriszta to get Erzsi to find out why Berta was in prison this time.

"She expects four months because she came into Budapest."

"Is that against the law?"

"For Berta it is. The judge who sentenced her last time ordered her to stay outside the city. She is a real headache to the cops."

I suppose since Erzsi had talked to her once, Berta knew she had an audience, so although Erzsi stayed away, Berta spent all one Sunday afternoon calling out the window. It began as chit-chat and progressed to a lament over her separation from her friend. If it had been a weekday, the *nevelőnő* would have punished her severely, but on this particular Sunday the guards on duty apparently didn't want to be bothered. They let her yell and would report it on Monday. Kriszta translated intermittently for me, with amusement. After an hour or so, Berta worked her emotion up to considerably more force.

"You know what she said this time," Kriszta laughed. "She said that human beings were created by God, but that policemen crawled out of the slime of Satan's womb."

"What does *Istenem* mean?" I had heard the word many times.

"It means 'My God,'" I asked about other phrases, and Kriszta and Erzsi snickered at my pronounciation. "You're learning,

Jeanette, very good." When Kriszta translated some of the blasphemy, I was sickened.

"It's sad that people use such filthy expressions," I commented, not so much out of condemnation as admitted shock.

"Nobody can use filthier expressions than the Hungarians. I'm not proud of it—some of it is even too disgusting for me—but maybe it's because no people has gone through so much hell as we have."

Since Kriszta could at times be congenial, I always seemed to lapse into thinking things were improving; then we would have another run-in. Sometimes it would be something almost too ridiculous for words, like the occasion on which Kriszta chose to forbid me to lean against the wall. "It is against the rules. The whitewash comes off, and the warden does not like the walls to look gray." Indeed it did come off, leaving its chalky white powder on my clothes, on Erzsi's, on Kriszta's, because everybody leaned against the walls, rule or no rule.

And there were other incidents, such as what happened on the Monday, a week or two after our bout over my shampooing my hair, that I came from the shower feeling half starved. I had had a particularly diarrheal night and had eaten only a few bites of bread for breakfast. We showered around ten, so there remained almost two hours until lunch. I was very hungry, so much so that I began to shake. The warm water had drained my energy. Ravenous for a piece of bread, I took my knife from the shelf and my bread from under the bed and cut myself a large chunk.

"Put that away!" Kriszta commanded. She must have had a bad night too, I thought, as I bit into the dry bread.

"I said put that food away!" she repeated sternly.

"I'm hungry."

"It's against the rules to eat between ten o'clock and eleven-thirty."

"Since when do you go so strictly by the rules?" I flared. "I've seen you eat at ten before."

"As cell supervisor, it is my job to follow the rules and see that the others in the cell do too."

"Congratulations on your sudden reformation."

"Put that bread away or I will have to call the guard and report you." She stood up and reached for a spoon from the shelf.

Astonished that she took it so seriously, I forgot about the bread in my hand and waving it at her, I retorted, "Go ahead, go right ahead!"

There was a pause as we glared at each other, neither of us being too sure of our footing.

"But remember," I added, grasping at any lever with which to fight back, "you will force me then to report the daily visits with the men at the window." I held my breath.

She toyed with the spoon in her hand. "So the big American is not so pure and innocent after all. You can play dirty too, can't you, sweetheart," she sneered, replacing the spoon and lighting a cigarette. We did not speak for two days after that.

At mealtime I tried to make it my habit to eat as much of the prison food as I could and then to cut a portion of the sausage or cheese from the supply the Legation had given me, just to leave a good taste. Naturally I shared with the others. With Anna and Julika it had been a pleasure, and it was even with Kriszta, in spite of our discrepancies, though she always insisted, "You shouldn't give your food away, Jeanette. Other people don't share, and you don't have to either." When Erzsi came, I reconsidered the apportionment, thinking to myself, "Why should I give that sloppy girl anything? She's too fat already," at the same time feeling guilty about my niggardly broodings.

What's happening to you, Janet? Prison changes people. I am growing miserly and selfish. By the time I get out of here I'll hate all communists, all Hungarians, all people—and myself most of all.

So I shared with Erzsi against my own will. Kriszta's outrage grew. "Why do you insist on giving all your food away? And to this big blubbery one especially? You need it a lot more than she does!"

"What are you so worried about? It's not your food I'm giving away," I retorted, perhaps to keep from exposing my own stingy thoughts. And perhaps, too, because of a certain glee I felt in the stupefaction it caused Kriszta. "I thought she was your friend," I criticized. "You should be glad she has a little food to enjoy here. I think you feel guilty because you never give anything of yours away."

"She is not my friend. I could not befriend anyone who has done what she has done."

I had asked once before what Erzsi had done, and Kriszta had replied sassily, "Ask her yourself if you want to know." I made up my mind that I would not ask again, but now my curiosity overruled, and I posed the question Kriszta had led into.

"She murdered her baby," Kriszta replied.

"Her own?" Instinctively I held my arms across my abdomen. "But why?"

"She has two children, two girls, ages three and five. Her husband left her over a year ago and married someone else."

"You mean she wanted the baby to have his father, and——?"

"I mean she doesn't know who the father is, or was."

I asked how it was done.

"She threw it down a well."

"Stillborn?"

"Alive."

I felt suddenly cold.

"Her brother came to see her the next day and happened to go into the back yard where the well was. He saw the baby floating on the surface and immediately called the police."

"He turned his sister in?"

"He probably didn't know it was her baby. She is so fat, she said nobody ever knew she was pregnant. The baby came a month early. She delivered it herself at home alone, and took it out and drowned it."

When I felt I could control the nausea that swept over me, I asked, "What will her punishment be?"

"Probably three years."

"But I still don't understand why. I mean, I thought abortion is legal here, isn't it?"

"It is. I have had six."

"Then why did she carry the child almost to term, and then —— Why did she not have an abortion?"

"She's so stupid." That was always Kriszta's answer, but I probed. "She didn't know until the fourth month. And I suspect that she was hoping her former husband or some other man would marry her again."

"What about her other two children? What will happen to them while their mother is here?"

"That's what she fears. Her husband has been trying to get custody of them, and now she's afraid he will manage it."

I could no longer look at Erzsi. Seeing the way she flirted with the men and left herself dirty, it was hard to imagine her as a mother, let alone a dedicated one, but she cried often, tears of genuine sorrow and fear for the two children she loved and was losing. She was a pathetic human being, to be pitied more than scorned, but I could muster neither empathy nor sympathy. She was more obnoxious to me than Crazy Mary had been. I just wanted out, away from the murderesses, the prostitutes, the thieves and liars, the guards and iron and cement.

I tried not to think about it; that would be the easiest. But for several nights thereafter I awoke, perspiring and gritting my teeth, from a dream about Erzsi tossing a baby down a well, my baby. When I tried to save my child, I fell too, waking before I hit bottom. Each time the dream was a little different, but each time I fell, and each time I awoke to find myself unable to rescue anybody, least of all myself.

Not long after Kriszta and I had squabbled over chess, she was playing a game of dominoes with Erzsi when the latter burst out crying.

"Is she weeping for her children?"

"No. She's blubbering because I told her she is too stupid to play dominoes, and it's the truth." Kriszta lit a cigarette in disgust.

"Like I'm too stupid for chess."

"I never said you were dumb. You were learning. You were beginning to make me a little nervous. I thought I was coming down with diarrhea too," she teased.

"Yes, I noticed the john was always occupied when I needed it during those last few games."

"Shall we play again sometime? Erzsi is lousy company."

"Sometime. Right now I'm too nervous. I keep thinking about the time I'm wasting here. I wish the trial would hurry up and get here. I wish——"

"Wishing is for children."

"I wish I had a cigarette."

"Well, I'll be damned. Here, have one, be my guest, please."

I had never desired a cigarette before, and I had assumed Kriszta only offered because she knew I would not accept. She had more cigarettes than any other prisoner I had seen, about twenty packages saved in her box under the cot, and she did not manage that by passing them out lavishly. Good sized *chicks* she often gave, but never a fresh smoke: it was quite an occasion in cell twenty-two.

28

I BEGAN SMOKING REGULARLY AFTER THAT, trying to limit it to only two or three a day because they were not my cigarettes, even though Kriszta was more generous with them than with her food. She had as much food as I did, or even more, but she did not share. When I ran out, she ate hers silently, not offering a bite. The motivation seemed not so much selfishness as an instinct for self-preservation. But she apparently enjoyed my smoking with her. I allowed myself one at mid-morning and one at mid-afternoon. There was no waste, because Erzsi got the *chicks* to roll into new cigarettes. "When you write out my next request slip, we can ask for my Kents and I'll pay you back." Kriszta agreed willingly for a change.

And so the time passed. Kriszta began talking to me more, telling me the local gossip. She told me the stories behind the murder cases, for instance, and pointed out the women who had confessed to committing them. "That little one with the crooked eyes and long hair killed her mother. She and her husband beat her to death with a bottle. They wanted the apartment her mother owned. Apartments are scarce here. The murder took place in the mother's living room. The couple killed her, pushed her body under the bed, then made love right over the corpse. Can you imagine?"

There was a lot of gossip of that sort to mold the atmosphere of prison life and distort the mind.

One afternoon during the *séta*, the captain of the guards, a man who looked like Horst Buchholz, the German actor, watched me so steadfastly as I passed by him that I almost stumbled. I had seen him before. He had an arrogant air that made me wonder just what sort of complex he was concealing beneath that attitude of self-importance. I could tell he was curious about "the American," as were all the other guards who peeked through the *spy* and whispered together about me, but I doubted that he would accommodate his curiosity that way. I was confident of my analysis of his haughty superiority, and when he walked up to me I was startled: it seemed out of character. He took hold of my upper arm and led me from the line. Inside the building I jerked free and stared at him, "Let go of me!" It may sound like a line out of an old movie, but it was the tone that mattered, not the vocabulary. He was not angered, but marched me down a corridor, around a corner, and stopped.

"What's this all about?"

He remained silent, took hold of my shoulders and turned me to face the wall. I began to shake. I dared not think what might happen. Footsteps could be heard coming in from the courtyard, but they continued on up the stairs, not coming in my direction. I waited. Nothing happened. I turned around and glared at "Horst Buchholz" who returned my gaze with a faint smile. "What's going on here?" This man was up to something queer, but what? He seemed almost amused. Abruptly, the guard pointed in the direction of the courtyard and indicated I should return to walk with the women. He did not touch me again, but walked behind me softly as if his job were done and he was relieved to be off duty.

Back in the cell, Kriszta said, "Did you see him?"

"Who? Horst Buchholz?"

"No, dumbbell, your husband. I knew it was your husband the instant I saw him."

"Damn it, it didn't work." Busso had waited for an opportune time to see me in the courtyard, but the guards had caught on and removed me from view. Even harmless attempts we made to relieve the desolate loneliness were aborted.

It was the very next day that excitement again stirred during the *séta*. In the stifling late-August heat, men from the adjacent courtyards sometimes collapsed from exhaustion, and they would be returned through our courtyard under guard to the building. (The men walked much faster than the women, and the younger ones did calisthenics.) Occasionally a man had to be carried, unconscious, into the building. I worried that the men had been beaten, but Kriszta assured me that since the revolution, striking a prisoner was forbidden, so now it was done only in secret, not in the courtyard.

On the particular day I remember, I was pacing idly along the cobblestones wondering how many more times I must walk that square, when the door of the men's courtyard opened straight

ahead of me. Four prisoners carried a man, and three guards surrounded the entourage, but as I passed, not three feet from them,
I caught a good view of the unconscious one. He was a boy, not
yet twenty, I guessed. I was relieved to know it was not my husband.

Suddenly a terrifying shriek came from the woman behind
me, so shrill that it paralyzed the entire courtyard.

"János! János!" she screamed, rushing to the side of the un-
hearing youth. She was a gypsy woman, a pretty one I had seen
often, about thirty years old with long, wavy, dyed-red hair,
wearing a brightly colored gathered cotton skirt and blouse. She
clung to the young man's body, clutching his white shirt with all
her might. More guards were immediately on the scene, and the
two on the bridge stood ready with their tommy guns. It took
three strong men, each twice the weight of the rampant woman,
to pull her from the boy. The young man was carried onward,
while the woman was led in restraint behind him, her cries echoing throughout the walls.

In our cell, Kriszta went immediately to the "telephone." The
gypsy woman's cell was next to ours, number twenty-one, and
her lamenting wails encompassed us in her agony.

"He is the gypsy's brother," Kriszta related. "She didn't even
know he was in jail." I asked if he was dead. "Could be, who
knows? We'll probably never know, and neither will his sister."

Subsequent to Busso's attempt to see me, the women's *séta*
was assigned to a different courtyard, one on the side rather than
in the middle of the area. As I walked from my cell one morning
I noticed a pretty girl coming out of cell twenty-four. Something
told me she was Western; certainly not her clothes, because she
wore stripes, but I was sure she was either Austrian or German.
Kriszta was the only person in line between the new girl and me,
and on the staircase I whispered, "Let me pass," but Kriszta pretended not to hear. In the courtyard she talked to the Westerner
while I fumed.

When we returned to the cell Kriszta reported that the girl was German and was in the Markó to appeal her sentence. "What else did you learn?" I had so many questions and ached to talk to the foreigner.

"Nothing. What else is there to learn?"

I had been angry with Kriszta before, but never so much as then. I attacked her with every word I knew, including the Hungarian profanities she had taught me. The next day, I got to walk downstairs behind the German girl.

She walked directly behind me. None of the regular guards were on duty that morning, a stroke of luck, because there were only three substitutes to cover six watchposts.

"Hello back there. How long are you in for?"

"Hello! What did you say?"

It was difficult to hear over the tramping, so we had to speak louder, always being careful to be quiet while passing a guard. "How much did you get?" I repeated.

"Eight months."

"Eight months!"

"*Nem szabad beszelni!*" a guard, a woman with black hair and red fingernails, shouted.

"Yes. I planned it all myself. I succeeded in getting a girl out of East Germany, and I told the court I was glad I did it," she said proudly.

"*Nem szabad beszelni!*" shouted the guard more sternly.

"I hate these swine here," said the girl behind me in reply to the warning.

"What prison are you in?"

"I can't hear you."

"What prison?" I spoke up.

"*Nem szabad beszelni,* Jeanette!" the red fingernails had detected me.

"*Szekesféhérvar.* An Austrian is with me. She got nine months. We're segregated from the Hungarians."

"Can you work? Is there anything to do?"

"Jeanette," the black-haired guard came toward me, shaking a threatening red nail and shouting into my ear. She dropped back to admonish the German girl too, waving her whole arm and spitting something to the effect that the *nevelőnő* would hear of our insolence.

The *nevelőnő* heard, and we heard from the *nevelőnő*, and Kriszta was called from the cell to report exactly what was discussed. "That ape," Kriszta described the "civil major." "Does he think I'm one of his kind? I told him you hardly spoke. It was that German girl who did all the talking. I said I couldn't hear what she said." When it came to choosing teams, Kriszta was on my side, and it did not matter to her who else lost by it. Her altruism had its own peculiar reasoning.

It was seen to from then on that there were about fifty women between the German girl and me, so that further conversation was impossible.

About eight days before my trial I was called downstairs. Instead of being taken to the usual lawyer's counseling chamber, I turned right and entered a small room near the main exit of the prison. The room was large enough for a table with a bench on either side. On the far side sat a man in "civvies."

"How do you do? I represent the prosecutor's office and am here to extend your official indictment." His accent made his English almost unintelligible.

"Please sign here." He placed a paper on the table and pointed to a line. Here we go again, I thought. Ten weeks previously I was thoroughly bewildered and had signed many papers. I had thought it would gain me something, my freedom or at least a visit with my husband. Since it had not, there seemed little reason to co-operate now.

"Please wait a minute." I ignored the pen he offered. "I didn't catch what you said."

"Pardon me?"

Because two people speak English does not mean they communicate.

I said, "Why should I sign?" No, that didn't sound right. I rephrased. "I mean, why do you ask me to sign? What is it?"

He adjusted his tie. "I represent the prosecutor's office and am here to extend your official indictment," he repeated verbatim.

"May I see it first? I requested that it be translated into English. Has that been done?"

"Yes, you may believe me that it has been translated into English," he withheld the papers. "Please sign."

"Will my husband receive a copy of the same?"

"Yes, as soon as you return to your cell."

"May I stay and see him, just look at him, for a few minutes?"

"I am not empowered to make such arrangements. You must sign and return immediately."

"But why must I sign? Does my signature mean that I agree with what you have written about me?"

"You must sign to show that you have received a copy of the indictment."

It was ridiculous to carry on. This man held my indictment, a paper I had long awaited, a notice of the formal charge against me, an indication of how atrocious my "crime" was as viewed by the peace-loving People's Republic of Hungary. I signed.

The indictment was printed in both English and Hungarian. I had never thought of myself as a criminal, and it seemed strange to read about myself as such. The charge was called "Unauthorized crossing of the frontier as indictable under Section 203/1 of the Criminal Code." Besides numerous misspellings, I was irritated by many discrepancies between the truth and what the prosecutor stated as being true. For instance, it was stated that Birke had informed us that they planned to travel to Hungary—worded as though Birke had chosen the country at liberty. They well knew that East Germans have no such choice.

The dates in the indictment were utterly confused. It was written that we had left home on June 13, 1966, arrived in Frankfurt am Main on the same day and also entered Hungary on June thirteenth. It sounded more like James Bond's agenda than ours. It also said we arrived at the border on the day of the escape at six P.M. I am sure that it was five. It's a minor point, I thought, but when they print, they should incorporate the facts. There was no hint of how they had managed to detect us, except that we had "behaved suspiciously."

In general, the indictment said that Busso was the "first charged," which meant he had taken the greatest part in the crime, and that I was the "second charged." It stated our plan briefly and said we had to pay all court costs. On the final page, I was amused at a sentence to the effect that the prosecutor recommended part of our punishment to be immediate expulsion from Hungary.

Most upsetting was the proposal to confiscate our passports. Busso and I had collected numerous stamps from thirty-two different countries as souvenirs of our travels. They held great sentimental value for us. Besides, my passport was not my personal property but rather the property of the United States of America.

At the bottom of the indictment was a list of names of people who should appear at the trial. It included Busso and me as the charged, and as a witness Andras Darazsi from Letenya, the officer we had hoped would help us at the border. It would be interesting to see what he had to say, and if he would aid us as he had promised.

I read through the pages twice and then, weary of it, handed it to Kriszta. All I could think was *please, get it over with.*

"Jeanette, this is wonderful!" Kriszta raved. "You aren't even charged with smuggling! You are sure to be set free soon. You will be home next week, I'm sure of it."

"Why the sudden change of heart?"

"What change?"

"Why all the good wishes and belief in my innocence?"

"You mean just because we disagree on a couple of things, I

should think you deserve to be convicted? Don't be silly."

"I hope they call you for jury duty."

"Pardon?"

"Never mind. Will you please help me get my garter belt from my suitcase so I can wear stockings and look presentable at the trial."

"Of course. Am I not always co-operative? Have I not written out dozens of request slips for you? What more can I do?"

"Not quite dozens. You can knock and tell the guard I want to see the warden." After much persuasion and against her better judgment, Kriszta knocked.

I was permitted to go to see the warden. We fenced lightly to explore each other's views—one of several debates we were to have before I departed that domicile—but whenever the conversation treaded too near to politics, he would ask if I spoke Esperanto or some such diverting question. On this day he was in a generous, almost jocund mood: I obtained the garterbelt, wondering if I would have the stockings to use with it, and pleased nonetheless, because I also managed to obtain my two cartons of Kents. Kriszta began to see that co-operation sometimes has its rewards.

The next day Dr. Nagy again visited me for a few minutes. He greeted me in a flurry, saying that he had to leave immediately but that he wanted to discuss one important point with me.

"I have read your indictment. I have read every word you said, every word your husband said, both to the investigator and to the prosecutor. I have found no sentence, no phrase whatsoever, to indicate that you," he paused for dramatic impact, "that you, my dear, ever took one active step in the action. You were passive the entire time. You did not obtain the passports. You did not stamp them with the false stamp. You did not make the plan. You did not drive the car. You see? You never took an active part in any of this!"

"Dr. Nagy," I interrupted, wondering who had put the bug in his ear. He had thought of all this both too suddenly and too late.

"Have you been talking to my husband?"

"Why, yes, yes—that is, I have seen his lawyer. The two of them agree this would be the best method of defense. Why?" He was injured that I did not commend his brilliancy and share his optimism. "Believe me," he chuckled happily, "we'll have you out of here in no time."

He had at last set a course of action and seemed so enthusiastic about it that I hesitated to infect him with my doubts. I had to think about it for a while. Just how active a part had I taken? It seemed so long past now. What had the others said to the prosecutor?

"Do not worry, *mein Goldiges,* you may soon walk out of these iron gates for good, ha ha ha. Yes, that's what we shall do. We shall plead not guilty."

What would a lawyer in the States do? What would a judge look for? Was such a defense possible in Hungary? "Dr. Nagy, how can I plead innocent? The Hungarian government has locked me up for two and a half months. They will never declare me innocent of the charge now. What would they say: 'sorry, our mistake'?"

"Quite true, quite true," he replied, undampened, "but they can declare you only a little bit guilty, just enough to merit the minimum sentence, don't you see?"

"Then why don't we plead that way?"

"My dear, you are so naive. Believe me, I know what's best. Your husband wants you out of here. You want to go home, don't you?"

"Of course."

"Then you must co-operate. It's best for both of you."

"What do you mean 'co-operate'?"

"You must agree to the defense of not guilty. Your husband has already consented. He will plead guilty, and we shall proceed from there."

"But I still do not see the advantage in it. I was in the car when we were all arrested together. How could I possibly be innocent?"

"It's a matter of technicality."

"I don't think the judge is concerned about technicalities. I think he is more concerned about appearances." I wanted to ask about perjury but didn't know the word in German. "But if I lie under—" I didn't know the word for "oath" either.

"Never mind, never mind." Dr. Nagy was not listening anyway. "This case is different. You are not European. We shall plead not guilty." He refused to hear any more objections. With a friendly little laugh, he continued, "Now, all you have to do is, when they give you a few minutes to make any comments, stand up and tell them that you personally never took an active part in the offense. You didn't even know about it until it was too late."

"I didn't? When did I learn of it?"

"Ummmm—" He thought for a moment. "Here, right here in Europe. Just say you did not plan it, you thought it was a vacation trip, and you were against it when you finally did learn what was going to happen. You therefore took no active part in the crime. Will you say that to the court?"

"No."

"But my dear girl, it's for your own——"

"I can't say that I was against it. I want that judge to know I favored freedom of movement before we got caught, and I still do!"

Evidently my voice had risen, because Dr. Nagy looked around to see if anyone had heard or understood. "No, no!"

"All right, I won't play the martyr, but I won't say that I did not foster the escape either."

"As you wish," he conceded. "Perhaps that is not necessary. Just say that you took no active step. Can you do that? Can you stand before the judge and say that?" He eyed me closely. "Your freedom rests on your own testimony." He paused to consider the slight overstatement. "Well, it *might* help if you testify."

"Yes, I can do that. We've all been here long enough."

"Good, good! It's all settled. You'll be out of here an hour after the trial. I'm confident of it." I asked the attorney why he didn't counsel me to this effect when he first met me at the *Stasi,* or at least before I had made the statements before the prosecutor. He disregarded the question altogether, saying, "Chin up, my dear. I'll see you in about a week. Oh, by the way, Mr. Gross gave me a package to bring to you. You will get it after it is checked."

Not much later, the things from the Consul were pushed through the hatch. "I like your Mr. Gross." Kriszta complimented my taste in representatives. He had sent two pairs of nylon stockings and an olive-green cotton shift, all of which fit perfectly. "He knows what to give a girl."

"Perhaps they belonged to his wife," I conjectured, ignoring Kriszta's one-track mind, "or maybe to a Hungarian secretary in the office. Whoever she is, I love her."

I told my roommate what Dr. Nagy had said. "Well that's the first time I have heard of a lawyer talking sense," she avowed, standing up to prepare for a speech. "Exactly what have you done in this so-called crime? Nothing. Your husband did it all: he planned it, he wrote the letters, he organized the car, the passports and the stamp, everything. He should never have taken you into Hungary in the first place. What did he need you for? He's to blame, not you." The usually cool Kriszta was getting excited.

"Hold on now," I corrected firmly. "Before you start attacking my husband, you had best get your facts straight. First of all, he did not take me into Hungary. I told him I wanted to come."

"You just want to protect him. You're always defending him. I don't believe you."

"Why don't you believe the truth? I came of my own accord."

"Why?" She spit the word at me, challenging me to answer. She was sure I could not.

"Because it never seriously occurred to me that we could fail!" I shouted. My skin was hot and I felt like slapping her. "Because I wanted to be there. I wanted to witness the success of a marvelous plan, a plan my husband had developed with *my encouragement*. The trouble with you, Kriszta, you have never had faith in anything or anybody—you don't know what the word means!" At that moment I hated Kriszta. It hurt to remember how much faith we had had, a faith that now seemed ridiculous, laughable. Why must she re-open that wound?

"Excuse me," she said almost inaudibly. "I know you believed in it. Even I would have."

I couldn't trust my ears. Had I heard Kriszta apologize?

"It was a good plan. Too bad it didn't work: I know of worse schemes that have succeeded. What they are doing here is inhuman."

With that, Kriszta unleashed the choler boiling inside me. "If I get angry enough in court, that's exactly what I am going to say to the judge. I'll tell him that being in a Hungarian prison has taught me more in two and a half months than I would ever have known if they had sent me directly home. I'll say that Communism is pure capitalism, only the money bags are in the hands of a few instead of the many, and the people know it. I'll say that now I know what a real police state is, and now I know what is great about America, great about all Western nations. It's only a matter of time until the people here rise up and demand liberty."

"Sure, you tell them that, Jeanette. Let them cremate you."

29

SEPTEMBER 16, 1966, at last arrived. I rose slowly and washed under the cold tap-water, feeling an uncomfortable sense of foreboding combined with an exhiliration that something was finally going to be decided. Today I would know.

Kriszta was excited too. Her unconcealed concern pleased me.

We crossed through a parking lot behind the courthouse and entered the back door. The woman put her finger to her lips to tell me she couldn't be seen allowing her prisoner to speak now. We co-operated.

At the door of the courtroom, Mr. Gross waited with Dr. Nagy and Dr. Kubinyi. He greeted us with a smile and a nod, not breaking the rule of silence. The hallway was crowded, and we were told to sit on a bench and wait. We sat close together, and the guards frowned, motioning that we must sit at opposite ends of the bench, but somebody came up and spoke to them so that they were distracted. "I have a letter for you tucked inside my waistband," Busso whispered. Dozens of people were milling around and shuffling past to see who we were. Many of them smiled and shook their heads back and forth in sympathy, knowing we were foreigners and were here for only one reason.

"On my side?" I whispered, not looking at Busso, but at the crowd, waiting for the right moment.

"No, in back. It will fall out if I stand again. I feel it slipping." The man talking to our guards pointed down the hall toward another door. As they all looked in that direction, I leaned closer and ran my finger quickly around inside the back of Busso's waistband. I touched the paper folded in a thick roll, and felt it drop down into his pants. My throat went dry as the guards glanced at us, but they turned away again just long enough for me to plunge my hand into the seat of his now-baggy britches and withdraw the letter. I clasped it in both hands behind me until I had a chance to put it into my raincoat pocket.

"You've got it?"

"Yes. What a funny place to carry a letter."

The woman's earrings glistened as she snapped her head around to glare at me for talking. I lowered my eyes appropriately, as a whipped animal should.

Court convened quickly in a small room at the end of the hall. It looked amazingly unlike what I had expected of a courtroom. There was no high judge's bench, no witness box, no bailiff, no court scribe. For a moment I thought there wasn't even a judge until I realized that the short young man who limped to the long desk at the front of the room was Judge Stefanics, the one Dr. Nagy had told me about. He was not wearing a long black robe. He did not even have a gavel, as I recall. To his right sat a man even younger than he, probably not over thirty, and to his left, a woman. Dr. Kubinyi and Dr. Nagy sat at a small table set at right angles to the judge's bench, and another woman sat opposite them across the room. She was the prosecutor, but not the same woman who had indicted us. Busso and I sat on a low bench facing the judge.

Dr. Stefanics said something, somebody else said something, and before I knew it, I was escorted from the room. I was surprised to find that I had to edge my way through to get to the door. The three benches behind ours were filled with spectators, and more stood in back, lining the room. The door was locked after my exit to prevent more onlookers from crowding in.

We waited in the hall, the guard with the gold earrings and I. The lights seemed abnormally bright, and people kept pacing by me for a second and third look. Hours seemed to pass. What were they asking Busso in there? What was he answering? One of the fluorescent lights began to weaken. It flickered on and off at irritating intervals. My mind seemed numb. I could not concentrate. I could not think. Why didn't somebody fix that damned light? I watched the door to the courtroom and started when it finally opened.

I stood before the judge with the little old white-haired interpreter at my side, the same man who had been present when I was allowed to see Busso six weeks before. He seemed like such a nice old fellow, but I seriously doubted that he could understand English well enough to interpret the proceedings. I watched the judge and the two assistants flanking him. Before any questions were asked, a recess was called.

Mr. Gross brought a box, and after asking the guards permission, opened it for us. "Here is some food for you. You are allowed to eat only during the recess. They won't let me give you the coffee, but there are sandwiches and grapes." He was not permitted to remain.

The room was cleared except for Busso and me and the guards. Busso's hands were again cuffed, so I fed him. "Not so much," he complained, "I have a lot to tell you."

"What happened?" I was surprised that the guards ignored our conversation.

"I said you thought you were on a vacation. You didn't learn about the plan until we got here. Honey, the warden insists you smoke. I almost hit him for his smart mouth. It's not true—is it?"

"Well——" Busso used to joke by saying he married me just because I was the only girl he had ever met who did not smoke. At least I had thought it was a joke. Now he took it so seriously. "I will quit the minute I get out," I promised.

"But Janet——"

"Please! the minute I am free." I again gave my word, pleading silently that he not make an issue and ask me to stop today. I needed a crutch, a time-marker, right now.

The judge returned to his bench then, and we fell silent. A few minutes later court reconvened.

I was summoned to stand before the bench and the man to the right of the judge watched me closely. Judge Stefanics and the woman hardly looked at me. Each was leafing through some papers on the desk. The judge did not look up even when he asked questions. The interpreter repeated each question to me in English and translated my reply back into Hungarian. He seemed to stutter on many of the words, and for his sake I felt obliged to be as clear as possible.

Judge Stefanics asked the same questions I had been asked by the officer at the border, the investigator at the *Stasi*, my lawyer, and the prosecutor at the Markó.

"When did you first meet your sister-in-law?"

"In December 1964."

"And you saw her again when?"

"In May 1965. We went to comfort her after her baby died," I said, but the interpreter replied only the date, that much Hungarian I understood.

"Your husband said it was June." I had known we would mix up our dates. "Were you present when her daughter died?"

"No. We were in the middle of a trip in North Africa at that time." The interpreter answered in Hungarian with "*nem*," and the judged asked the next question before he could continue.

"When did she die?"

"I think it was in March. We heard about it in Nice, France. No, maybe it was closer to February."

"What did she die of?"

"Pneumonia. Pneumonia of the lungs."

"Did you make plans for your sister-in-law's departure from East Germany when you were there in June?"

"Not definitely. Nothing was definite. We daydreamed together, saying 'wouldn't it be nice *if*—' " I felt uncomfortable when the Hungarian version of my answer once again amounted to not more than three words. Wasn't the interpreter supposed to translate exactly?

"Did your sister-in-law attempt suicide?"

That happened before we visited her. He was not following the chronological order, mixing things up to confuse me. "Yes."

"Why?"

"Because of the death of her daughter." What a stupid question.

"How? How did she try to kill herself?"

"She turned on the gas in the kitchen."

"How do you know that, and your husband does not?"

"He doesn't?" I looked over my shoulder at Busso. He shrugged helplessly. "I guess I was alone with his sister when she told me.'"

"Exactly when was the plan made?"

"The actual planning? It must have been after Christmas, at the beginning of this year."

"How did you communicate?"

"You mean my husband and his sister?" I was trying to point out that I had not done the writing, but the interpreter obviously did not translate word for word, and such nuances were lost. "By mail."

"You speak German, do you not?"

"I speak it now, but I have learned much of it here in jail."

"But you read the letters, did you not? You knew of the plan through reading the letters."

"No, German handwriting is too difficult. My husband read them to me. I knew only what he chose to tell me." That was true.

The prosecutor, a lean, vigorous woman with sharp black eyes, stood, first addressing the chair and then the interpreter, who looked at me. "She asks if you understood everything your husband and your sister-in-law said when you traveled to Berlin."

"When we traveled to Berlin?" I repeated, perplexed.

"Yes, when you drove from Vienna to Berlin, did you understand what was said?"

"But my sister was not with us from Vienna to Berlin." How could they ask such a question? If Birke had been with us in Vienna, what would be the point in taking this God-forsaken detour via Budapest?

The interpreter repeated my reply being with, "*nem*," and I was sure he followed with "She didn't understand everything that was said," completely oblivious to the absurdity of it.

I was asked to verify the next statement. "You stayed two nights in Hungary the first time, isn't that right?"

"No, just one night."

"*Igen*," the interpreter said to the judge.

"No!" I stopped him, careless of the disgruntled judge, "I said no, we only stayed one night," and the interpreter said something which I had to presume was the correct translation of my answer.

"When exactly did you learn of the plan?" the interpreter inquired softly.

Did he mean learn of the intention, of the goal? Or did he mean learn the specific details of procedure? I assumed the latter. "I learned of the plan in detail in Europe as we carried out the steps." Busso had given me only an outline before we left the States. The prosecutor listened impatiently to the translator's repetition of my reply, then fired the next few questions at me.

"Not before?"

"Not in detail." I looked at Dr. Nagy, hoping to find some evidence in his expression as to how I was doing, but he was looking at the table top.

"Why, then, did you state in earlier testimony that you knew of the plan, that you knew in detail?"

"As I said, I learned as we carried out the steps together. What I didn't understand, I learned from my husband while we spent two days together at the border just after they caught us. Up to now, nobody has asked exactly *when* I learned the details. The misunderstanding must be due to the language difficulty. When I was asked 'did you?' I thought they meant 'you' in the plural. It was not made clear that 'you' in the singular was meant, except a couple of times. I always answered 'we,' not 'I' " With the wording of the questions, they made it easy for me to be truthful, but did they understand my answers?

"But you told the officer at the border that it was a mutual plan."

"Yes." Oh God, I'll never be able to explain my involved reasoning, "but that was because he advised us to let *one* take the blame. I didn't trust him, so I did the opposite."

For the first time the judge looked directly at me. I returned his gaze, hoping he would at last see me as a human being and not a personification of the Enemy. I felt a strange mixture of anxiety and placidity, ready to face any question now, ready to battle for my liberty. "Please tell him," I said to the interpreter, "that the plan would have been carried out exactly as it was even if I had not been present. It mattered little that I was there."

"Yes, I understand," replied the interpreter, but he did not translate my words.

"Please, tell him," I urged.

"Yes, well—" He remained reluctant. The judge was talking to his assistants when he noticed with irritation that I had spoken without being asked to. He inquired of the interpreter what I wanted, but as the latter began talking, waved his hand to silence him in a manner that said, "yes, yes, I know, never mind." He did not like being interrupted while conferring with his associates.

Then something was said in Hungarian, everybody rose, the judge and two assistants stood, collected their papers together, and everybody in the room began talking at once. Mr. Gross pushed his way to us to say, "There will be a recess while the decision is made. We can go into a nearby room together."

"That interpreter is terrible," Busso complained as we were bustled into the hallway, the guards nudging us on so that it was hard to hear what Mr. Gross replied.

"Mr. Gross, I don't think that interpreter translated half of what I said," I called out. "The judge doesn't let him."

The Consul managed to step alongside my guard in the hall and answered, "I know, he did an appalling job of translating, completely distorting your testimony. If it's any consolation, I'm sure the case was pre-determined long before this, as I indicated earlier, so it is doubtful that your words made any difference."

We entered a room several doors from the courtroom where Mr. Gross and Mr. Peel, a representative of the Canadian Embassy in Prague, sat beside us on a bench and the guards stood watch before us.

"What are our chances?" Busso and I asked. "How does it seem to be going?"

"It looks pretty good. Better than I had anticipated."

"You mean Janet might go home?" Busso queried.

"Don't get your hopes up," Mr. Gross said noncommittally.

"I have a letter here from your parents in Seattle," Mr. Peel said. "Shall I read it?"

Before he had completed the second page, there was a knock on the door and a man stuck his head in to call us back to court.

We assembled and remained standing before the judge while he said a few words, and court was adjourned.

"Hey, what's going on? Aren't they going to translate? What was the verdict?" Busso and I stood confounded as the guards again tried to bustle us from the courtroom. What about our defense? Neither Dr. Nagy nor Dr. Kubinyi had said a word. Dr. Nagy came toward me and said something in German, but I was looking for Mr. Gross and did not concentrate to understand the lawyer.

"Mr. Gross?" I saw him elbowing his way through behind Dr. Nagy. "What's happening?"

"There has been a postponement," Mr. Gross explained as Dr. Nagy and the others made way for him. The guards blocked him from coming directly to us, and he called louder, over the throng of Hungarian, "The decision has been postponed. There is some question about your testimony."

"But when? When will we know?" Disappointment stabbed through me.

"It won't be much longer."

"But——"

"Don't worry, this may be good. I'll try to see you before then."

"But—" Before I could finish, we were marched back to the Markó, back to waiting.

30

"WELL?" Kriszta asked even before I stepped inside the cell.

"Well what?" I asked, teasing her.

"You know. How many months did you get?"

"None."

"Don't play games. How many? It can't be too good, or you couldn't hide the grin. Is it more than three?"

"Got a cigarette?"

Kriszta clicked her tongue irritably and handed me the cigarette she had been just about to light. "It couldn't be bad news or you'd be screaming." She waited while I tapped the cigarette to pack the loose Hungarian tobacco.

"Got a light?" I asked, smiling in open amusement—for a change it was Kriszta who was anxious. "Hey, where's Erzsi?"

"She was transferred."

"What a blessing."

"That's for sure. What about your verdict?"

"What about that light?"

"You do not get the matches until you tell me," she clasped them, determined to beat me at my own game. "How many months?"

"None."

"You mean they are releasing you?" she let the matches fall on the table without notice.

"I mean they didn't sentence me."

"What?"

"They liked me so much, they want to see me again."

"*Istenem*, I give up. You're not funny, you know."

I told Kriszta what had happened. "What do you make of it?"

A guard came to the hatch. "Jeanette," he called, and Kriszta translated, "September twenty-ninth, three-thirty P.M. That is your next trial date." The guard left, and Kriszta exclaimed, "That will be your last day in prison, I know it will. Why else would they schedule it for the twenty-ninth, the very date you would be released if you got three months?"

When the hallway sounded clear, I removed Busso's letter from my pocket. The pages could be concealed behind an open book so that a passing guard would not discover my treasure.

"How is he?" Kriszta asked, leaning close.

"He has lost a lot of weight, probably thirty pounds, but he still has a lot of fight in him." The letter was on toilet paper, and I read it over and over, letting my cigarette burn away unsmoked.

Kriszta was as patient as she could be, "What does he say?"

"He says he loves me," I answered, smiling in spite of myself.

"Is that all?" she asked as though it were hardly worth reading if that were all.

"No," I said, making her wait a minute to hear the rest, "he said to give his love to my cute cell partner, too."

"*Istenem*, you're unbearable today."

Busso had actually written about how he felt and how he cursed our captors. Most important, he wrote, "I met a guy, a Hungarian-born German, who says there is hope even now. I'm not sure I can trust him, but it's worth checking out. I've got to talk to you before you go home. It's urgent. Don't leave until you talk to me." I did not tell Kriszta about that part.

The letter made me happier than I had been in a long time, but it did not calm me. I told the doctor about my nervousness, and he said that the aide would come with a tranquilizer for me. On the way back from seeing him, I managed to get into line next to the woman I had met earlier and ask her if she was really a nun.

"Kriszta," I reported back excitedly, "you know that young woman with the brown sweat pants and glasses?"

"Ja, what about her?"

"I met her on the stairs. She's a nun."

"Sure, and I'm Queen Elizabeth."

"Don't you believe it?"

"A nun? Are you kidding? There is no such thing in Hungary."

"She is. She really talks like a nun. I met her before and I asked her more about it today."

"She's lying. What did she say?"

"She said she was in prison once before for teaching her belief to a class of young people. She got four years then and will probably get another four years now. Isn't that awful?"

"Don't let her worry you. She is making up that story. Why does she say she is here this time?"

"Because she sent for a book written by the Pope. I believe her."

"Man, you are naive. There is no such thing as a nun in Hungary. It's against the law. We used to have them years ago, but then they were ordered not to congregate more than once a year, and now not at all. They don't exist any more."

"That's probably what the nuns say about the prostitutes; and that's what the government says about both."

Dr. Nagy came to see me on the nineteenth, a Monday.
"How did I do in court?"

"You did just fine, very well, in fact. The chances are better than ever that you will get no more than three months."

"Dr. Nagy, I would be forever grateful if you could get me off now."

"Ummmm." he said, distracted by the several matches which had failed to light the cigarette hanging from his lips.

When one held fire, he seemed to be better able to concentrate on the matter at hand. "You know," he began, "your husband paid his lawyer two hundred dollars for his defense. I think that's a fair sum if— Of course you do not have to pay me; I am glad to take your case without gratuity, but usually a client likes to express his——"

"You told me the State pays you. Besides, that two hundred dollars was for both of you."

"Oh, no, neither Dr. Kubinyi nor Dr. Paulinyi mentioned anything about dividing the money," he said in a low voice. He expected me to promise the money willingly, and when I said nothing, it flustered him. "No, your husband made no such provision, for I am, after all, your lawyer and not his, you see. But, of course, I make no demands. I just thought that you would wish to, after you are free, since it is, after all, a matter of life and death, so to speak, and——"

"Dr. Nagy, my husband told me that that money was to go to both his lawyer and mine. You will have to settle it with Mr. Kubinyi, or with the woman if she happened to take it to Vienna with her. My husband specifically told me not to pay anybody. Besides, I don't have much money of my own here, only a few dollars, so it would have to come from him."

"My dear, I know your husband, I know the type. He is a shrewd and cunning man who cheats his way out of paying whenever he can. I'm your lawyer and he should——"

"I don't think we have any more to say. I told you the first time we met——"

"Now, now, *mein Goldiges,* there is no reason to get excited. I didn't mean it about your husband. I just mentioned it in passing. Of course I will defend you gladly, even without pay. Now let us leave it at that, shall we?"

"But if you want money——"

"We can discuss that after you're out, all right? Now, as I was saying, the trial went well."

"Why didn't they sentence us?"

"Well, they want time to study it a bit more. You did just fine. Keep up the good work. We will prove that you had nothing to do with it whatsoever, neither physically nor psychologically; no active part."

"But they think that because I speak to you in German, I knew the language when the plan was made. I didn't."

"Don't worry, don't worry, I will tell them all that. I must rush now. *Adieu,* my dear. *Adieu.*"

Although middays were still warm, the mornings and evenings were suddenly cooler, and I was grateful to Mr. Gross for sending two sweaters for me. After the first trial I thought a lot about Gretchen: if I had not met her, if I had not learned so much German from her, I would not have been able to understand Dr.

Nagy, and maybe the court would be convinced that I could not have done much. Gretchen was probably out with her boyfriend now, or home drinking a good cup of hot coffee and eating meat for dinner, and chocolate. It would be fun to meet her in Vienna.

A day or two later, as I stepped out into the courtyard one morning and felt the crisp dewy September air pleasantly nip my cheeks, my eyes passed as usual down the line of women ahead of me, and I saw a short, blonde girl in worn high-heeled sandals and a wrinkled lavender dress. Here? What happened? I thought the officer—she was so sure—she was always so much more in command than I. The figure ahead of me who walked in line with the women from cell two had changed from the girl I had known at the *Stasi*. Her hair had been washed too often with the crude brown soap, so that it hung formless and unpretty. It had grown out and the bleached part made an ugly line where the brown began. Most startling was her figure. The lavender dress had hung nicely before, but now, even though she wore a sweater in the cool morning air, I could see that the garment strained to cover her increased waist and thighs. She must have gorged herself on bread for lack of something better to do, I judged—bread and as much chocolate as she could buy. I tried to get her attention, but she did not seem to be the cocky little imp I had known, one who would have glanced about inquisitively with a child's curiosity. Finally, as the line ascended the stairs, I called her name, "Gretchen!" She looked down the stairwell and when she saw me smiling up, returned only a faint flicker of recognition. My God, what have they done to her? For the first time, I believed with certainty that Gretchen was real, that she was not a spy, and that she was not any more invincible than the rest of us; she had simply held to her resolution longer.

Through Kriszta, although she accommodated begrudgingly, I asked Szemetria, I asked the *nevelőnő*, I asked other guards to please put Gretchen and me in the same cell. We had a free bed, we had two free beds; she could come to cell twenty-two. I implored the doctor to help. It was all to no avail.

"Why don't they put her in our cell?" I complained to Kriszta.

"They don't need a reason." She shrugged, and it made me angry that she did not care. "We get along fine with just the two of us here. It's peaceful," she said.

Mr. Gross came on September twenty-second for one hour. We met in the same prosecutor's office as before. I thanked him for the clothing and for the food he now spread like a feast before me: thick ham and cheese and tuna sandwiches, many fancy cakes dipped in chocolate, and a large thermos of hot, black coffee. When my eyes adjusted once more to the sight of normal food, I asked what he thought about the trial. "Why did they postpone the decision?"

"There was some question about your testimony. Did you make contradictory statements at previous interviews?"

"Not exactly. I was pretty confused most of the time, and only once did I have an interpreter who spoke some English—at the prosecutor's office. Dr. Nagy did not make it clear how I should defend myself until the week before the trial. It had never occurred to me that he would advise pleading not guilty. I thought there was no such thing here, especially where foreigners are concerned."

"That's about it. I wish I could tell you something more optimistic, but I don't think you should get your hopes up."

"I know. I'll try not to." He knew how much I wanted out on the twenty-ninth, but, wisely, he cautioned me against too much optimism. "How did Busso's testimony go?"

"He is rather caustic. He is sure to get at least six months, maybe seven or eight. There is reason to hope he won't get more, because it is really a simple case of border violation as far as Hungary is concerned. The whole thing amounts to the maintenance of good relations with East Germany."

The Consul gave me messages from relatives and friends while I gulped down sandwiches, cake and coffee. I asked about our rented car.

"As far as I know, it is still in the Markó yard. I haven't heard from the agency in Frankfurt, but the people here say they won't release it to anybody right now, anyway."

"And Kurt and Birke?" I had waited before posing the question, leaving ample time for him to convey possible good news.

"I'm sorry. We have been unable to learn anything through channels, but your mother managed to have a letter translated to send to your mother-in-law. There has been no reply as far as I know."

How could the hours be so long in the cell and so short outside? "I'll see you on the twenty-ninth," my guardian assured me as we parted.

31

SEVEN MORE DAYS. One week exactly. There was no way of rushing it; I resigned myself to waiting it out as I must, trying to make it a little less tortuous than the weeks past, trying to be positive. Without expectation, I continued the effort to see Gretchen. One evening Szemetria came to our hatch—he had developed a habit of coming by every time he had night duty, to chat. I decided he asked too many questions, even if he did no harm, and I answered the inquiries he put to me through Kriszta as briefly as I could. On this particular evening he began with the usual, "*Hogy vagy*, Jeanette?" (How are you?). "Are you comfortable? Did you get enough *tészta* to eat today?" And then he came to the point of his visit. Did I know Gretchen in cell two? She was from Austria, wasn't she? How and where did I get to know her? She helped somebody escape too, didn't she? Did the escapee make it out?

"If you want to know about that," I replied, "ask her, not me."

"He did," Kriszta told me, "and he says she told him all about it. He thinks she's a smart girl, rather pretty too, he says. He is just checking out her story. He declares that although she has only been here a few days, she can practically speak Hungarian like a native." I agreed that Gretchen was an intelligent girl, even if her instant fluency was something of an over-statement, and that she was pretty.

"I don't believe anyone can learn a language so fast," Kriszta inserted her own opinion. "He's full of monkey shit. He says a smart girl like that would not involve herself in a scheme that would get her into prison for nothing, and he wants to know your opinion."

"Tell him he's a better judge than I. I mind my own business."

Szemetria didn't seem to mind my retort and leaned closer so that his face covered the hatch opening. "Tell me, Jeanette," he said, via Kriszta, "I won't say anything, I'm just curious. How much did she get for it?"

"How much did who get for what?"

"You know, how much is Gretchen getting for sitting it out? You can tell me."

"Nothing," I said, blowing smoke accidentally in his face. "She did it because somebody needed help. She did not know it would be so dangerous. Tell him I want to wash now, and he'll have to leave." That wasn't true, and Szemetria knew it. I had already washed and was wearing my nightgown, Busso's pajama top.

"He has a lot of nerve asking me to inform on a friend. He's supposed to be the prisoner's buddy? What a rat." Kriszta agreed, and there were no more "chats" with Szemetria—and no more extras at mealtime when he was on duty.

The *civil major* amused himself by coming around too, and he was far less endurable than Szemetria. Often he brought someone from outside to view the American specimen. Everyone had comments to make, with the wet-lipped pansy-faced major leading the way by ever encouraging me to engage in conversation with him. From the little bit Kriszta was willing to translate of his remarks such as, "You must eat more. You are becoming so skinny your husband will look elsewhere for his mattress," I found nothing to be gained by conversing.

Kriszta and I agreed on Szemetria and the major, but on little else. We argued intermittently for days about the nun, about getting Gretchen into our cell, about Julia, about anything and everything. A popular topic of dispute was love, and the lack of concurrence spurred us on to stronger debate. "How can you believe there is love?" Kriszta asked more than once, throwing up her hands in dismay. "It's like believing in fluffy white clouds. The clouds are pretty on sunny days, but wait until the bad times come. The pretty clouds and the sun disappear without a trace, and all you have left are black thunder and rain. When the going gets rough, love disappears and leaves only misery and hate."

"How can you believe in hate without believing in love?"

"Because I can feel hate. I've seen it often and know what it is." Her cynicism was no pretense.

"And I've known love."

"From whom?"

"From lots of people, from my husband, of course, and——"

"Was it love that made him bring you here?" she interjected.

"It wasn't hate, and he didn't make me come. We've been over this subject before."

"But if you had not married him, you would never have had all this trouble."

"Then I would have married someone else and had other problems."

"Such as he might not wash enough so that he stank when he came near you," she hypothesized.

"That could be a problem," I laughed.

"It's no joke. That was my problem. One of the main reasons I decided to leave my husband." She had not talked much about her marriage. I was curious, but Kriszta could tell you to mind your own business without saying a word.

"He never bathed?"

"Only once a day."

"Wasn't that enough?"

"Of course not. A person should wash himself all over at least twice a day. Three times if he can shower at work."

"Isn't that rather extreme?"

"Not when a person stinks. But my husband refused to wash more than once a day—and I had to fight with him to make him do that."

"Why did you marry him?"

"He was different from me. I thought he would be good for me. I met him just after I was released from reform school: we've been married now almost five years, but after three I knew I couldn't stick it out for a lifetime. I left him over a year ago."

"What was he like?"

"Quiet, agreeable, easy-going, not like me at all; I like action. His intelligence impressed me at first, until I found out he had no ambition to use it. He was content just to work in the factory at whatever they told him to do. He didn't want to think for himself." She stood gazing idly out the window as she talked. "I wanted more than that. I bore his son the first year we were married. Maybe that's where the trouble really began. Sandor, my husband, was always jealous of our son."

"Maybe you gave the baby more attention than you gave your husband; did you?"

"I don't know. I don't care. I had no time for my husband, and I never loved him. I only love my son."

"Notice, you do know love."

"My son," she sighed. "He'll be past five by the time I'm out of here."

"Does your husband know what you did after you left him?"

"That I'm a whore? Of course. He comes to my place almost every week, pretending to be visiting his son, but he really wants to see me. He still wants me back."

"How did it start, Kriszta? How does a girl decide to become a prostitute?"

"I was fifteen. I had known the facts of life for a long time. I met a boy. He was Austrian, but he lived with his family in Hungary. He was tall, blond, beautiful; four years older than I. As soon as I met him, I knew what he wanted and I was ready. I was tired of being a virgin, even a little embarrassed about it. All my friends had had boyfriends already. I felt overdue to give up my virginity. Why should I shield myself from it? Why should I let my body waste uselessly away? I wanted to see what love was like." She stopped staring out the window and lit a cigarette. "The blond and I did it twice the day after we met. I didn't see him for a couple of days after that, so I went to his house to find him. He and his family had moved back to Austria, and he had not even told me he was leaving. The landlady gave me an envelope he had left with my name on it. I thought it was a letter, a love letter." She paused to inhale the smoke deeply and let it slowly out through her nose. "There was no note, not one written word in the envelope. There was just money."

I couldn't think of anything to say.

"You may think I have thick skin, Jeanette," she continued with a faint tremor, "but this payment for—for—I was hurt, very hurt. It made me feel dirty."

The way she said it, the unperturbable Kriszta, was agonizing. I joined her in a cigarette, taking the light from the end of hers to conserve matches.

"But I got over it," she said slowly. "I was developing into a woman. Wherever I went, especially when I was dressed up and looked older, men in the coffee shops watched me. I enjoyed it. By the time I was sixteen, I had decided to make the most of my talent. The men made proposals. I accepted one and then another. It was easy from there."

"For how long before the police caught up with you?"

"Almost a year. I landed in the reform school before my seventeenth birthday and stayed fourteen months. It was nice. I liked it there." She put her cigarette out and went to use the toilet, continuing her story. "It was not like prison at all, more like school, only I didn't have to go home to my bitchy mother after classes. She and I never got along very well and it was good to get away from her. Did you and your mother fight much?"

"No." How different people can be. "Did your mother have a career?"

"She was a whore too, until she married my dad. But they never got along well, and it folded after eleven years. When I was in the children's prison, Mom met and married my stepfather, the nicest guy she ever could have found. Too bad he wasn't my real father." Kriszta flushed the toilet, washed her hands, and sat across from me at the table. "Too bad he died."

"I'm sorry to hear that. He might have been good for both your mother and you."

"He sure was. We were great friends, and he was good to my mother too. Why couldn't it have been my father who died instead of my stepfather." It was a statement rather than a question. "My stepfather and I understood each other. I remembered once I saw him at the movies with another woman."

"Before he married your mother?"

"No, after. He winked at me and I shut my eyes for a second, and we never talked about it after that. We got along just fine."

I nodded, trying to reason as Kriszta did. "What does your mother say about your selling your body for a living?"

"She was against it. She kept telling me it would land me in jail. She always nagged until I told her to shut up. Then she would be still and sulk. She knew what I meant. How could she tell me what to do after having whored around herself?"

"Maybe she just wanted to save you from making the same mistakes," I suggested.

"Sure, sure, but she didn't want to save me all that badly," she said with a sneer. "I support her. She lives off my body too."

Kriszta now had no reluctance to answer my questions, and I was fascinated. "What's the daily routine of an average prostitute? What does she like to do? What does she care about?"

"Every prostitute's interest is money: money the easy way," she answered simply. "We're a lazy bunch, really. We hate to work. We hate factory life, and there is nothing else to work at, so we do what comes naturally. Why waste your time sleeping with the same man all the time when you can sleep with a different one every night and make money at the same time?"

"That's one way to look at it. But ugh," in my mind I pictured homely, unclean, awkward men, "how can a girl sleep with a man who doesn't appeal to her, with just any old man off the street?"

"I cannot answer that. I am very selective about my clients. Only young men, handsome men, tall men from the West can share my bed, for the price, that is."

"What's the price?"

"Two thousand forint."

"Two thou—on the black market that's a lot of money!"

"At least forty American dollars, yes. About a month's wages in the factory."

I gave a faint whistle.

"But few girls are as strict as I am. They aren't professional about it, like that hook-nosed thing in nineteen; she'll lay for any slob just for a glass of beer. Or that redhead in eighteen, she and I were in the reformatory together. That was after the revolution of fifty-six, but the Russians still had camps in Hungary. There was one not far from the reform school. The redhead, we called her Piroska, would slip away at night, go to the camp and earn a fistful of money, and be back by two or three A.M. to catch some sleep. She didn't care who she laid for, as long as he had money."

"And you?" I asked. "Did you earn money from the Russians?"

"No, never. I told you, I can't stand dirty men."

I asked about some of the others in the Markó. "What about the black-haired girl, the one who serves the food at noon and gives us extra helpings. Is she in for prostitution?"

"No. She's in for something even more foolish," Kriszta laughed. "I don't know what you call it in German. She was married to two men at the same time. That's what I call really overworked!"

"Bigamy. That's the word in English and it might be the same in German." I stood up to stretch. Your muscles can turn to marmalade in a cell, and still they get cramped. "What do you do in the daytime, Kriszta? Sleep?"

"I'll tell you," she began, "my work day begins between nine-thirty and ten o'clock or so at night. That's when I go to the bar."

"Always the same bar?"

"No, not always. There are several good ones, the Pipacs [White Poppy] Bár, the Vörös Csillag [Red Star] Hotel, and quite a few others. But a girl can't operate just anywhere. The police watch most of the big hotels pretty closely. I have my favorites, and my customers know where to find me. Just the good bars, mind you." She enjoyed talking about her work, emphasizing that she was strictly a high-class call-girl.

"There must be other girls there too, whores I mean; what do you all do?"

"Some sit at the bar. Your friend Julia liked to sit at the bar, usually with another girl or two. Me, I prefer a table to myself. One where I can see the whole room. I usually drink one, two, occasionally three drinks, and by then, most days, a man comes and asks to join me. Often the waiter is sent to ask if I am busy or waiting for someone; that way, the man will not embarrass himself by being turned down," she explained, "and I like it better too because then I can ask the waiter to point the man out. If I don't like his looks, it's easy to say I am busy."

"Did you often have open competition with the other girls for a man's attention and money?" I wondered.

"No, I kept clear of most of that. I let the customer choose me. But your Julia," a sneer formed on her lips, "she competed with everybody, even with the wives and girlfriends of men who weren't even looking for a bed partner. She thought she was so pretty she could make every man fall at her feet."

"I'll bet some did."

"Yes. I've seen more than one guy take his date home, then come back and take Julia out. That's rotten. I wouldn't do that."

"Was Julia known to be good, special in bed, I mean?"

"She was known for her looks. She's such a tall thing, I couldn't see it myself. She dressed sexy, as you say, but she was straight up and down naked—well, you saw her, didn't you? What did you think?"

"As a matter of fact," I said slowly, deciding whether or not I wanted to anger Kriszta, "I didn't think she had a bad figure."

"Not bad?" she howled. "Not bad for a lamppost."

"Come on Kriszta, Julia has a nice figure, so what?" There was no comparison in beauty between Julia and Kriszta. Julia's body was slim, firm, smooth, so pure white that one had the impression she knew nothing of the depravity of the world. Kriszta's body, with its scarred abdomen, sagging breasts, and skin that looked like it needed a breath of fresh air, was a carcass in comparison. But Kriszta had something else, a certain character, a certain coarse charm all her own, a certain reality in her cynicism, an honesty that could be very attractive. "That's not what I asked anyway. I asked if she was good in bed."

"How should I know?" she flung at me. "I never slept with her!"

"That's good to know. Now I feel safer."

"All I know is," Kriszta continued without a smile, "I had a lot more steady customers than she did. She took Hungarians too, anybody. I only took foreigners."

"All right, all right." I wanted to change the subject. "Never mind that. After you had a customer, what did you do? Go to his hotel?"

"No. That's risky. You can get caught too easily. The cheap girls do it, but not me. That's why it was so important to me to get an apartment. They are extremely difficult to obtain here, you know. I was lucky, very lucky, to find two. My mother lives next door, so she does all the housework for me. She has to earn her way a little bit. She cleans her two rooms and my two rooms and takes care of my son. He sleeps at her place so he won't be disturbed at night."

"That's a good arrangement," I agreed. "So you bring home some strange foreigner. Then what?"

"First we have a couple of drinks together at the bar, so he isn't really a stranger. Then we take a taxi to my place. We put on some records, Al Hirt, Harry Belafonte, or somebody good like that, and play cards or chess. That's where I learned to play. Or we just talk if he wants to, and later, about three or so, we go to bed." She sounded like that was the conclusion.

"And then?"

"You're married. You figure it out."

"What about undressing? Do you have special music or what?"

"Man, you do want to know every detail, don't you?" she laughed.

"Sure," we were both amused at the conversation, "I just might consider a new occupation. Watch out, Kriszta, when this bombshell walks into the Pipacs Bar," I threatened. "If you're not careful, you might lose every customer." I smoothed my eyebrows and patted my hair. "You haven't seen me in action yet."

"Ya, you're right: I'd lose every customer, because one look at you and they'd all be scared clear out of Hungary," she scoffed. "If you really want to know, I always go into the bathroom for a new customer so that he can get into bed while I'm getting ready. I don't care where I undress——"

"I believe that."

"——but it's more comfortable for the man that way."

"What about the money? Do you demand cash in advance or what?"

"That's the rule. But there is never any problem: that's another reason I am selective. Most of them just lay the money on the dresser at night. Regulars sometimes pay the next morning."

"And then?"

"And then?" she repeated blankly.

"And then are you madly passionate, or what? I should think it would be exhausting trying to keep a different man entertained every night."

"Sometimes it's passionate, if he wants it that way. Many don't. Many men just want someone to lie beside. They make easy love, it goes fast, and then they sleep like babies. Some don't want to do it at all."

"That's the business for me. They pay me forty dollars for playing chess (I'd even let the man win) and rental of a warm blanket. Tell me," I asked, "what about kissing? I once read that prostitutes don't like to kiss a man on the mouth. Is that true?"

"If I like a man, I kiss him. Why not?"

"I'm asking you. What about other things, deviations from the standard—positions?"

"Whoa, now, you mean perverted things? No, I don't go in for that. There are girls who specialize in that. I don't, I'm old-fashioned. Is that what you wanted to know? You should be in cell twenty-eight. That's where the specialist in perversion is. She does acts in front of the customer to get him excited. She'll do anything out of the ordinary that the man asks for. I hear her favorite is playing with a dog. She likes to do it to monkeys too. You could ask her questions that would embarrass you blue just to think of. But she doesn't speak German. Too bad."

"And I'm not in twenty-eight. Too bad. What's the matter with her?"

"Nothing. She likes to excel, that's all. She earns double the money per act, and she commonly does more than one per night."

I digested eighty dollars, and double that, for a minute, and then asked, "What do you do in the morning? That would be the hardest for me. I'm not fit to live with until I've had two cups of coffee."

"It's not as difficult as having a husband. Most of the men are businessmen who have come to sell something in Budapest. They usually get up about seven without disturbing me, go to a restaurant to eat, and go about their daily routine. Sometimes, when they have more time, they stay for breakfast with me. If I can, I like to sleep until noon or more. Then I get up, eat, shower, and play with my son until around six."

"What happens at six?"

"I shower, change clothes, and go to the hairdresser and cosmetician."

"Every day?"

"Of course every day. I have to look good."

"Tell me, Kriszta, don't you feel bad sometimes? I mean guilty about making love to another woman's husband?"

"Not at all. I'm doing the wives a favor. I'm taking care of their men without trying to steal them away. If he did not have me, he would take someone else, probably a streetwalker who'd steal him blind or try to make him fall in love with her, or give him a disease. I think every man should have a whore, don't you?"

"Not my man."

"Why not? Making love is healthy, and a wife needs a rest or even a little variety herself sometimes."

"Maybe that used to be true in the days when sexual enjoyment was considered for men only, not now."

"Why don't you become a nun, Jeanette?"

"I guess I'm just a misfit, Kriszta. I'd feel miserable as a whore and out of character as a nun."

"Actually," Kriszta admitted, "once I did feel bad. The man was very nice, and after he climaxed, he said he loved and missed his wife terribly and that he should not be with me, and then he wept."

Kriszta thought about that for a long time and then I asked, "Do you plan to go back to living the same way again? What do you want out of life?"

"No, I don't want to go back to it. I'm almost twenty-five, and if I don't find a good man by the time I'm thirty, I won't have much chance after that. I want to marry an intelligent, respectable man who will take me to the theater. I would be true to him, very true. And I want to have time to spend with my son." It wasn't often my roommate revealed her dreams. "Jeanette, I never met anyone who asked so many questions."

"I never met a classy call-girl before. I'm learning. Remind me to send Kadar a letter of thanks for the education. I don't even have to pay tuition."

"Oh yes, you do. You pay for every stinking day of board and room in this hotel."

"What? I refuse! I never heard of such a thing."

"They won't let you out of Hungary until you've paid your bill, that's certain."

It was interesting learning about Kriszta's life, learning how different we were, and how alike in many ways. I was amazed at how basically unshocking, unglamourous, unexceptional her story seemed when one knew the beginning and the end.

We were comfortable together, Kriszta and I, and we jointly planned ways to improve conditions. Because washing in cold water was a displeasure, I complained to the doctor and he saw to it that, "to protect my health," cell twenty-two received a *kana* of warm water nightly. To soothe my aching stomach, he issued orders for "the diet" for me, pronounced "dee-ate." "All the foreigners prefer it," he said. "It is blander."

The diet consisted the first day of green peas in a sweet flour sauce, then carrots in a sweet flour sauce, then both peas and carrots in a sweet flour sauce. Once I was very hungry and washed off the peas in order to eat them, but otherwise, the course was completely unpalatable. After four straight days of sweet sauce I received a variety of grain cereals, plain potatoes, and on Sunday a slice of cheese and a shallow pan of warm milk. Kriszta and I shared the prison food equally so that on a few occasions, when we both received something edible, our table looked quite festive.

I continued to ask a lot of questions, and Kriszta wanted to know about me too, but there was a limit to how much we could entertain each other. A hundred, a thousand times a day I was reminded that I was in prison, and all I could think of then was "I want out!'

32

ON SEPTEMBER TWENTY-NINTH, I was disappointed not to be guarded by the same woman as before, the young one with the tiny gold earrings. This time my warder was a tube-like female who must have been created by a cement mason, I was sure. She acted even more coarse than the *Vipera*, and the same lines of contempt for humanity shaped her mouth. As we passed the open door of the black cell, where a prisoner on cleaning duty washed the floor, the squat guard stopped and said something to me. Many guards had spoken to me this way, rattling in their own tongue, knowing I did not understand and putting me in the position of an ignorant toad. As always, it made me furious. She shrugged and shook her head, commenting on my intelligence to the *Vipera* and other nearby guards, and then demonstrated exactly what she had asked by jutting her hips forward and holding her hand in front as if she were a man holding his penis. "No," I replied, "I don't have to go."

As before, I walked behind Busso to the courthouse, but it was not possible to talk, because the guards kept us at a distance. We were immediately ushered into the main courtroom—I recognized it as the one Julia had described to me—a large room that looked more like what I had expected at the first trial. There was a raised desk for the judge, the same judge as before, Judge Stefanics, and his two assistants, not the same two as before. Busso and I were separated by a new interpreter, who sat between us, a kind-looking man with gray hair and keen eyes, and I decided he was Jewish. There was a different prosecutor, the third we had had, a white-haired man who sat on the left side of the room. Dr. Kubinyi and Dr. Nagy shared a desk to the right. Directly between the judge and us was a three-sided box resembling an anchored chariot, made of wood and without adornment—the witness stand.

Maybe because the room looked more like a traditional courtroom; or because of the stillness that surrounded us in the large space, even though some fifty spectators shuffled in to occupy the rows behind us; or because of the spectators themselves and my surprise that so much of the public was admitted before the doors were secured; or maybe all of these things combined excited the awareness in me that, in spite of my efforts to be calm for fear I might be sick, today was the culmination of three months of waiting; today I could be allowed to go home.

I knew Mr. Gross was present, because I had caught sight of him in the hall, but I didn't have a chance to survey the other people in the room much.

The trial began without delay. I thought I would again have to leave the room and looked at the guard sitting to my left, but she did not know what I meant and motioned impatiently for me to sit still and quit turning my head.

Instead of asking Busso questions, the judge's attention was at once directed to me. I started to stand as was the apparent custom, but the interpreter said, "No, that is not necessary. Sit down."

A woman and a man entered the room. I recognized them as the stocky female prosecutor who had composed our indictment and the interpreter who had also been present at that time. The prosecutor was called to the witness box. She stood with her back to me and answered a few questions put to her by the judge. Evidently she was asked if she thought I had understood her interrogation of me. Naturally, she replied *"Igen,"* and she stepped down. The young interpreter took the stand next, but stepped down shortly to face me.

"Do you remember me?" he asked in German.

"Yes, I do."

"Didn't you understand the questions I translated to you on August fourth?"

"I thought then that I understood, but I see now that there must have been some misunderstanding. You see, when you spoke to me in the polite or formal form, I thought you were using the plural because it is the same word. I always answered in the plural by saying 'we,' don't you remember? Since the four of us acted as a group, I didn't know you were asking me as an individual."

The judge did not like my speaking so long and called the interpreter back to the stand. Maybe he thought I was confusing the witness, but he need not have worried. From what I gathered, the judge asked the witness if he thought I had understood him and the man replied he did and stepped down. I kept asking my present interpreter what was being said but, with a certain dismay in his voice, he said only, "I am sorry, I cannot talk at this time. We must be still."

If they're calling witnesses, I wondered, where is the witness for the defense, one who will testify that we are not professionals, that we were not trying to undermine the commune, that we are merely a family? Who will assert that we carried no weapons, made no malevolent attempts to escape, injured no one?

The judge spoke to Dr. Kubinyi, who rose, said a few sentences, and reseated himself. Dr. Nagy then spoke. It was no surprise that he had the style and tone of an eighteenth-century orator. I caught the word *kedves*, dear, and knew he was telling the court what a nice, dear girl I was, so I could not possibly have done such a dastardly thing, which seemed the wrong way entirely to approach the defense, and I was glad when, after four or five tedious minutes, a great yawn by the magistrate caused the lawyer to end his argument, and he sat down.

Inside me a trace of fire began to rekindle, a fire of anger and indignation that I thought had died for lack of air or strength inside prison walls. What the devil was going on here? It all appeared so artificial, so phony. Where was that officer from the border, Mr. Darazsi, or whatever his name was, the one who would "do all he could to help" us? Why wasn't he called?

The judge said something to the interpreter then, and the man looked at each of us with his keen, gentle eyes and said, "You have the opportunity to speak now. My advice is to say nothing or else to make it concise, because the magistrate is short of patience today. Do either of you wish to say something?"

"I do. I have a hell of a lot to say," Busso answered emphatically.

"Yes, I do too," I said, "let Busso be first."

"Do not take too much time," the interpreter cautioned.

Busso stood, and as he spoke I watched our tribunes. Dr. Stefanics was leafing through some papers. The woman, her hair piled festively in great curls on on top of her head, was playing with a pencil, and the other man was surveying the audience behind us.

Busso had written his speech out, and I wondered where he had obtained the paper and pencil. He glanced up intermittently and spoke with passion. "My sister is not a strong girl. She needed our help." He continued speaking with his heart in his throat and tears in his eyes. "My wife did absolutely nothing to plan the escape. She knew of the general outline, but it wasn't until we spent two days at the border together that she learned the details from me. It would have been carried out exactly as it was if she had not been there. She was unaware—" The judge's glance slid past Busso and halted to meet my eyes. His expression did not change, nor did mine. Busso was talking about love for one's family being unbound within political restrictions, and though he stumbled for a second, his words were filled with significance and urgency.

Suddenly, seeing the judge's eyes, I knew what the outcome of this circus would be. I knew without a doubt that I would not go home today, or next week, or next month. I had tried to brace myself for it before, but knowing it was different. It didn't matter what Busso said. It didn't even matter what Dr. Kubinyi and Dr. Nagy said. Mr. Gross had tried to tell me, but gently, so that I would not collapse without my snowflake of hope. It was all an act, an off-Broadway, way-off-Broadway performance, a showpiece of hypocrisy. If they had wanted to listen to our pleas, there had been no reason to adjourn the first time. The question was not what we did, or how or why; we had already confessed to that ten times over. The question was how to build it into an immoral felony, how to etch it unmistakably into everyone's mind—the minds of the audience, the judge's mind, and even into Busso's mind and my own—that we had committed a major *crime*. The best way to inscribe the lesson was to play-act a genuine prosecution.

Busso had been speaking for perhaps three minutes. The judge looked at his watch, leaned over to say something to the man on his right, then interrupted Busso. "But I'm not finished," Busso argued.

"Your time is up, I am sorry," the interpreter said. "You must sit down for your own good. Do not anger the judge."

The old man looked at me, "You could say something if you insist, but——"

"Busso has said everything, but they don't *listen*," I flared. "Will it do any good? I would like to——"

"I think you would be wise to be still. It will do no good now. There is no use repeating what has already been said, and if you say the wrong thing——"

"I would like to tell that Stefanics exactly——"

"Your anger can only do you harm," he said urgently. The judge said something to the effect that my time was up and the interpreter replied, he told me a minute later, that I request only that the court weigh carefully the sincere words of my husband.

The prosecutor made several firm statements and I cursed myself for not understanding Hungarian. It all went so fast, I felt confused when a recess was soon called. Mr. Gross generously brought us some sandwiches, as before, but he could not come near, since the guards were more strict than ever. A man in the audience managed to get close enough to our bench to hold his hand out to me. I reached to touch it and he pressed four wrapped, hard candies into my palm. He said something in Hungarian to wish us well, and I wanted to hug him, but of course could say only, *"Köszönom,"* thank you, before he was shoved away.

Busso and I were able to speak only a few sentences, and we tried to reassure each other that the separation would not be much longer. The judge did not leave the room but sat casually in his chair talking animatedly to his associates. He was smiling broadly, and I had the distinct impression that he was talking about his recent vacation, or maybe about a new show in town, anything but our case.

Barely had we sampled the good sandwiches when they were taken away and the trial was reconvened. My husband and I stared at each other, wondering, dreading, hoping; acutely aware that the murmur of voices around us now fell silent, sharing our apprehensive expectancy. A statement was read in Hungarian, the accusation against us, I presumed. Following it, also in Hungarian, the decision as to our penalties of which I understood only, "Busso Lemmé—*nyolc honap*. Jeanette Lemmé—*hat honap*."

The interpreter translated the verdict, adding, "You may appeal the decision if you wish." Court was adjourned.

"Thank you," I replied. "It was nice meeting you. I think an appeal would be just as useless as this trial was, don't you?"

"It would be an unnecessary repetition of the strain on your emotions, I'm afraid," he replied candidly. "Good-by and good luck," he shook Busso's hand and mine, and it was then, as I thought about what a good man he seemed, that he leaned heavily on his cane, and I noticed his crippled leg. Dr. Nagy and Dr. Kubinyi came to us to say good-by, and the interpreter limped away.

"He is very nice," I said pointedly to my lawyer, "too bad about his leg."

"Ah, yes, of course," he replied absently, and made some standard apology about the decision, saying that I was young and the time would go by rapidly for me, and besides, "we shall definitely appeal, and you'll be home before you know it."

"No, I don't want to appeal," I said flatly. "If you really want to help, please arrange a good long visit with my husband," I entreated. "I am now entitled to it by your law." I turned to find Mr. Gross. "What a farce," I said, shaking my head, but smiling, and it seemed that I had just discovered the word, just uncovered the root of its derivation. He had no time to reply, because I was pressed to walk ahead through the door. It seemed that everybody wanted to exit at the same time I did. In the doorway a woman squeezed in front of me, and in an angry, anguished voice she whispered in English, "You are right. That is exactly what this is, a farce! I am sorry." I was astonished and touched by her apology for her country and replied rapidly, "Good luck."

"And to you, *barátnöm* [friend]," she replied, her eyes authenticating her sincerity before she had to fall back with the assembly to make way for Busso and his patrolman behind me. Several sharp jabs to my ribs made me stumble on down the corridor as my husband and I were led back to prison.

Minutes later I sat in cell twenty-two, calm for the first time in months.

"Well?" Kriszta probed.

"Well what?" I asked. It was more fun to tease her now than it had been the first time.

"You know what." She was not angry about the game this time and played along.

"Do you have any cigarettes left?"

"The Kents are gone. Have one of mine," she offered a *Munkas* ("Worker's" cigarette). She tossed a box of matches to me, a new one, and I examined it idly. On the face of the box was a picture of the American flag. One of the red stripes extended out beyond the border of the flag, and on it were written the words Ku Klux Klan. Another red stripe extended vertically through that to form a cross. The face of a negro was pictured in the bottom right hand corner with the words, "TILTAKOZZ a *fajüldözés ellen!*" I requested a translation.

"It says, 'Down with racial persecution!' Isn't that stupid?" Kriszta snatched the matches back. "Don't let it bother you." She handed me her cigarette. "We need to conserve matches anyway. Draw from mine."

"Thanks. We've learned to tolerate each other quite well these past few weeks, haven't we?" I observed. "Now I have to go somewhere else and begin all over to learn to live with strangers."

"Maybe that is what prison and punishment are: forcing us to do what the rest of the world cannot. How much did your husband get?"

"Eight months," I swallowed hard and felt a pain in the bridge of my nose that predicted a flow of tears if I didn't inhale hot smoke quickly.

"And you got four, it couldn't be more than four."

"Yes it could. I'll give you a hint: I'm halfway through."

"Six? Three more months? But they should at least give you one third off. They give one third off to all Hungarians on their first offense. Don't you think they will?" I responded with a "now-what-do-you-think" glance, and she abandoned the idea, saying, "Too bad it couldn't be less, but you will make it all right. You'll be home before you know it." The same prediction that had irritated me when Dr. Nagy said it sounded reassuring now from Kriszta. "After all this is over, what will you do?"

"All this," I repeated, contemplating the quantity of experience those two words encompassed. "The failure at the border. The abrupt separation, the imprisonment—it seems like years ago. The solitary confinement that all but drove me insane. The insufferable eyes watching day and night. The pointless isolation from

Busso and the agony of knowing how my parents have suffered, the loss of my job, and decline of our business."

"The education you got here in the Markó," Kriszta contributed, "with lesbians, whores, murderers, and thieves who even steal from their own kind."

"The ever-present fear that predominates every breath one takes, the fear of silence, the fear of the unknown, and especially the fear of time lost, wasted in physical and mental decay and personal anonymity." I paced the cell, hoping to walk the next three months away. "I just hope they set me free on December twenty-ninth as they have now promised. My first day in freedom will be a day in heaven. What will I do when it's all over?" I repeated Kriszta's question.

"This must make quite a change in your life," she mused.

The future had seemed so cloudy before, so distant and uncertain. All at once, the fog cleared. There was one easy, vivid answer to that question.

"In a way my life has been altered, I suppose, but then," I asked in reply, "what has actually changed?"

"Wait a minute, are you still thinking of your——"

"They are behind bars too. And even when they are released, the land remains their cell, the government their jailer. They still need help."

"After all this," she enunciated slowly, as though giving up on a lost cause. "You are still a dreamer, Jeanette. You are still very ——" she hesitated, not wanting to hurt my feelings or our last day together.

"Naive," I finished for her.

"Very naive. I wish you luck, *barátnőm.*"

Epilogue

BIRKE AND KURT ARE FREE. After our capture, they were sent back to East Germany, where Kurt was sentenced to two years six months and his wife to two years one month. They served fourteen months before they were both released directly from prison to West Germany, and they are now happily accustomed to the pace of progressive Western living. Ironically, only by being imprisoned for a crime that was never brought to fulfillment did we learn the right sources, the contacts, the channels through which two people could have their liberty; and our objective was accomplished. Those who made it possible have asked that the details not be published in order to preserve the same path for others still captive behind the Iron Curtain.

Gretchen, incidentally, received a sentence of five months. I saw her briefly in Vienna, but unfortunately our dream of a day on the city never materialized, because of interfering circumstances. Freedom itself was so delicious, however, that we needed no ornamentation. The two Westerners—the German, and the other Austrian woman—served out their sentences of eight and nine months, respectively, and are safely back home.

Busso and I were sent to different prisons after the trial, and during the remaining months, our petitions to have the same two-hour visitation privileges accorded other prisoners were continually ignored. In spite of my initial objections, an appeal trial was arranged late in November, even though I never saw my lawyer to discuss it. It was, like the first, strictly for appearances. At the appeal, during the recess, Busso whispered his urgent message to me. It pertained to the definite possibility of securing Kurt and Birke's release. Even when I left Hungary after serving my six months, I was not allowed to visit my husband.

I was not pregnant while confined. Perhaps my body knew that certain functions serve no purpose in prison, and it rested temporarily. Since then, Busso and I have returned to good health and now have a delightful little daughter.

My husband and I are deeply grateful to the many friends, neighbors, and concerned strangers who made efforts to help us in our trouble. To each one, our sincere thanks. Not unappreciated were the many letters and steps taken by Senator Jackson, Senator Magnuson and Representative Pelly.

I have attempted here to describe what I saw as I saw it. The book does not answer many questions involved, I am aware: questions of philosophy, questions of moral principle, questions of civil or criminal law. Such questions are complicated by evolution: each problem changes even as each of us is changing.

I have changed since that first day in prison, and since those first days in 1967, after my release, when I answered reporters' questions. My attitudes, my judgments have altered, some of them making a full one-hundred-and-eighty-degree turnabout. Six months no longer seems like a lifetime—but I do not plan to forfeit it soon again! And in retrospect, my opinion of Hungarian lawyers was altered even before an old cliché, quoted to me by Mr. Gross, took on new meaning as stated by a Communist attorney: "A defense lawyer in a Communist trial just spits against the wind." That man and I understand each other. Even my judgment of my own lawyer has changed. Mr. Gross described him in a letter as "zealously and aggressively presenting the best case he can"; partly, I suspect, to console my parents, but partly because there are many who would have cared much less about my defense. At the time I thought him a State's simpering Simon, and now—now I wonder, did I ever know a Hungarian lawyer? Whatever for?

One question I remember in particular, put to me by a reporter immediately after my release, may yet be unanswered,

"Do you feel grateful for getting off with only a six-month sentence?"

I do not remember my exact reply, but I know what my feeling was at the moment, a feeling that for my health, my country, my family, and my daily life, I thank God. Millions of people have endured a great deal more suffering in confinement than I, and there are innumberable books which recount the terrors of war, concentration camps, and thousands of other horrendous human agonies. I am thankful that my tale cannot out-stock these tragic events. In direct answer, I would respond to the reporter's question by saying that then, in the same sense that a man is grateful whose hand has been chopped off instead of his whole arm or leg, I was grateful. Come to think of it, "grateful" may not be quite the right word.

Hungary is a picturesque country with an intriguing heritage. If you can see it without using hotels, restaurants, and night spots, you will learn much of interest. I strongly recommend, however, that Americans and other Western tourists do not donate their hard currency in support of governments that leech our gold for a system of one-way tourist trade.

If, on the other hand, present attempts by Willy Brandt and other western leaders to open communication links should succeed, and if Eastern Bloc leaders should recognize the eminent advantages of free exchange between nations, travelers the world over would rejoice in the dissolution of barriers. It would seem time to me now, after a quarter of a century, with due negotiation, to acknowledge the German Democratic Republic. I think, by looking forward rather than backward, it could be done with dignity on both sides. Do you agree, Mr. Ulbricht?

Good subsists within the Communist Bloc nations: good people, good ideas, and in some leaders, good will. But when a basic right, the right to move freely and to determine one's own destiny, to seek out a new existence in distant lands, is denied, then the evils of that society override the good. When the foundation of a system relies on human bondage, far more is sacrificed than is gained.

My heart goes out to the yet millions of good people helplessly incarcerated in Communist nations for purposes of economic experimentation. As long as there is indiscriminate mass imprisonment by such totalitarians, let the yearning people under their rule know that there is a free West to come to, one they may leave at liberty; and for them, let there always be new paths of liberation. I wish them, all who dare search for a better life, good luck and safe journey.